HIGHWAY TO HELL

The Life and Death of AC/DC Legend Bon Scott

SECOND REVISED EDITION

Clinton Walker

Verse Chorus Press

Published in the USA by Verse Chorus Press,
PO Box 14806, Portland OR 97293, www.versechorus.com

This book was first published in 1994 by Pan Macmillan, Australia.
Revised edition first published in the USA by Verse Chorus Press in 2001
Second revised edition first published in 2007

Front cover photograph © Philip Morris
Design and layout by Steve Connell
The editor and the publisher wish to thank all those who supplied
photographs and gave permission to reproduce copyright material in
this book. Every effort has been made to contact copyright holders,
and the publishers would like to hear from any copyright owners from
whom permission was inadvertently not obtained. In such cases, we
will be pleased to obtain appropriate permission and provide suitable
acknowledgment in future printings.

Printed in China by C&C Offset Printing Co., Ltd.

ISBN 978-1-891241-23-9
Library of Congress Control Number 2007931765

CONTENTS

PREFACE TO THE SECOND US EDITION

I've always said it was easy to write *Highway to Hell*. I mean, with material this good it'd be hard to fuck it up. When I started work on the book in the early '90s, I remember feeling I should be looking over my shoulder all the time, because this amazing story was just sitting there, untouched—I couldn't believe I had it to myself, as I did at the time. The book has struck such a chord that it's never been out of print, and since it seems to have taken on a life of its own, I've been disinclined to tamper with it as it went through its various editions, even though it has faults I now find glaring.

For this new edition, however, it became necessary to go beyond the usual bit of panel-beating and significantly rewrite the last chapter and the epilogue. For one thing, while my original reconstruction of Bon's last hours was essentially correct (and I take some pride in that), despite the pressure exerted by various conspiracy theories over the years, I was able to confirm and flesh out the details in the book's final chapter after mystery man Alistair Kinnear (who had been with Bon that night) issued an important public statement in 2005. Furthermore, as *Back in Black*—AC/DC's first post-Bon album and their tribute to him—has grown in stature over the years, the questions that still surround its genesis have become more pressing; I've examined these questions more closely here than in previous editions.

Ultimately, though, as I re-read the book I was struck all over again by this amazing character and his amazing story. I am confident that new readers will find the same—the power of it is such that it can survive any of my inadequacies as a writer. There's no doubt—Bon (still) lives!

C.W.
Sydney, 2007

PREFACE TO THE FIRST US EDITION

Rock'n'roll was invented in America, for sure—but it was quickly appropriated by the British. And then, in Australia, it was appropriated all over again. For years our music—like so many things in Australia—was only an "equivalent" of something American or British.

In some ways, despite our isolation, our tiny population, and our colonial inferiority complex (what we refer to in Australia as "the cultural cringe"), it is not so surprising that this English-speaking country should have become the world's third-largest producer of rock music. But because it largely mimicked US and UK models for so long, audiences in other countries have only recently become aware that Australian acts are, in fact, Australian.

As a music writer who started out in the late seventies when punk was reinventing rock'n'roll, I saw members of my own generation—the Saints, the Go-Betweens, Nick Cave, and their successors—play a leading role in a worldwide uprising. Having this year produced a book/film/soundtrack called *Buried Country: The Story of Aboriginal Country Music*, I remain committed to telling the stories of the emergence of original Australian music.

In Bon Scott, I found a legendary character who already had a grip on people's imagination, and whose career with the Spektors, the Valentines, Fraternity, and then AC/DC encapsulated virtually the entire narrative of Australian rock's evolution. After seeing the early AC/DC constantly on Australian TV's *Countdown* in 1975-76, I had tended—like many other observers—to write them off as some sort of teenybopper boogie band. And then they left the country, to seek success on a bigger stage. Meanwhile, the late seventies seemed to flash by—it was an incredibly exciting time for all of us. Then suddenly, in 1980, Bon Scott was dead. He was 33.

Twenty years later, having survived many rock'n'roll indulgences myself, I know how young 33 is. Yet I am still astonished at the amount of life Bon Scott packed into those years. His life, career, and death had all the drama, comedy, and tragedy of a classical narrative.

Highway to Hell was written with the belief that it could go around the world despite the "cultural cringe," so I'm delighted to see it published now in the USA. Compounding my joy—as well as having actually received an advance!—is the fact that, though revised and updated with new information, it remains an Australian story told from an Australian perspective. Great credit and thanks, then, go to Verse Chorus Press.

From the response to this book's original edition in 1994 I learned the power of a single personality. Bon Scott touched so many people in his life that my attempt to portray him touched people too. Those I relied on as sources also gave me praise for having accurately captured something of him, while Bon's parents, as I'd feared, didn't like seeing his seedier side aired so publicly; and the AC/DC machine, inevitably, remains unmoved-.

After an unsuccessful referendum in 1999, Australians are still debating their future as a nation. There is a growing movement that will sooner or later succeed in transforming this country—a onetime penal colony still nominally ruled by the British monarch—into a republic. The whitefella who first arrived here and stole the land from its Aboriginal inhabitants was a British convict. So when it's time to choose a new national anthem, I'll be pumping for AC/DC's "Jailbreak"—because all of us in Australia, black and white, need to break the shackles of the recent past we all have in common. In his own way, Bon Scott tried to do this, too.

I believe American readers and rock'n'roll fans will respond to Bon as a character in the same way Australians already have: his human qualities are universal. Beyond that, I hope new readers will discover the things that Australian rock'n'roll has in common with its American and British cousins—and also what makes it unique.

C.W.
Sydney, December 2000

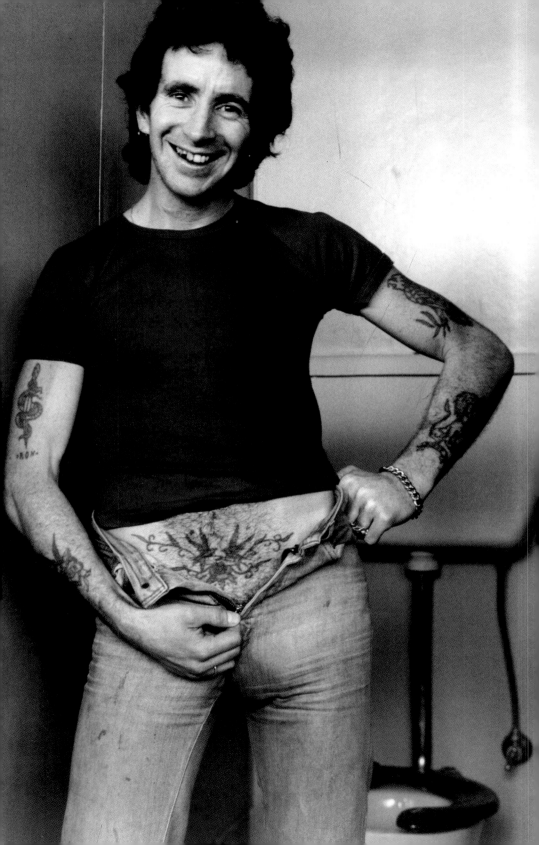

INTRODUCTION

When Bon Scott died in London in February 1980, AC/DC was on the verge of the breakthrough that established them as one of the most popular rock'n'roll bands of all time.

AC/DC was then still a new band on the world stage, as the schoolboy get-up of spotty young guitarist Angus Young emphasized. But Bon himself was a veteran, the self-confessed old man of the band, a 33-year-old who had already been around the block twice since the sixties. When he was pronounced dead on arrival at Kings College Hospital, the cumulative grind of nearly 20 years on the road had finally caught up with him.

Bon Scott was a man who lived for the moment. And when those moments had run out, his reputation solidified into legend—this was indeed one of the last true wild men of rock. The graffiti *BON LIVES!* is still to be found scrawled on walls all over the world.

Dead rock stars are often deified on the basis of martyrdom alone, however senseless. But Bon Scott was a working-class hero in life, and he became an icon in death.

AC/DC carried on after Bon died—as he would certainly have wanted them to—but while the later line-up of the band, with singer Brian Johnson, has enjoyed the greatest success, it is impossible to shake the feeling that it ain't what it used to be. The Young brothers, Malcolm and Angus, who formed AC/DC and still run it, have acknowledged it was Bon who set them on their path, and the band today has only a faint echo of the earthiness, humor and honesty he invested it with.

AC/DC's back catalogue has never been out of print, and is still selling. In 2003, when the band was inducted into the Rock and Roll Hall of Fame in the US, AC/DC could claim worldwide album sales of over 120 million, making them the fifth-biggest rock act of all time behind only the Beatles, Led Zeppelin, Pink Floyd and the Eagles (and ahead of the Stones, the Bee Gees, everyone). "I'll go on record as saying they're the greatest rock'n'roll band of all time," says Rick Rubin, arguably the most important record producer of the last two decades, and a man who measures all his work against one album—Bon's swan song, *Highway to Hell*.

By 2005, by which time streets had been named after AC/DC in Madrid and Melbourne alike, and Bon's grave in Fremantle was listed as a heritage site by the National Trust following the 25th anniversary of his death, AC/DC's influence was so pervasive that new Australian band Airborne incited an international bidding war on the basis that they sounded more like AC/DC than all the other young "new rock" bands trying to sound like AC/DC. Like Bon-era AC/DC, of course.

But beyond the shiny garlands and concrete monuments, beyond his musical legacy, beyond even the timeless appeal he exerts on successive generations, Bon has an iconic status which is intangible, a given in our popular cultural heritage. As an Australian musical icon, he has a wider appeal than Dame Nellie Melba, Johnny O'Keefe, Nick Cave, even Slim Dusty. Appellations like "an Australian Jim Morrison" are simply degrading—Bon is the world's one and only Bon and nothing less.

Bon embodies the tearaway spirit, and no one he's touched—even though they may "grow up" and leave rock'n'roll behind, shear their greasy locks and trade their denim jacket for coveralls or a shirt and tie—will ever forget his example, the mischievous glint in his eye and the screeching call to arms.

Bon's image was not so emblematic that he might now be mass produced like a Ned Kelly or a Kiss or Elvis doll, or even an Angus Young doll; nor does he exist in the Australian collective memory as faded black-and-white newsreel footage, like, say, that of cricket legend Donald Bradman cutting an English field to pieces. Nor is he a still photograph, even for all the forceful motion it might capture—as so many indelible images of Elvis do. No, we are more likely to remember Bon fleetingly, flashlike, mercurial. He will be performing, on TV's *Countdown* maybe, or at a show you went to but can't fully remember after all those years and the rush and haze it was at the time anyway. He will be a splay of elbows and skin and tattoos, grinning with evil intent, grabbing at the microphone, screeching in his inimitable fashion, the center of a driving storm of volume, rhythm and blues that enveloped everything, that simply lodged itself in the atmosphere as part of the air you breathed and so to which reaction was involuntary, the body jerking in tandem motion. This was rebellion and release superior to any other available in spiritually bereft suburbia. And Bon was its advocate, a denim-clad Pied Piper with a bottle in his hand, a lady in waiting and the hellhounds on his trail . . .

Bon updated the Australian larrikin archetype. He was "the original currency lad," as Sidney J. Baker defined him in *The Australian Language*: "tough, defiant, reckless," plugged into the urban, electric twentieth century. Part of Bon's appeal was vicarious, as it always is with rock stars—they live out our fantasies for us, and Bon very much lived the life of excess his audience could only dream about. But his immortality is not the result of nostalgic yearning. Even after his death Bon remains potent, the brute poet of the inarticulate underclass, a spokesman for not a generation but a class, a class with little influence or barely even so much as a voice. In railing against conformity, mediocrity and hypocrisy, Bon's rebellion was blessedly not nihilistic, however, but rather the opposite—it expressed a lust for life that knew no bounds. With a disregard for all the niceties—even though, ironically, an impeccable politeness was one of Bon's endearing personal traits—he might have been saying nothing more than, Believe nothing they tell you! Break free! Find out for yourself! Live life!

Bon regarded AC/DC's 1976 hit single "Jailbreak" as one of his best songs, and indeed it might well stand as his most succinct autobiographical statement—jail being a blunt metaphor for the straight life.

It's true that Bon himself grew up hard, even served time, but he had no chip on his shoulder. Nor was he motivated by the short man's syndrome that seems, at least in part, to drive an Iggy Pop or a James Brown. Like Elvis, Bon loved and respected his parents; it was just that he rejected their way of life, as he saw it, the slow quiet suburban death of stolid conformity and insincere gestures. No gesture was ever so sincere as the finger Bon gave to all of this—to polite society, the silent majority, which, with its blinkeredness and apathy, was to Bon the antithesis of what life was all about.

Bon surmounted the odds to become a rock'n'roll star, a singer and songwriter. He wasn't so much a singer as he was a screamer. He could play drums, as he did with his father in the Fremantle Pipe Band. But leaving school at 15, he hardly had any grand plans. It would probably have been enough that he stayed out of trouble. It is testimony to Bon's strength of character, his pure desire, that after his stint behind bars he never went back there.

Bon Scott was the personification of the old adage, "It's the singer, not the song." He was never more at home than on stage, and perhaps more than his abilities as a singer and songwriter, he was great as a performer. His brilliance was that you believed in him; that, as they say, he could sell a song. Maybe it was his refusal to take anything, himself especially, too seriously—maybe it was just his impishness—but there was something conspiratorial in his grin that encouraged people who might otherwise never have stepped out of line to join with him in giving the finger to everything dull and constraining.

Something touched a nerve, made a connection. Journalist George Frazier, on the occasion of Janis Joplin's death in 1970, wrote a eulogy to her in the *Boston Globe* which uncannily evokes Bon: ". . . an unkempt, vulgar, obscene girl (though never malicious and with a certain sweetness) who, given a microphone and an audience of her peers, became a wild child. She really couldn't sing very well and she was far more gamin than graceful, and yet the young, as is their way these days, responded to her because of her shortcomings, because of her desecration of discipline. She was marvelous because she was so dreadful, so much animal energy and so little art."

That Bon too was, and still is, reviled almost as equally as he's adored only confirms his potency. There is perhaps a little bit of Bon in everyone, only some people don't want to admit it—people who don't like getting their hands dirty.

Bon's old friends like to say his life was a success story because, it would appear, he got exactly what he wanted. He was initially driven not so much by the need to express himself as the desire, simply, to become a rock'n'roll star, to escape that monstrous suburban straitjacket—and he achieved precisely that.

Vince Lovegrove, who was co-vocalist with Bon in the Valentines in the sixties, wrote in an obituary to his old friend: "To Bon, success meant one thing—more—more booze, more women, more dope, more energy, more rock'n'roll . . . more life!"

They say that being in a rock'n'roll band is a sure way of prolonging adolescence, of putting off growing up—and it is. But by the time AC/DC started to become really successful, Bon had been around for so long that the success only served to illustrate to him what was really important. Fame and riches, in themselves, are empty. The tragedy of Bon's death— along with the fact that in so many ways he died alone in the world—was that he was only just starting to come to terms with a life that had to be lived—which he found he needed to live—beyond rock'n'roll. Off the road. He had always been so busy chasing his dream that he never stopped running. His only refuge was in alcohol and sex. When late in the piece he did find the space and time to glance over his shoulder, or stop at a byway and look at his life, at life in general, he realized what he was missing: a home. It doesn't matter who you are, you need a home to go to.

Bon was a wild man of rock, it's true; but the Bon Scott behind the image was a different person, as is so often the case.

"I encountered Bon Scott a number of times during the seventies," wrote Australian Rock Brain of the Universe Glenn A. Baker, "and each meeting served to increase my incredulity that a performer's public image could be so at odds with his real personality. Bon really was a sweet man. He was warm, friendly and uncommonly funny. He did not breathe fire, pluck wings off flies or eat children whole. And while his daunting stage persona was by no means fraudulent, it was most certainly a professional cloak that could be worn at convenient moments."

Nobody who knew Bon can find a bad word for him. He had great generosity of spirit, perhaps too much. But while he was a consummate professional, as everyone who worked with him testifies, he always leaned heavily on the bottle. The monotony of life on the road ensured it was so. Alcoholic death crept up on him.

Being in a rock'n'roll band is also akin to being adopted by a surrogate family, and to Bon "the band"—whichever band he happened to be in at any given time, from the Valentines in the sixties, through Fraternity in the early seventies, to AC/DC—was always the closest thing he had to a home.

Bon got married during the heady early seventies. But just as the hippie dream went up in smoke, Bon's marriage too fell apart. Bon was torn during those days, to a point where, literally, he almost killed himself. It was only AC/DC that saved him.

AC/DC provided Bon with a new purpose, a new family. With Malcolm and Angus' big brother, former Easybeat George, presiding over AC/DC from his studio lair, the Youngs were a tightly-knit Scots clan that worked on an all-or-nothing, us-against-them basis: Bon, who had the talent they needed, and happily also happened to be a Scot, was accepted as one of them, a blood brother, and that was that.

Bon, however, was a quite different type of person to any of the Youngs. He was outgoing, good-humored, and trusting, while the Youngs were a closed shop, uniformly suspicious, almost paranoid, possessed of the virtual opposite of Bon's generosity of spirit, and prone to sullenness. Just as nobody can find a bad word for Bon, few people who have had dealings with the Youngs can find a good word for them. But Bon was united with Malcolm, Angus and George because they let him in, as they did so few others, and they shared a common goal—the music—and if nothing else, a ribald sense of humor.

Gradually, though, as the band became more successful and the mood within it more businesslike (if not downright venal), and as everyone cultivated their own individual personal lives, Bon found himself more alone than ever. In the end, he really did have nowhere to go.

The other tragedy in Bon's death was not so much that he didn't live to make it (*Highway to Hell,* his last album with the band, was big enough, and after a certain point the magnitude of success becomes academic); it was rather that as a writer, he was only just hitting his stride.

AC/DC never received their critical due during Bon's lifetime. Bon was contemptuous of the critics who didn't even try to understand AC/DC; nevertheless, while there are few artists who don't crave success on both critical and commercial fronts, what was most important and satisfying to Bon was that people simply "got off on it."

But if it's true, as Matisse contended, that an artist's greatness is measured by the number of new signs he introduces to the language, there's no doubt that AC/DC are one of the great rock'n'roll bands.

There's something about listening to old AC/DC albums now, as if, even with all the vitality they still exude, they're preserved in amber. At the time the band was making those records, however, there was nothing else that sounded like them; that so much sounds like them now is testimony to their greatness.

The crosscut riffing which soon became AC/DC's trademark—due to the telepathic communication between the two guitarist brothers, the Gibson and the Gretsch—had a seminal influence on rock as it lurched into the eighties. AC/DC laid the blueprint for what would become known as stadium rock—but also for its official antithesis, the grunge of the '90s (not to mention contemporary "new rock"). The grunge-metal axis which revitalized rock in the nineties owed as much to AC/DC as it did to Led Zeppelin, the Stooges, the New York Dolls, the Velvet Underground, the Sex Pistols, Neil Young, the Ramones and Black Sabbath. Kurt Cobain, after all, taught himself guitar by playing along with AC/DC records.

Critics were slow to acknowledge all this. It's ironic though perhaps understandable, that Brian Johnson, as an outsider who joined AC/DC at a time when they were a fully realized band, has become their one spokesman capable of self-analysis. As he told *RAM* in 1981, ". . . with AC/DC it's so easy and simple, critics can't get into it and therefore they can't describe it." He's saying that AC/DC have none of the identifiable elements that critics like to latch onto, whether they be literary—lyrics that beg to be analyzed—or the obvious signs of traditions inherited, sources updated.

The wordy Bob Dylan is the orthodox rock critic's yardstick against which all else is measured. Dylan invested rock with meaning, made it something "serious" (like it's not serious when Elvis declares, "You ain't nothin' but a hound dog," and turns the entire Western world upside down!). But too many critics suffer from an inferiority complex in the face of their "high art" brethren who look down on rock'n'roll; they seem to think rock'n'roll needs elevation. What they fail to realize is that rock'n'roll was born of base instincts, of disposability and banality—the commercial imperative—and it's still at its glorious best when it revels in these qualities, accepts them only to transcend them, becomes like the brilliant implosion of a dark star which itself dies but burns an indelible mark on those who see it.

It is pretension, not intelligence or sensitivity, that is rock'n'roll's worst enemy. A pretension that is ashamed of rock's gutter origins.

Music, by definition, transcends the literal, and rock'n'roll is at its best when it springs purely from instinct, uncluttered by intellect. Simple and direct, it can have an immediate power that doesn't have to preclude resonance. If Bon fails to fit the orthodox Dylanesque measure of a great rock lyricist, then more power to him. The real point is a matter of attitude, tone, and honesty. Bon was a storyteller who had a terrific eye for detail yet liked to get straight to the moral of the story, and who also, importantly, rejected self-censorship (he was aware, for instance, of the inflammatory nature of a song like "She's Got the Jack" even when he wrote it, but he still went ahead with it).

In a way, AC/DC never fitted in. Clearly, they're not heavy metal, as they're commonly described. Few heavy metal bands have a sense of humor, to start with. AC/DC developed in isolation, in Australia in the mid-seventies, citing only pure, classic fifties rock'n'roll as a source—Little Richard, Chuck Berry—and it's perhaps because they sprang so directly from this untainted well that, whilst their sound might have seemed generic, it was actually because it was so original that it defied description.

Even Britain's *New Musical Express,* AC/DC's erstwhile critical arch-enemy, had to admit upon the release of *Highway to Hell,* "By taking all the unfashionable clichés and metaphors of heavy rock, discarding every ounce of the genre's attendant flab, and fusing those ingredients with gall, simplicity and deceptive facility into a dynamic whole, they have created an aesthetic of their own."

Says Rick Rubin: "When I was in junior high in 1979, my classmates all liked Led Zeppelin. But I loved AC/DC. When I'm producing a rock band, I try to create albums that sound as powerful as *Highway to Hell.* Whether it's the Cult or the Red Hot Chili Peppers, I apply the same basic formula: Keep it sparse. Make the guitar parts more rhythmic. It sounds simple, but what AC/DC did is almost impossible to duplicate. A great band like Metallica could play an AC/DC song note for note, and they still wouldn't capture the tension and release that drives the music. There's nothing like it."

There is something uniquely Australian about this. AC/DC's down-to-earth, no-frills style—a sense of modesty almost, even in their arrogance; a passion more appropriate to amateurs, and a disdain for self-indulgence—coupled with a spirit of belligerent independence, a devout work ethic, and a profound sense of irreverence, has provided a model, one way or another, for practically every other Australian rock'n'roll act that has subsequently succeeded overseas, from INXS to Nick Cave to Silverchair to Jet.

Bon was color to the band's movement. As such, as a rock'n'roll star, he was granted license to exercise a total lack of restraint, in both his life and art. His fans admired him because he wasn't afraid of anything; it seemed that he never stopped to think, just leapt straight in—he gave. He drew his art from life, the rampant fornicator stripped bare. The classic bluesmen addressed many of the same issues, only with more finesse—as does a contemporary black artist like Prince—but Bon, free of all artifice and pretension, talked plain to such a point that it went under the heads of many.

But even if Bon might have had better writing ahead of him, that he still left us with such classics as "High Voltage," "Long Way to the Top," "Jailbreak," "Live Wire," "She's Got Balls," "Ride On," "Let There Be Rock," "Whole Lotta Rosie" and "Highway to Hell," is enough. Certainly, AC/DC has produced little of equal stature since; to this day, the guts of their live set derives from their first six years with Bon.

By 1979, AC/DC was an altogether different entity to what it once was. Torn by ambition, paranoia and betrayal, the band had become big business. Bon's de facto family had left home. Both Malcolm and Angus were buying houses and had girlfriends, whom they would eventually marry. Bon meanwhile, on a return trip to Australia, bought a motorcycle. With customary bravado, he joked that he wasn't ready yet to settle down. But in reality, unimpressed by all the glittery excess and phoniness of stardom, and, if nothing else, just plain tired—or maybe, just finally starting to become a little jaded—he was determinedly trying to remain in touch with his roots, with the old friends he had who he knew were true friends. That he lacked the soul mate he so desired ate away at him. The bottle, and rock'n'roll—always the music—was all that sustained him meantime. He was working on new material for an album he knew would be as huge as *Back in Black* turned out. He was excited at the prospects. But then, suddenly, surprisingly, his life, his body, demanded its own back.

For too long, Bon had pushed himself too hard. He could give no more.

"The trouble with eulogizing a Janis Joplin," concluded George Frazier, "is that, in doing so, we are eulogizing not achievement or artistry but a lifestyle that did no one any good, neither her nor those who idolized her. To try to pass off as art what was merely drunk and disorderly is to mislead the young. There are times when to speak ill of the dead is not to do a disservice, but to endow a wastrel existence with a certain significance—a cautionary memento mori to would-be disciples. In other words, what comfort is Southern Comfort when it contributes to the early end of a foolish little girl? Sometimes the young are very stupid."

"Jailbreak" became a self-fulfilling prophecy. Like the song's hero, Bon broke his shackles—but only to be shot down in flight.

Up in the hills: Bon helps prepare the site for the Myponga
Pop Festival outside Adelaide, January 1971.

1. ADELAIDE, 1974

Well, I feel like a shirt that ain't been worn
Feel like a sheep that ain't been shorn
Feel like a baby that ain't been born
Feel like a rip that ain't been torn
     Wish I'd done something so I could boast
But I've had one less than the Holy Ghost
And I hear that he's had less than most
I been up in the hills too long
     That old sow's gettin' too old now
I been up in the hills too long
Ain't a thing on the farm that's safe from harm
I been up in the hills too long
     Well, I feel like a song that ain't been sung
 I feel like a phone that ain't been rung
I feel like a barrel that ain't been brung
Feel like a murderer that ain't been hung
     Wish I'd done something so I could brag
I feel like a squirrel that ain't been bagged
25 years and I ain't been shagged
Been up in the hills too long
     Well, I feel like an egg that ain't been laid
I feel like a bill that ain't been paid
I feel like a giant that ain't been slayed
I feel like a sayin' that ain't been sayed
     Well, I don't think things can get much worse
I feel my life is in reverse

One more fuck it'll be my first
I been up in the hills too long.
                    —Bon Scott, "Been Up in the Hills Too Long" (1974)

FEBRUARY 1974. Bon Scott was working on the weigh bridge at the Wallaroo fertilizer plant, down by the docks at Port Adelaide, South Australia. Loading trucks. Unloading trucks. It was backbreaking work, but Bon had never been afraid of work. He was a Scot, after all, and the Scots virtually invented the Protestant work ethic.

He sweated it out in the heat and grime, listening to a transistor radio. Bon was a small man—5' 5"—but somehow he was imposing. He had an implacable sort of frame. It took punishment well. The tattoos completed the picture.

No, Bon wasn't afraid of hard work—Bon Scott wasn't afraid of anything—it was just that he preferred not to have to do it. That, after all, was why he had got into rock'n'roll in the first place. It wasn't even so much for the chicks, because Bon could always score—women just seemed to like Bon, and Bon loved women. It was work Bon wanted to avoid, the daily, nine-to-five grind of selling that too-large a piece of your soul in return for what? A nagging wife, an interminable mortgage, screaming hungry mouths to feed? The last thing Bon ever wanted was to feel a yoke around his neck.

Bon wanted to be able to wake up when he felt like it, wherever he found himself. He wanted to do as he pleased, see the world, try everything. He wanted to be able to get on stage and strut his stuff and feel people appreciated it. He wanted to be able to believe in himself.

But Bon's rock'n'roll dream had recently gone wrong. He'd just returned from England with, or rather without, Fraternity, the band he'd joined after the Valentines broke up. A wastrel tribe of spoiled hippies, Fraternity had gone overseas expecting success to land in their lap. When that didn't happen, they were stumped. Eventually they straggled home, embittered and in disarray.

With his young marriage also in tatters, Bon was altogether without a rudder. It was the first time since before he joined his first band, the Spektors, in 1964 that he was not in a band; and being in a rock'n'roll band that was going somewhere, or at least entertained the hope of going somewhere, was what justified Bon's life. Not since the Spektors turned pro had Bon worked a day job. He didn't even have his wife Irene to support him now.

Bon was crashing at a tiny place former Fraternity leader Bruce Howe had in Semaphore. He was getting around on the new bike he'd bought—a Triumph, which everyone told him was just too big—and seeing Irene and squabbling with her.

To keep himself out of any more trouble, and just to keep his hand in, Bon was mucking around with an outfit called the Mount Lofty Rangers, and it was then that he wrote "Been Up in the Hills Too Long." A bluegrass stomp, it referred nominally to the farm in the Adelaide hills that had once been Fraternity's communal home. But with its mood of discontent, it was perhaps more prophetic than literal.

One Friday night in late February, the Rangers were rehearsing at the Old Lion Hotel in North Adelaide. Bon arrived on his bike, late, and a bit pissed. There was nothing unusual in that. Bon was always running late, and he always carried a flask of Johnnie Walker or Southern Comfort in his pocket. The heady days of tripping were over, but the scene had now become a pretty heavy drinking one.

Bon was upset and angry. He'd had a tiff with Irene. That wasn't unusual either—Bon and Irene fought all the time—but this time Bon had been tipped over the edge. Bon's fuse was by any standards a long one; but that night, with all the energy that had previously found an outlet on stage pent up inside him, he snapped.

Bon got drunker and more agitated, and took it out on the musicians. The musicians responded in kind. Absolutely blind, Bon stormed off, telling everyone to get fucked. This was his dark side, when he didn't care even for his own safety, when his recklessness became purely self-destructive. Everyone told him, Don't get on your bike, Bon, you're too pissed to ride. Bon told them to fuck off. He furiously threw an empty bottle on the ground, and, amid smashed glass, roared off.

The hospital rang Irene in the early hours of Saturday morning. Irene rang Vince Lovegrove, one of Bon's oldest friends, who lived just around the corner. Calls from his friend at all hours were not unusual, Vince later recalled in the obituary he wrote to Bon, but this time Vince knew something was wrong as soon as the phone woke him. He too had watched Bon ride off into the night.

"I went and picked up Irene and we went down to the hospital," Lovegrove said. "Bon was a mess. All his teeth were wired up, he was on a respirator, and he was abusing the nurses, abusing them through this respirator!"

A report ran the following day in the *News* under the headline SINGER

INJURED. "Well-known Adelaide pop singer Bon Scott has been seriously injured in a motorcycle accident," it read. "Scott, who suffered a broken arm, broken leg, broken nose and concussion in the accident at Croydon, is in a serious condition at the Queen Elizabeth Hospital intensive care ward."

After three days in and out of consciousness, and then four weeks in traction, Irene finally took Bon home. He had almost died; but maybe, as things so often are, the accident was meant to happen. Bon was certainly one to believe in fate. Mobility was central to Bon's philosophy of life: it was just, keep moving. And here he was laid up with his leg in a cast, with wires through his jaw, resenting the hell out of his condition, but finally being forced to stop and think.

He decided that he had to leave Fraternity, Adelaide, even Irene. He didn't want to give up on his marriage, but he had to. His calling was somewhere out there on the road, and Irene just wanted to settle down. And while he appreciated the fact that Fraternity had opened his musical horizons after the shallow Valentines, he realized he'd had enough of this serious shit. He wanted to rock'n'roll, pure and simple.

Bon had to find a ticket out.

When he got back on his feet, Vince, who was working as a concert promoter, gave him some odd jobs to do—putting up posters, driving around visiting bands, painting the office. In August, Vince brought a virtually unknown band by the name of AC/DC to town.

It was the answer to all Bon's prayers.

Vince kept telling Bon how good these kids were, and urging him to come down and have a look at them. They wanted a new singer and Vince had the idea of putting them and Bon together. Bon was skeptical, but he went along to see them one night anyway.

Hobbling into the Pooraka Hotel, Bon had no idea he was staring his future in the face. But AC/DC was everything he could have asked for—a gung-ho young rock'n'roll band in need of a front man. If Bon had any doubts about himself—that he wasn't fully recovered from the accident, or that at 28 he was getting on a bit—they were swept aside. AC/DC and Bon were made for each other.

Within weeks, Bon was playing his debut performance with the band in Sydney. The Youngs had found the link they were after. AC/DC were on their way.

Inspired though he was, Bon knew it was still going to be a long way to the top, but he was prepared to give everything he had. For the old man, as his new young cohorts called him, it would be third time lucky.

High Street, Kirriemuir, in the late 1940s.

2. SCOTLAND

An Arctic wind whips across the Roods on the upper side of the small Scottish town of Kirriemuir, where Bon Scott spent the first six years of his life.

Kirriemuir nestles in the foothills of the Grampians, low in the highlands in the county of Angus, in southeast Scotland. Known as the "gateway to the glens," it is today a town of barely 5,000 inhabitants—a quaint, rustic, tiny network of narrow streets and lanes onto which red-stone buildings crowd for frontage.

Kirriemuir grew up around its sole industry, jute-spinning (jute is a flax-like fiber used in canvas manufacture). In the eighteenth century, with the arrival of the loom, the town was thriving. But by now, Kirriemuir has outlived its usefulness. It is notable only as the birthplace of J.M. Barrie, creator of Peter Pan. Bon doesn't get a look in.

It's a little more sheltered down in town, on Bank Street, where Bon's father Chick worked with his brother George in the bakery owned by their father, Alec. Alexander Scott had started the business in 1920, two years after Charles, to give Chick his proper name, was born.

It was warm in the floury air of the bakehouse, where the men worked long and hard. But the days seem short when you get up in the middle of the night to start baking for dawn, when dawn itself is late and sunset early, and you're a young man who likes a bit of a lark. Chick had wanted to go to sea with his friend Angus, but his parents wouldn't allow it. Instead, he served an apprenticeship at the bakery, and joined the local territorial Citizen Military Forces (CMF).

When the Second World War broke out in 1939, Chick was one of the first to go. He was 22. He served in the army as a baker, in France initially and then Ireland, North Africa and Italy.

Before he was sent to France, Chick was stationed in Kirkcaldy, a seaport just across the Firth of Forth from Edinburgh, and it was there that he met Bon's mother, Isa. Isobelle Cunningham Mitchell was one of the four daughters of George Mitchell. Her family was, as she put it, just "ordinary folk, workin' folk." She was lean and small, a pretty girl with strong bones and sharp eyes. Chick was a bit of a wag, with tattoos on his forearms and a gaunt handsomeness.

Isa and Chick both enjoyed music. "I met him at the dancing," Isa remembers fondly.

Music has always been common ground in Scotland, a country otherwise almost schizophrenic in character. With the sort of puritanical religious heritage that can only be divisive, Scotland is governed by tensions. The tension between arrogance and modesty, material poverty and cultural wealth; between dependence and a rebel streak, stoicism and wild release; between those who drink too much and those who don't touch a drop—and worst of all, between getting drunk and getting sober. Scotland still has more deaths due to drinking than just about anywhere else in the Western world—and just as many wowsers to shake a finger at the fact.

Chick and Isa Scott maintain their own balance. Isa, who disapproves of drink, buzzes with nervous energy, chattering incessantly. Chick is more reserved, laconic. As a youngster, he admits, "I just liked to get out and have a good time, be a bit of a delinquent."

Music ran through life in Scotland after radio and before TV, and so it did through both Chick and Isa's families. Chick's father used to do a bit of singing, and his mother, Jayne Belford Nielson, encouraged musical activity. Five years Chick's senior, his brother George played piano in local bands, and George's children would go on to play various instruments as well. Chick had taken lessons on piano and fiddle, but he never stuck at it.

Isa's family was musical too: "We just loved music. Mum would play the piano. Dad played the piano, and the organ, had a lovely operatic voice."

Scotland was little affected by the war and life for Isa went on as usual in Kirkcaldy. Just no lights at night time. And the fact that her man was away fighting.

Chick and Isa married in 1941 on one of his leaves from Ireland. Chick's mother didn't exactly approve of the marriage—she felt Isa's social station was beneath the Scotts'—but Chick was determined. In 1943, Isa gave birth to a son, Sandy. He died nine months later. Chick never saw him.

LEFT: Bon at one, with Isa. Chick in the background. Kirriemuir, July 1947. RIGHT: The young Ron: "He was into everything."

Chick was demobbed on the very last day of 1945 and he and Isa moved to Kirriemuir. Chick's father bought the couple the house in the Roods, which Isa named Raymondscraig after a park she used to visit in Kirkcaldy. It was a small terraced house, but it was plenty for frugal people.

Chick and Isa would go out to the dancing. Isa would go to church on Sundays. Chick was a member of the local amateur light opera company (Gilbert and Sullivan), and played drums in the Kirriemuir Pipe Band.

ISA: "There was a pipe band nearly every week, every Saturday night, marching through the square."

So the world that Bon entered as Ronald Belford Scott, on July 9, 1946, was a happy one. The war was over and, as Chick recalls, "I was in business with my father, and my brother, so we hadnae money troubles or anything."

The young Bon, or Ron, as his mother still calls him, was a typical tyke: "He was into everything. A mind of his own. He went walking himself, I never had to do anything, he just walked in one day."

By the time Bon started school he was already displaying errant traits.

ISA: "He used to never come home from school. He'd just go off with some of his little mates, and never think of comin' up the hill. I used to have to go chase him. So it started young!

"He was mischievous, I would say, more than anything. Not naughty. He just had a mind of his own and if he wanted to do something, that was it."

He had also started to display an early musical bent.

ISA: "Mad on drums, he was, mad on drums. Played on a biscuit tin. Or the bread board, he could practice on a bread board. He loved it. People heard him practicing, and they knew."

And so when the pipe band marched through the town square every Saturday night, the peeling of the pipes rising into the Scottish sky, silver in the summer's twilight, "Ron," Isa still huffs exasperatedly, "had to get and march up and down with them."

Life was steady for the Scotts. Isa had given birth to another son, Derek, in 1949. But, as Chick says, "You get a bit unsettled after six years in the army."

Scotland has long seen its sons and daughters migrate to greener climes, and never more so than in the fifties and sixties. If there was a postwar boom going on, it certainly wasn't happening in Scotland. It was happening in places like America, Canada, New Zealand and Australia. This was a time when the New World was encouraging migrants from its British forebear, when it needed people to build a future. Australia was offering assisted passages, which meant British families could travel, by boat, for a mere ten pounds. And Scotland was never going to get any warmer.

ISA: "My sister lived in Melbourne; they migrated about a year before us, her with her husband and her little girl, June, and that put us on edge then. We thought, Oh, I'd love to go out there too."

Australia was a new frontier in the 1950s, a huge underpopulated continent bursting with potential wealth. Since it had escaped the war relatively unscathed, the emphasis was not so much on rebuilding as on simply building. But even before the war Australia had believed, as then prime minister Billy Hughes put it, that it had to "populate or perish" in the face of Asia's teeming millions. So in 1947 Australia embarked on a massive immigration program.

Of course, it was based on the so-called White Australia Policy. Australia's ideal migrant was exclusively European, and preferably British. Australia offered a fresh start, a sunny, open vista for those prepared to take the plunge—and thousands of Britons were happy to leave behind their gray, wartorn homeland.

The number of British migrants fell short of expectations, however—mainly because there weren't enough ships to transport them—and

Australia, still in need of people, then opened up to refugees from camps in Southern Europe. By 1951, these displaced people comprised half of the migrant intake.

By 1955, Australia—a country with a prewar population of barely seven million—welcomed its millionth migrant. If "welcomed" is the right word. "Wogs" and "dagoes" were openly resented. Not even the English were unreservedly accepted; Australians could never quite shake their suspicion of "whingeing Poms." They liked to pour scorn on the Irish, too, but for various reasons the Scots were embraced unqualifiedly.

Australia and the Celts generally have much in common. Australia's roots, as a British penal colony, are as Irish as they are English, after all. And just as Ireland and Scotland have long been downtrodden by England, so too has Australia. Australia shares with the Celts a rebel streak and a wry, laconic sense of humor, not to mention a terrific thirst. But while Australians felt threatened by the Catholicism of the Irish, they could readily identify with the Scots and their Protestant heritage.

It's unlikely, then, that the young Ronald Scott ever suffered racial taunts in Australia. And if he did, well, he was a tough little nut, who could always stand up for himself with a belligerence that belied his small stature.

The Scotts arrived in Australia in 1952. Bon was six.

ISA: "Coming out on the boat I used to sing to Ron, I used to learn him tunes, all the words. Just singing them over. He picked them up good."

They landed in Melbourne, and moved in with Isa's sister, who lived in Sunshine, a suburb in Melbourne's industrial west. Then they got their own house at the bottom of the street. Sunshine is situated next door to Footscray, helping to form the wrong-side-of-the-tracks enclave that is western Melbourne. In the early fifties, the area was a haven for migrants—Italian and Greek as well as British—who lived in rows of terraced houses and worked in local factories.

Life in Sunshine was rough and tumble, but in an era of full employment, few went without the necessities. Chick got a job as window-framer. The future was wide open.

Bon was enrolled in Sunshine Primary School.

ISA: "He even played on little drums when he went to the first school at Sunshine. The kids used to march to school and Ron was at the end of the line playing the drums. It kept everybody in step.

"I used to go to church on a pushbike in Sunshine. Ron used to like going to church. Not that there was anything in it, he just liked the singing. But that was as far as it went. Oh, they all went to Sunday school when we first came out here, until they got old enough to say, Oh, I'm not going back there."

In 1953, a fourth son, Graeme, was born, a baby brother for Bon and Derek. The red-haired, freckle-faced Bon was in grade one at the time.

ISA: "Ron loved music. He started off in school with a recorder. He wanted to learn piano, we had a beautiful piano, he was seven years old at the time, but he wouldnae go to the lessons. So after a while, he wanted an accordion. So what did we do, we sold the piano and bought an accordion, and he went to lessons for that. That lasted a while. Ah, but he wanted to play the drums. We sold the accordion and he got his first drum set. Of course, he picked that up himself then. You never had to tell him to do that, it was just natural to him."

At the same time, Bon's tearaway spirit was starting to take flight.

ISA: "He used to go to Footscray baths, and come home and tell me he'd been jumping from the highest diving board. That's just the kind of person he was. You wouldnae have to dare him to do it."

When Bon learnt to swim, he was extremely pleased with himself. He liked the feeling of weightlessness, of drive, as if he could break away from all earthly bonds. But of course, that wasn't enough. He had to scale the high-diving board. He would properly fly now.

Everybody would be watching, all the girls as well as the boys, and they would have to be impressed by anyone so brave. So Bon climbed the tower, and standing up there, on the end of the board where it's springy and slippery, he might have felt a twinge of fear if he wasn't already consumed by his own performance, aware that all eyes were upon him. From way up above, he could see the other kids standing around the pool's edge, teeth chattering in the cold, but transfixed by him. And then the lifeguard noticed, and shouted, Hey, come on now, you come down from there this instant; and that was all the encouragement Bon needed. It was then and only then that he commenced his descent. He paused for the beat—an early indication of his natural sense of timing—and then he leapt. And as he flew through the air, he felt a rush of blood through his small tensile frame and he felt more alive than he ever had in his short life.

He hit the water with a belly-flopping splash. His flapping around as he broke the surface was equaled only by that of the lifeguards at poolside. He climbed out of the water, and now he maybe even felt more alive, as his body reverberated and he was at once chided by the adults and had all the kids wide-eyed and open-mouthed. The boys were full of admiration and envy; the girls, fear and wonder.

Bon had just taken his first curtain call, and he liked it. It was the sort of high he would spend the rest of his life chasing.

In 1956, Graeme was diagnosed with asthma and the family moved to Perth, 1700 miles away. The doctors said the hot dry climate of the west would be better for him.

Bon was going on ten. Rock'n'roll had just hit. The world would never be the same again. Bon's world was about to change, too—for that reason as well as others.

Scotland's *Fife Free Press* reported in 1962: "One of the side drummers in the Fremantle Pipe Band, who played at the opening ceremony of the Empire Games in Perth, was Ronald Scott, son of Mr. and Mrs. Charles Scott, who formerly resided in Roods, Kirriemuir."

3. FREMANTLE

Standing at the mouth of the Swan River, some 12 miles south of Perth, the port town of Fremantle has a sandy, windswept beach front typical of the Western Australian coastline. Established in 1829, Fremantle remained a busy port until after the Second World War, when the wharfing tradition worldwide went into slow decline due to the effects of containerization. Fremantle was nonetheless still the docklands, the dangerous, bustling stamping ground of sailors, spivs, prostitutes and all manner of hard men.

In the fifties, the town was boosted by the construction of the Kwinana industrial complex some 15 miles to the south. People started to make their homes in Fremantle, among them the Scotts.

Chick went ahead of the rest of the family. He had a job lined up with the same firm he'd worked for in Melbourne. Chick would find a place for the family to live, while Isa packed up house in Sunshine. He signed a short lease on a house in South Fremantle, before he found one to buy on the other side of the river.

ISA: "North Fremantle was a nice place when they were growing up, it used to be like a country town."

The Scotts' home, on Harvest Road, was a big red-brick Federation house that stood on the peak of a rise overlooking the river.

ISA: "I joined a Scottish club in Fremantle, and my husband joined the Caledonian Society, and that's why we got to know people."

Chick also joined the Scots pipe band which was a good part of the pride of Fremantle. Bon tagged along with his father, and joined the band too, as a side-drummer.

"Before TV, we used to sit around and listen to the radio," said Bon's youngest brother Graeme. "My dad and Ron used to go out to practice for the pipe band, drumming. It was a big occasion when the bands played, the whole family used to go out, put on their kilts, strap the drums on. Me and Derek would follow behind. Those were the big occasions, Scottish things."

Bon and Derek attended North Fremantle Primary. Bon was never greatly enamoured of school, but he got by, and didn't get into any more trouble than most headstrong boys.

Chick and Isa were dedicated parents. They pretty much allowed the three boys the run of the house, but when they did say jump, they meant jump! The boys, in turn, respected their parents' authority, and didn't push them. It was this upbringing that taught Bon the good manners that never deserted him.

Outside school, Bon had his musical pursuits, and the river was nearby.

ISA: "You never needed to worry where they were, they were always down the river. All the time. They'd just walk down—didn't need a car, we didn't have a car at that time, it was just two minutes away—so then they'd come home for something to eat, then they'd go down again . . . Derek was a quiet kid. Ron was more outgoing, he had a lot of friends."

Bon appeared on stage for the first time at North Fremantle Town Hall, when he played a recorder duet with a friend in a school concert.

In 1959, aged 12, Bon started secondary school at John Curtin High. He also started to get into the more serious sort of mischief that boys of that age will. As his adulthood friend Pat Pickett put it, "When you're a kid, there's always one guy who did it when he was 12, you know—Bon was that guy."

Rock'n'roll was also starting to set a bead on Bon's mind.

Australia's first baby-boom teenagers were knocked for six, as they would have put it themselves, when in 1956 they saw *The Blackboard Jungle*, the film that sported Bill Haley's "Rock Around the Clock" as its theme. It was the first rock'n'roll song Australia had heard.

Isolated Anglophile Australia could not have even begun to anticipate rock'n'roll. In the United States, rock'n'roll, for the early fifties, was a thundercloud brewing on the horizon, the music and the attitude of the urban black ghetto and rural white trash alike. In Britain, restless kids—tomorrow's teddy boys—were just waiting for something like rock'n'roll to come along.

In the early 1950s, however, Australia still clung culturally to Mother

LEFT: Harvest Road, Fremantle, 1956. Bon (right), younger brother Derek (center).
RIGHT: In fancy dress. Graeme Scott: "He loved the attention."

England's apron strings. Accents and attitudes on the radio assumed British parentage. Australian country music was a unique, indigenous innovation, but it meant little in the cities.

Australian kids at the time, to borrow Nik Cohn's description of pre-rock'n'roll English teens, "shared everything with their parents . . . danced to the same music, sat through the same films, [wore] the same clothes." Bodgies and widgies were inner city toughs who had emerged during the war in response to visiting American servicemen and all the cultural baggage they carried—the stylish cut of their clothes, the music they liked to dance to, their exotic slang—but even after the war, bodgies were still reveling in archaic swing jazz. There had to be something more than Frank Sinatra.

"Rock Around the Clock," then, was a revelation. Elvis, not much later, sealed it. Overnight, a Sydneyside Frank Sinatra/Johnnie Ray imitator, Johnny O'Keefe, became a Bill Haley imitator. Haley himself was nothing more than a second-string hillbilly singer who got lucky on a black R&B trip. And this was the very birth of Australian rock'n'roll—an imitation of an imitation.

Both Britain and Australia produced little first generation rock'n'roll of much worth because neither country had any tradition in the Ameri-

"Old Year's Night," 1957. Bon and Chick dressed up to play. Isa: "He was mad on pipe bands until he got to 17, and then he went right against the kilt."

can roots of the music. Britain went on to produce great rock'n'roll in the sixties—in contrast to Australia's very erratic output—because young British musicians sought out those roots and consciously emulated them. Australia, on the other hand, was denied the opportunity to hear the great body of American black music because local record companies, colonial outposts to British head offices, refused to release it.

Johnny O'Keefe couldn't help but be a mere facsimile of rock'n'roll, an entertainer sooner than a singer, who simply changed his stripes. But even if O'Keefe started a long way from the source, and even if he admitted himself he was a limited singer, he became a convincing enough rock'n'roll performer because he found in rock'n'roll something that aligned directly with his own larrikin spirit. O'Keefe became a star for the very reason that Australians identified with him as one of their own—and that was an epochal transcendence of the "cultural cringe," Australia's traditional inferiority complex. For perhaps the first time ever, urban Australians embraced a musician because of his Australianness.

In O'Keefe's wake, rock'n'roll stormed the barricades. It was grappling in the dark—guitarists had to build their own instruments, copying designs out of photographs of American bands—but it was naive enough not to become discouraged.

Said Bon himself in the film *Let There Be Rock*, "Back in about 1957 or '8, I used to sing in the shower, and my mum used to say, Ron, if you can't sing proper songs, shut up; don't sing this rock'n'roll garbage."

Australian kids had got a hold on rock'n'roll, even if it was only a toehold, and they weren't going to let it go. Bon was absorbed by the drums.

CHICK: "What was he, novice champion at 12? And then he was under-17 champion for five years."

GRAEME SCOTT: "He played on TV one time, he went on and played drums while there was this girl who did the highland dancing, there was a piper there.

"He loved the attention from the girls. He was in the paper one time, in the Scottish get-up, with two highland dancers, about the same age as him, 12 or 13, and he had this big smile on his face."

But even as Chick and Isa took pride in the lead Bon set, he was courting disaster. Going down to the river now was a less innocent exercise. Boys would be puffing on cigarettes, and sneaking off behind the bushes with girls. School was a meeting place that was only barely neutral. Kids in gangs from surrounding neighborhoods converged at school, enacting an uneasy truce which would be broken as soon as they were out of their school uniforms.

To grow up working-class in Australia in the fifties was to grow up tough. You had to be able to fight, and if you didn't keep your guard up vigilantly, you would be knocked down. To be knocked down was to be weak, and being weak meant you were the lowest of the low.

As William Dick wrote in *A Bunch of Ratbags*, his classic documentary novel of growing up a bodgie in mythical Melbourne suburb Goodwood, a thinly disguised version of Footscray: "If you didn't belong to a mob, you just didn't belong. The kids in mobs picked on you and you got belted up and made to fear them. But if you belonged to a mob, you were given a certain amount of respect."

GRAEME: "Ron and his friends Terry and Moe formed the nucleus of a gang, and once they got their cars, they were full on."

Bon was drumming, swimming, learning to fuck and learning to fight. School came a poor last and he left as soon as he legally could, when he turned 15 in 1961. He got a job as a farmhand on a market-garden, driving a tractor. Later his friend Terry got him a job on the crayfishing boats, as hard a way to make a living as there is.

Being a fisherman proved too much even for Bon though, so he quickly chucked it in and got a job working for Avery Scales, as an apprentice weighing-machine mechanic.

Bon was a rocker. Rockers superseded bodgies. Bodgies had abandoned Johnnie Ray to jump on the rock'n'roll bandwagon, but the move—to rockers especially, who, as their name suggests, were born of rock'n'roll—was typically transparent. Rockers could be identified by their slicked-back hair, leather jackets and skintight pants (as opposed to bodgies' preppier Tony Curtis crew-cuts and cardigans), and they were into Elvis, Little Richard, Jerry Lee Lewis, Chuck Berry. Buddy Holly, Fats Domino, and the like were considered weak, far too tame and clean cut. It was the bad boys that rockers like Bon were into.

Perhaps only the details distinguished one cult from another, however. Sidney Baker's definition of the archetypal larrikin could equally be applied to bodgies, rockers or mods, and would certainly seem to apply to Bon. "He dressed with exaggerated precision, he extracted comfort from being a member of a gang, he was alleged to have too much money and to lack parental control, he looked upon refinement in social conduct as a form of weakness ... he was given to spasms of violence ... [he had] contempt for anything effeminate."

"It was all rock'n'roll, jiving," said Maureen Henderson, who hung around with Bon and her brother Terry, Bon's best mate. "Me and Bonnie, we were a couple of the best jivers in Fremantle. He was a good jiver."

Movies, which Bon went to see at the drive-in, were a primary source of inspiration—*The Girl Can't Help It, Hot Rod Gang, Jailhouse Rock, King Creole*. All things American, like rock'n'roll itself, were exotic and attractive. Everybody was especially into the cars. Befinned and chromed American tanks were a symbol of everything truculent young Australians aspired to—they were flash and fast and dangerous.

Bon was thumbing his nose at authority. Although there was an impishness about his defiance—a bravado that rather innocently asked, who says I can't—Bon could turn nasty when provoked, striking back with unforgiving viciousness. He was only small, but he had a fearsome reputation as a street fighter, who could not only tear a bigger man apart, but would himself refuse to be beaten.

MAUREEN HENDERSON: "They went up to East Perth to get tattoos. Terry got "Death Before Dishonour" on his arm, and Bonnie got that one, just above his hairline, when he pulled his jeans down. Terry was sitting on one side of him, I was on the other side, and tears were just rolling down his face. He couldn't do his jeans up for weeks, he had to stay at home.

Because he used to wear these ... we used to call them stovepipes, and his were so tight, he put them on by turning them inside out and rolling them up his legs."

GRAEME: "In those days, in Fremantle, it was all gangs. Gangs were pretty hard in those days. There was nothing else to do. Other gangs didn't come into your neighborhood unless they wanted to fight."

Said Vince Lovegrove, who would later form the Valentines with Bon, but then lived in the more sedate, semi-rural Applecross: "I used to play football, when I was about 14 or 15, and we used to be shit scared of going down and playing South Fremantle, because they were the rough team.

"Fremantle was always looked down upon by the rest of Perth. It was a scary place. There was a picture theatre there, and I went to see a movie there one night, I had to get a bus, and I remember my parents giving me this lecture, Come straight home, don't hang around, there's a lot of bodgies and rockers there, just be careful."

Bon's gang consisted of him and Terry, his best mate, and Moe, Dave, Archie and Dick, plus Maureen and a couple of other girls. Girls were very much second-class citizens. The gang cruised, and hung out. On weekends, they went to dances, which were as good for blues as they were for sheilas, for fighting and fucking. They seldom went to pubs; occasionally, they'd down a couple of bottles, or pass around a flagon of port, but drinking was not a priority. The big thing was just hanging out, in Fremantle, at the Cafe de Wheels. The car park would be packed with Customlines, Ford single-spinners, Chevys, Dodge Customs, and all the boys would be milling around them. Brawls erupted like flash fires, over nothing—it was merely testing your mettle. At other times, down dead-end back roads or at deserted beaches, there were gang bangs.

It was a lifestyle uncannily similar to that described by William Dick's hero Terry in *A Bunch of Ratbags*:

We'd been running with the pack for nine months or so, and were we tough! We had proved this in our many street brawls. I hadn't had so much fun in my whole life since I had become a bodgie and joined the boys. We had plenty of sheilas knocking around with us, and there was always one of them willing to indulge in love play with us. There were also the other real tough widgies, who thought nothing of taking on a dozen or so of our boys in a back-up [gang bang]. I had been in a couple of back-ups since joining up, and I thought they were terrific fun.

All the boys reminded me of a lot of dogs chasing after a bitch that was on heat when they were arguing about who was next and worrying about missing out on a turn.

Like they'd seen in the movies, Bon and his mates further tested their mettle by racing their cars.

MAUREEN: "There was one time, they had this drag down at Port Beach, Terry had this car, it was a Ford, single-spinner. They were mad on cars. They used to pinch them too, go for a ride. Anyway, there were dragging, and Bonnie hit this FJ, a ute [utility van], split it in half. Oh, they used to drag down there all the time.

"They used to go out and knock fuel off. I would have to go look-out while they siphoned it."

In early 1963 Perth was experiencing what *West Australian* columnist Athol Thomas said, "appears to be one of Perth's worst outbreaks of larrikinism." Bodgies "plagued" the Windmill Tearooms, forcing it to move from the city to Subiaco, and finally to close. Police were called in to break up, as the *West Australian* reported, "between 150 and 200 youths [who] caused an uproar in a North Fremantle snack bar on Sunday morning."

Bon and Terry were well known, by the cops and everyone else alike, as two of the toughest kids in Fremantle. When you're boss cocky, someone's always coming along who wants to try and knock you off your perch, so Bon and Terry had to fend off challengers all the time; fight them and beat them. They also had to put up with the constant attention of the police. If anyone was going to get pinched for anything in Fremantle, Bon and Terry were the first suspects. One time, Terry copped a hiding off the police for something someone else did. Things were starting to get serious.

Bon was running wild in the streets and local legend had him responsible for the vicious beating of a copper.

At the height of this war of attrition, Bon moved in around the corner with Terry and his family. Whether he jumped or was pushed is unclear, but even if his parents weren't entirely naive, Bon wouldn't have wanted them to know the worst, and so he may well have left of his own accord. Either way, he wound up with the Hendersons, where he was accepted unquestioningly. Olive and Jim Henderson already had nine kids, and so with a few other extended-family members also floating around their big house, Bon was hardly noticed.

Bon was drawn to danger; it got the adrenaline flowing and attracted attention in the same way that diving off the high board had all those years

Bon listed as his previous occupations: weighing machine mechanic, crayfisher, postie, farmhand. As a postman, 1965.

ago in Sunshine. But even as he ran by night with the boys, by day he was a diligent worker, and he won Avery's Best First Year Apprentice Award.

ISA: "At that age, you couldn't follow him. He had a mind of his own, that lad. He was mad on pipe bands until he got to 17, and then he wouldn't wear a skirt no more. He went right against the kilt. We just had to go along with him because it was his way. We never said, Don't do that, Ron—if I did say, Don't do that, he would just go out and do it.

"So after he gave up the drums in the pipe band, well, that was all he thought about, music, he wanted to get in a band."

GRAEME: "He knew he wanted to do something with music, but I think he just didn't know how to do it."

Rock'n'roll, by the early sixties, was dead in the water. Elvis was in the army, Buddy Holly was dead, Chuck Berry was in jail, Jerry Lee Lewis was in disgrace and Little Richard was in church. The music business was back in charge. Clean-cut teen idols—all of whom seemed to be named Bobby (Vee, Vinton, Rydell)—were the order of the day.

However, the one new white innovation that did emerge during this period—and hit Australia—was instrumental rock'n'roll. British band the

Shadows inspired young middle-class boys all over Australia to pick up electric guitars. It was a style Australia was better suited to. After all, it was surf music as much as anything, and in the early sixties, beach culture was growing as rapidly and naturally in Australia as it was in California.

Vince Lovegrove was a 14-year-old at Applecross High in 1961, when he joined an outfit called the Dynells. "They were friends of mine, who had a Shadows-type band, because that was the go then, it was just pre-stomps. But they were still mainly surfies we played to. We used to play all the surf clubs down the coast.

"We used to put our own shows on in the beginning, hire a local hall, buy a couple of crates of soft drink, throw them in a tub of ice, charge double, you know. This was just pre-Beatles. What would happen was, the band would go out and play their instrumentals, and everyone would be up dancing, and then half way through the night, the singer—that was me—would get up to do a few songs. That was when everyone would take a break and go and get a drink!"

CHICK: "Ron used to go down to Port Beach, they used to have dances down there, and they used to get up and sing there. But he wasn't in a band then."

The Port Beach dances were run by their star, Johnny Young, who would sing a set or two in front of his band, the Nomads. (Young would go on to become one of Australia's biggest stars in the 1960s.)

MAUREEN: "We all used to go to the stomps down at Port Beach, but we didn't like Johnny Young, we thought he was a poof or something, so we used to call out, We want Bonnie! We want Bonnie!"

Bon would jump up and have a sing, but he wouldn't do some wimpy ballad, rather a rock'n'roll song, like "Long Tall Sally" or "Blue Suede Shoes."

MAUREEN: "All the girls used to go wild over him, and I think that caused a bit of trouble. Johnny Young used to get pretty upset."

The first Beatles single "Please, Please Me" was released in Australia around this time, in February 1963. It stiffed. It would be almost a year before their second, "She Loves You," went straight to number one.

Bon, meantime, had been to hell and back.

CHICK: "Evidently, someone assaulted a girl at the dance . . ."

ISA: "And he retaliated . . ."

CHICK: "And the police came . . ."

An item ran in the *West Australian* on March 13:

A 16-year-old youth pleaded guilty in the Fremantle Children's Court yesterday to charges of having given a false name and address to the police, having escaped legal custody, having unlawful carnal knowledge and having stolen 12 gallons of petrol.

He was committed to the care of the Child Welfare Department until he was 18 with a recommendation that he be kept in an institution of maximum security.

He was put on a five pound bond to come up for sentence if called on in the next two years on the unlawful carnal knowledge charge.

What happened was that Bon had "gone for a walk" with this girl, who was under the age of consent, and when they got back to the hall, some other guys wanted a piece of her too. Bon launched into them. When the police showed up Bon tried to put one over them—and almost succeeded. He took off in Terry's car, only to be apprehended trying to get away with some petrol.

Later, Bon would never much talk about this episode in his life, but he did confide in Silver Smith, a woman with whom he lived for several years. "Something really worried him personally," she recalled. "He had this thing that he had to make it up to his parents for something that had happened way back when. Part of his drive to be successful was to do it for mum and dad. His grandparents came out from Kirriemuir when he was 15 or 16, and this was a big thing for the family; and Bon got into some sort of trouble, and he ended up in remand at this boys' home, and when his parents went to see him, he wanted more than anything to go home, but he was so ashamed that he refused to see his parents—he just wouldn't face up to it. And so he had a choice of either being remanded into his parents' custody, and it all being forgotten, or going through the legal process, and he made the choice of going through the legal process.

"By the time he got out, the grandparents had gone home, and of course, they subsequently died. So he always wanted to do something to rectify that."

Fronting his first band, the Spektors, in 1965. Bon: "I was a drummer in those days, and I used to play half the night on drums and spend the other half singing. The singer also played drums—but not as good as me! Then I got an offer from the Valentines as drummer. But I wanted to be a singer so I joined as singer. It wasn't because I wanted to be up front—it was because the singer used to get more chicks."

4. THE VALENTINES

Wake-up was at six a.m. The screws would come by and rouse their charges. Bon jumped to. He quickly made his bed, folding the blankets just so, army-style. His cell door was opened and, inspection passed, he joined the other boys as they filed down to the showers. Many of them were already puffing on a cigarette. Riverbank was a juvenile institution—the youngest inmates were 14—but they all received a weekly tobacco ration. It was pure horseshit, something called Waldon, but it was something to suck on, something to break the monotony. Butts were saved. The showers were cold.

The day ahead held little brighter promise, maybe dinner if it proved any good, or a sing-along after that. But there were more pitfalls along the way. A cross look, a slip of the tongue, could get you into all sorts of trouble. At worst, you could end up in the box for fighting—and fighting was par for the course.

Riverbank wasn't any ordinary boys' home; it was a prison for boys. It was where the really bad boys went. Bon served nine months there.

Newly built in the early sixties, situated at the base of the scrubby hills on the northeast edge of Perth, Riverbank was a modern brick structure which at least allowed for some light and air and decent facilities. But still, it was a dark, hard place. Kept under lock and key rather than in open dormitories, these boys didn't need too much prodding to become violent. Sexual favors were taken, not given.

During the week, the boys worked in craft shops or around the place in the kitchen or the laundry. Bon would never forget the hours spent on his hands and knees, scrubbing. He missed the fresh air. And it was always cold, freezing cold.

In the evening, after dinner, the boys congregated in a common room. They played cards, listened to the radio. They were encouraged to read, or sing, or play musical instruments. Any activity, in fact, which didn't result in a fight was considered fruitful.

Saturday was a lay day, usually given over to sport. On Saturday night, maybe there'd be a movie. On Sundays, chapel was compulsory, and then after lunch, visitors were allowed. Sometimes a concert was staged for visitors.

Bon decided early on that jail was a mug's game. He was no fool; it was obvious there was no percentage in a life outside the law. He could see that most of his fellow inmates were going to spend the rest of their lives in and out of jail. And that wasn't for Bon. He owed his parents better, if nothing else. He was going to keep his head down and his nose clean—do his time and get out as soon as possible.

The silver lining to Bon's time inside was that he started to take seriously the idea of getting into a band. He was hearing the Beatles on the radio; a change was in the air. He took to spending his recreation periods mucking around on drums, with a couple of other boys. They learnt a few songs, and called themselves a band.

ISA: "We went up to a concert one day there, and he was playing, and he said then, Oh, I'm going to be famous. And I just . . . Anyway, he was keen, he knew that's what he wanted to do. But as a drummer, not as a front man."

Bon was released by Christmas 1963. The carnal knowledge charges would not be proceeded upon. It was deemed that Bon had learnt his lesson. As Isa said, it "mebbe did him the world of good." Bon moved back in with his family.

CHICK: "When he came out of Riverbank, his parole officer said, 'The best thing you can do is get into the CMF [Citizen Military Forces], so I took him up, and I don't know what happened, the parole officer went with him, but they just didnae want him."

Australia was involved in the Vietnam War by then, so Bon had to register for National Service. He was never called up. Later, he would claim, in an interview with a German magazine, "I was rejected by the army, because they said I was socially maladjusted."

Bon put his time at Riverbank behind him. That he was able to do so, when most juvenile offenders return to incarceration, is testament to the firmness of his resolve and his strength of character. All he now wanted to do was get into a band. He could channel all his energy into that.

If Bon had ever had a nasty streak, prison scared it out of him. "Bon didn't have a mean bone in his body," said Wyn Milson, with whom Bon would shortly form his first real band. "He never looked for trouble. But if it happened, he wouldn't walk away. The trouble was, that was when girls started going for guys in bands, and the other guys didn't necessarily appreciate that. I was a little guy myself, and if anyone was harassing me, Bon would always step in. So he got branded as a troublemaker, when in fact he was probably the only one standing up."

Bon got back on the straight and narrow. He got a job as a storeman with the egg board. He was flailing for sweet life at the drum kit he had installed in the bay window of his mother's living room. He met two boys who worked at the Kwinana oil refinery—Wyn Milson, who played guitar, and John Collins, who was a singer—and roped in his friend Brian Gannon, who played bass, and the Spektors were born.

Born in Wales in 1948, Wyn, who lived in Medina, beyond Kwinana, had picked up a guitar after hearing the Shadows. Then the Beatles hit. And then the Stones. And as Wyn put it: "The Shadows were square. Even the Beatles were guys in suits. But the Stones . . .!"

The Spektors were a weekend band who played around on the Perth circuit for a year or so in 1965 before merging with their top rivals the Winztons, fronted by Vince Lovegrove, to form the Valentines.

In the reflected glow of the Beatles, a beat music scene sprang up in Perth, as it did in practically every other city in the Western world. Its king was Johnny Young. Young was training as a DJ when he started playing dances as singer with the Nomads in 1962. In 1965, he was made host of a new local TV show called *Club 17*.

The Spektors played their first performances at the Medina Youth Club in early 1965. This gig was momentous not only for that reason, but also because it was how Bon met a pretty 17-year-old blonde called Maria Van Vlijman, with whom he became infatuated, and spent the next four years in an on-again-off-again relationship. Bon had had girlfriends before—he had had plenty of girls, period—but none was like Maria.

MARIA: "I think it was one of those police club dances, on a Friday night; there would have been about a dozen people there. Anyway, out through the back door comes this guy, small, with tattoos. Well, I didn't know anybody with tattoos. And his mother was in tow, being really quite bossy. It turned out it was Bon, and she had to drive him there with his drums, because he'd lost his license or something. I became secretary, or president, or whatever, of their fan club."

Maria was from the right side of the tracks, a good Catholic girl of solid Dutch parentage. To Bon, she was a cut above all the slack molls and dirty scrags he used for what he could get, and he courted her and wooed her with all his worldly wiles.

MARIA: "He was going to marry me; he wanted to marry a virgin, and I was going to be it. But I knew for a fact, behind my back—I learnt later on—there was those gang bangs. But I never saw anything like that. Maybe I was just naive. Bon was very experienced, but to me, he was this nice boy. You couldn't swear around me. And there was no drinking."

Apart from the fact that the rampantly lascivious Bon managed to keep his hands off Maria, their relationship was also bizarre because at the same time Maria was also seeing bass player Brian Gannon, unaware that he was barely over 15. As Maria herself put it, she was 17 going on 12; Brian Gannon was 15 going on 21. It was a ménage à trois which existed with its participants' full knowledge, and which they all somehow managed to cope with, if only just.

MARIA: "If we were going out to a gig, I would be holding Bon's hand, with the rug over my knees, and holding Brian's hand as well. I kissed both of them, but didn't go to bed with either of them. It was a wonderful time for all of us."

Through 1965, the Spektors played weekly gigs, or stomps, held in halls and surf clubs like the Cave, the Shakeway, the Big Beat, the Z-Club and the Rendezvous. They would get 20 minutes or so in the middle of the bill with half a dozen other bands like the Johnny Young-less Nomads, the Dimensions, the Triffids, Russ and the Little Wheels, and the Winztons. Their set consisted of Stones' songs, Them's "Gloria," and the Beatles' "Yesterday." Stomps were dry, though the boys in the band always had a bottle of ale or two stashed out the back.

WYN MILSON: "The whole problem with being a band in Perth back then was the search for material. It was a consuming process, because you just couldn't get anything, no blues, or anything like that. You used to have to dig for it."

Bon would borrow his father's new Falcon station wagon to lug his drums around. That lasted until he fell asleep at the wheel one night. The paper reported that Ronald Scott (19) "was taken to hospital with facial injuries after the car he was driving hit a light-pole on Stirling Highway, Claremont." It added that Brian Gannon (15), "a passenger in Scott's car," suffered "concussion and cuts." It was the first of many injuries Bon would

LEFT: Bon met his first serious girlfriend, Maria Van Vlijman, in 1965. He always carried this photograph with him. RIGHT: Maria and Bon in their best mod finery, 1966.

inflict on himself.

The band was back on deck the following weekend. Bon was a hard man to keep down. An appearance on *Club 17* in October was tangible evidence that the Spektors were indeed as the *West Australian* put it, "one of Perth's top five rock groups."

The band continued playing into 1966 without making much greater headway, though they could hardly have complained. The Spektors had started out as a fun thing, and they were having the time of their lives. The band was often billed as John Collins and the Spektors, though Bon would occasionally step up to the mike to sing a song or two. He was learning to like the applause, to like being a center of attention. He didn't find it difficult.

Bon won out over Brian Gannon for Maria and the couple reveled in the throes of puppy love. Maria got a job in the pay office at the Fremantle docks, and since her parents had moved further away into the country, she took a lease on a flat in east Fremantle with her brother Joe, despite her tender years. This meant that Bon, who only lived across the way in North Fremantle, was able to spend all the more time with her. He had by then tossed in his job at the egg board and was working as a postman.

He reserved all his most gentlemanly charms for Maria. He would dress up just to have lunch with her every day, then return to work. Both their families disapproved of the relationship. To Maria's parents, Bon was an undesirable, a larrikin; to Chick and Isa, Maria was stuck-up, snooty.

MARIA: "Every night, we'd do something, even if it was just watch TV. I would be out with Bon till three or four o'clock every night, and then have to get up at seven to go to work. I was always late.

"It was a ritual every Saturday to go to a place called Musgrove, where all the new bands would play. We used to go to church on Sundays.

"Oh, we'd go down to the wharf, and Bon would buy fish'n'chips, and we'd watch the waves."

Maria would attend Spektors' gigs and rehearsals alike.

ISA: "They used to practice in my house. The band, in my lounge! We all had to clear out and go into the kitchen when they practiced."

The scene was still growing. Johnny Young joined new local independent label Clarion Records, and released the single "Step Back," an Easybeats song. It went to number one nationally in June 1966.

When Johnny Young predictably set out for the brighter lights of Melbourne, he left behind a big gap in Perth. Neither the Winztons nor the Spektors, the next two best acts in town, were quite equipped to fill it, and they might well have cancelled each other out in the attempt. But if they joined forces, there would be nothing stopping them.

The idea to form the Valentines was hatched by the Winztons' Vince Lovegrove in cahoots with 6KY DJ and music director, Allan Robertson. Robertson, who named the band and could see the potential of an act with two lead singers. After all, it had worked for the Twilights, Sam & Dave, the Righteous Brothers.

Vince had known Bon for a while. Vince had left school to take up a journalism cadetship at the *West Australian,* but threw that in to concentrate on music. After the Dynells he fronted the Dimensions before forming the Winztons. In the obituary to Bon he wrote for *RAM*, Vince recalled, "Bon was the cute little drummer with cute little eyes, pixie-like ears, a cute, turned-up nose, a cute little Scottish accent, and about four very obvious cute little tattoos. In rock'n'roll in those days, you could go a long way being cute. We became friends."

The Winztons hit a peak when they played at the Capitol Theatre with Billy Thorpe and the Aztecs (the biggest band in the country alongside the Easybeats), then riding high on hits like "Mashed Potato" and "Poison Ivy." There was a party afterwards.

VINCE LOVEGROVE: "We got invited to this party; it was our first real rock'n'roll party like we thought they must have all the time in the eastern States. Bon and I went, and I remember being really intimidated by Billy Thorpe, afraid to talk to him, and he was only a year older than we were. But we just thought, Right, well, this is it, this is what it's all about, this is for us!"

Vince was then working as a sales assistant at Pellew's Menswear in Fremantle, and Bon would drop in on him away from his postman's rounds. "[We] realized our ambitions were the same. To go to Melbourne and be the best band in the country," Vince wrote. "Bon didn't want to drum anymore, and as I was the singer in my band, we decided to be democratic and have two singers."

ISA: "Ron liked being up front. I don't think it suited him being behind the drums."

The formation of the Valentines sorted the men from the boys, or at least those that had steady girlfriends from those that didn't. The Valentines' plan was to turn pro and it's near impossible to combine a career in rock'n'roll and marriage. John Collins and Brian Gannon gave up music altogether and both soon settled happily down to married life. But Bon—Maria or no Maria—was going to do what he was going to do. He insisted on bringing Wyn Milson into the band with him, which suited everyone fine, as Wyn was quite serious about his music.

From the Winztons came guitarist Ted Ward and bassist John Cooksey, whilst drummer Warwick Findlay was recruited from Russ and the Little Wheels. Cooksey was replaced a short while later by Bruce Abbott.

The band was driven by a calculated careerism. Bon and Vince had together seen their future—their names in lights in the eastern States—and they were prepared to do anything to get it. They were turned on in the first place by the Beatles and the Stones, but it was Australian acts that really inspired them to give it a serious go. They'd seen the success enjoyed not only by the Easybeats, who were their godhead, but also Ray Brown and the Whispers, Billy Thorpe and the Aztecs, and then the Masters Apprentices and the Twilights. And if Johnny Young could do it too, then surely so could they.

A hierarchy evolved within the Valentines that saw Vince emerge as the band's leader and premier sex symbol. Bon deferred to Vince, for the time being at least, because he knew Vince could get them what they wanted. Vince was a smooth operator. His experience at the *West Australian* had taught him media savvy, and his charm and cleverness made him a natural at public relations and promotion.

At any rate, Bon always had Wyn's ear, and it was Wyn who emerged as the band's musical director, for what that was worth—the whole band was still grappling in the dark for a real musical sign.

But even if Bon was prepared to hand the reins over to Vince—and he didn't want to know about administration or money—the pair's rivalry colored the Valentines' personal dynamic, and certainly affected their own relationship, though they remained friends, till the day Bon died.

One of the first edicts brought down in the new regime was that girlfriends at gigs were a no-no. This meant that Bon had to tell Maria she couldn't come to the band's debut at Broadway. Maria was horrified, not least of all by the fact that Bon was prepared to pass on Vince's demand, and even while she conspired with Bon to buck Vince, appearing at every subsequent show (there was no love lost between Maria and Vince either), she was plotting to get her own back on Bon. She wanted to see him squirm, make him beg.

The Valentines took over all the gigs and fans that the Winztons and Spektors had previously divided, and that immediately made them top dogs in Perth. They were heavily rotated on the 6KY "Big K" dance circuit—it helped that they were nominally managed by DJ Allan Robertson. They also played licensed discos like the Top Hat, North Side and Trend Setter, which were raking it in thanks largely to the Western Australia mining boom.

The Valentines' repertoire consisted mainly of soul covers—Sam & Dave and Wilson Pickett (the roots of the Rolling Stones)—plus songs by mod staples the Who, the Small Faces and Spencer Davis.

WYN: "We used to sneak into the 6KY record library late at night and go through the old stuff looking for singles that had the big hole in the middle. You'd find something and say, Who's this?"

With their matching blue sharkskin suits, the band was also developing a sensational stage act which would soon even incorporate flashbombs.

In January 1967, the Valentines played in front of their biggest ever crowd—over 3,000 teenagers—at a concert for Torchbearers for Legacy in Perth's Supreme Court Gardens. The *Sunday Times* praised the band: "with lead singers Bon and Vince clearly demonstrated [sic] their vibrant personality."

Life, then, for the band was good. They'd all quit their day jobs. There were always parties, and everyone was young and pretty. Bon and Maria made a handsome couple, even if they squabbled a lot. Maria liked to play cat and mouse with Bon. But when the games became too much to bear,

Bon took up overtly with a go-go dancer by the name of Lyn. Maria soon lured him back though.

"Now established as one of the star attractions on the Perth scene," as a 6KY fan club flyer put it, it was inevitable that the Valentines would link up with Clarion Records. Headed by Martin Clarke and distributed by Festival (Australia's own major label), Clarion was one of the many independents that sprang up and fostered local talent in Australia in the sixties. The Valentines thus went into a primitive studio off Hay Street in the center of Perth very late one night, and emerged the following morning clutching a one-take, two-track tape of two simple tunes.

"Everyday I Have To Cry" was a rolling, melodic song originally cut by black US country-soul singer Arthur Alexander; while "Can't Dance With You" was a B-side for the Small Faces, a prime slice of proto-funk/rock. As a debut single by a band from the backwoods of Perth, it wasn't bad, and when it was released in May 1967 it duly climbed into the top five in the Western Australian charts.

The Vallies, as they were affectionately known, were on a roll. When the all-conquering Easybeats played two shows at His Majesty's on June 12 on their return tour from England after the worldwide success of "Friday on My Mind," the Valentines supported. The Easys took a real shine to them. It was likely on this occasion that songwriter-guitarist and fellow Scot, George Young, first noticed Bon, how reminiscent he was of his own band's front man, "Little" Stevie Wright. Of course, of all the Easybeats, Bon idolized Little Stevie particularly, to the point of consciously aping his moves.

The Valentines partied with the Easybeats back at their hotel, as hordes of screaming teenage girls littered the footpath below. The two bands swapped shirts like opposing Grand Final football teams, and the Easys even knocked up a song on the spot for Vallies. Not much of a song, it's true, but one that would constitute the Valentines' second single.

"She Said" was the first of three songs the Easybeats would give to the Valentines, and it was the start of the lifelong relationship George Young would have with Bon.

Bon and Maria had kissed (at most!) and made up, but just as soon, Maria was taking off for the big smoke, Melbourne. There had to be something more there than working in the pay office at the Fremantle docks.

MARIA: "I was ready to go, but I don't think I would have gone if I didn't know that somewhere down the track, Bon was going to come too."

Wyn Milson, by this time, had effectively moved into the Scotts' North Fremantle home, rather than having to commute all the way to Medina all the time. "Bon just said, Come and stay at my place; didn't ask his parents, and basically, they just accepted me. When I think about it now, if someone lobbed at my house, and was coming in at three every morning making hot chocolate, leaving burnt milk in the saucepan, and then went to bed in the lounge room so you couldn't go in there till one in the afternoon, I would throw them out. But they never said a word."

"She Said" was released in July, backed with a lame version of Phil Spector's "To Know You Is To Love You." It was a step back for the Valentines, probably only recorded because it was penned by the Easybeats. Bon blew a recorder, presumably just because he could. Not even all the Valentines' hometown hero status could save "She Said." It stiffed.

The irony is that even as the single couldn't get out of the blocks, the band won the State final of the Hoadley's Battle of the Sounds. The Valentines flew to Melbourne to compete in the national final, and though they were beaten out of first place by the Groop, they made a good impression. Tastemakers Ian "Molly" Meldrum of *Go-Set* and DJ Stan "The Man" Rofe both gave them the nod. Vince, of course, got in some serious networking during the visit; and so, flying home, the Valentines had no second thoughts as to where their future lay.

The band's plan was to get together the money to pay for the move to Melbourne. They got onto a winner in an all-day every-day gig at the State Fair, with visiting Victorian star Ronnie Burns.

WYN: "You'd do a half hour on stage, then go out the back so they could throw everybody out, and then you'd go up and do it again."

Bassist Bruce Abbott fell victim to the dreaded fiancée disease, and decided to stay behind in Perth and get married. He was replaced by John Cooksey. Bon wrote to Maria just a week before the band was due to leave for Melbourne:

> We have had no end of complications with our trip. It looked almost as though we would have to call it off till we got more money. Vin and I are going to Perth tomorrow to sell everything we can lay our hands on . . .
>
> I guess that you're having a great time going to all the new places. I hope we can both have a good time together when I arrive. I hope that it works out this time. If it doesn't I don't know what I'll do. I'll be so flippin' lonely.

VINCE: "No one in Perth could understand why we wanted to leave. They said, It's paradise here, it's sunny, we've got all these beautiful beaches. What could you say?"

The band finally got it together and they all met at the station to catch the train. The scene was like something out of *Exodus*. Mothers were sobbing, fathers stoic. The boys were beside themselves.

They felt like explorers or crusaders. The trip across the Nullarbor Plain was all of four days—somehow they would have to contain their excitement—and at the other end, Melbourne was still very much an unknown quantity. But they were blessed with the hope of the age, the confidence of their youth and their innocence.

If and when they returned to Perth, it would be as stars, conquering heroes. And so it would be.

Be Our Valentine in '69

The Valentines go bubblegum. Left to right: Vince Lovegrove, Doug Lavery, Wyn Milson, Bon, Ted Ward, John Cooksey. Vince: "Melbourne was a lot more teenybopper oriented, which we foolishly catered to because it was good for the ego. But it wasn't really doing us much good musically."

5. MELBOURNE

The Valentines arrived in Melbourne on Friday the 13th of October, 1967—drawn inextricably to the city which was at the time indisputably Australia's pop capital.

The rivalry between Melbourne and Sydney is one of Australia's oldest. Sydney, city of water, speed and light, is the New World to Melbourne's Old, with its long winters and its somber, more rarefied air. The rock'n'roll scenes in the two cities have always been as distinctly different as those of Los Angeles and London, and have always vied for supremacy.

In the very early sixties, both Sydney and Melbourne played host to thriving teenage dance circuits. The music was almost entirely instrumental rock'n'roll—surf music in Sydney, while Melbourne bands had a brassier sound. When the Beatles exploded and every instrumental band in the land scrambled to find a singer—not to mention grow their hair—it was Sydney, for some reason, that produced the first rush of hits, via the Easybeats and the Aztecs. But Sydney's dominance wouldn't last long. By the end of 1965, the emphasis had swung to Melbourne. It would not return to Sydney till the start of the eighties.

Success in rock'n'roll, like most fields, takes more than talent, and Melbourne had more than just bands. It had the Anglophile mod look that sunny Sydney could never quite approximate. It quickly became Australia's media capital, too, the home of *Go-Set* magazine, the weekly bible of the sixties Australian pop scene, and of TV's *Go!!* show and other national shows like *Kommotion* and *Uptight*.

Melbourne also boasted a whole new breed of young entrepreneurs who helped build up its live circuit. Although Australia is now famous for its bands bred in pubs, pubs didn't really open up to live rock'n'roll until the licensing hours were extended in the early seventies. In Melbourne in the sixties there were two types of gigs, neither of which allowed alcohol: teenage dances in the suburbs, held in halls, church halls, town halls; and, for the older, more sophisticated audience, late-night clubs, called discos, which were unlicensed too (licensed clubs remained the preserve of adult entertainment, jazz, cabaret or comedy). With varying degrees of success, bands straddled the two circuits, from, say, the Q Club, a dance in suburban Kew, to city discos like the Thumpin' Tum, or Sebastian's in St. Kilda.

Led by the Loved Ones, Bobby & Laurie, the Groop and Ronnie Burns, a second wave of acts exploded out of Melbourne in 1965, leaving every Sydney band except the Easybeats eating dust. Further strengthening the scene, the Masters Apprentices and the Twilights moved to Melbourne from Adelaide, and then Johnny Young arrived from Perth.

Little of the music itself was actually very good—Australian musicians, without any background in blues-based rock'n'roll, were still just trying to get a handle on it—but the seeds of something greater were being sown.

When the Valentines pulled into Flinders Street Station on that Black Friday morning late in 1967, they had no tangible plans.

VINCE: "We had Ronnie Burns's phone number. We called him from the station. He came and picked us up and took us to a Chinese restaurant. We stayed at a hotel that night."

The *West Australian* had reported on the eve of the band's departure, "The Valentines are willing to start at the bottom and work hard and these qualities have proven to be most necessary." Indeed the Valentines would struggle for some time yet.

Within a week of arriving in Melbourne, the band was being man- aged by former Loved Ones singer Gerry Humphries, in partnership with Johnny Young's drummer Don Pryor—for what it was worth. The pair threw a generous reception to launch the band along with "She Said," but then . . . nothing. Humphries and Pryor's interest dropped off. On the rebound, the band signed on with AMBO, the Australian Management Booking Agency, which farmed out the talent to a large proportion of Melbourne's discos and dances. But with "She Said" going nowhere, getting gigs wasn't going to be easy.

As if by way of a rude baptism, the Valentines were sent bush, on a tour of rural Victoria. They got around, gear and all, in a Kombi van they'd bought and daubed in psychedelic colors.

Renting a house in the far eastern Melbourne suburb of Burwood, the band almost literally starved, earning barely enough to cover costs from unattended midweek gigs. They would go into supermarkets and eat in the aisles, or steal milk money on the way home late at night. Though most of them were in their early twenties, the Valentines were still boys who had barely broken away from their mothers' apron strings, and they had no idea how to look after themselves. Female fans helped.

Vince wrote: "Bon was the only guy in the band unruffled by our seemingly hopeless situation. He was a great positive inspiration in those days when we needed it most."

Bon would occasionally stay with Maria, who had a flat in the same block as Humphries and Pryor, in swish South Yarra. But their relationship would always be problematic. Bon had chosen his path in life, and Maria seemed unwilling to accept the reality that it entailed—that he would be away a lot, on the road; that he would attract a lot of attention, particularly female; and that he would make no money, at least not initially. They were always arguing. The rest of the band, in turn, resented Maria for the hold she had on Bon. However, even with her taunting, Bon was hopelessly romantically in love. Whenever he was away, he would write her love letters, sometimes several times a day.

MARIA: "He used to talk about how when the group was successful and it would be on the road in Australia, and America, it would have a tour bus, and on the back would be a little caravan attached for he and I!"

Bon was possibly a little intimidated by the sophisticated, cliquey Melbourne scene, and so was happy to put his faith in Vince, who seemed capable of scoring the necessary social points. It suited Vince's ego to be making decisions for the band. Strangely, there was a quite subservient streak in Bon. It was not so much that he craved acceptance, rather that he wanted to please people, and at his best he could be quite unselfish. So for the meantime at least, he was bowing to both Maria and Vince.

VINCE: "It was a confusing time anyway, for guys. Bon always seemed troubled by something, whether it was his creative desire as opposed to feelings of inadequacy due to his working-class origins, or lack of education, I don't know. But there was some sort of conflict there, where he was unsure of himself. He had a lot of bravado, but really he was a softie underneath."

Vince pulled off a coup when he managed to sell the band away from AMBO to Ivan Dayman. Dayman was the agent behind Sunshine Records and Normie Rowe; from his base in Brisbane he controlled a circuit of venues all over Australia.

As Dayman booked the band into Adelaide for a week in February, Clarion released a third Valentines single, "I Can Hear The Raindrops"/ "Why Me?" These were the first two original songs cut by the band—written by Vince and Ted Ward—but both were eminently forgettable, and the disc, again, died a death.

In March, the band ventured for the first time to Brisbane, then to Sydney and then back to Melbourne. It was an experience that taught them just how grueling life on the road could be. They lived, collectively, on a bare $300 a week, which was what Dayman paid them. They traveled by bus, train, car—however they could. They lugged all their own gear; they stayed in boarding houses and seedy hotels, and they played dives. But they wouldn't have changed things for anything. This was the life they'd wanted.

By the middle of April, they were back in Sydney for an extended eight-week stay. This was a turning point for the band and for Bon.

Staying at the shabby Americana Hotel in the red-light district of Kings Cross—then buzzing like a boom town, due to the influx of American servicemen on R&R leave from Vietnam—the band was still strapped for cash, pooling funds to eat fish'n'chips. But they were getting somewhere at last. *Go-Set* stringer David Elfick proclaimed that the band's "performances at Sydney's Op-Pop disco justified their rating as Perth's number one group . . . They have a distinctive sound . . . they play Pickett, Redding type numbers, straight top 40 and comedy ('Would You Like To Swing On a Bra?')." No band, at that time, played its own material on stage, unless those songs were already hits.

Bon wrote to Maria that posters for the band were plastered all over Sydney, and that while they were going down well—had even drawn "the biggest crowd in six weeks at Op-Pop"—it "could be a lot better", and so the band was "going to have a meeting to try to find out how we can best improve ourselves". The band was geed up in anticipation of going into Festival Records' Pyrmont studios with ace producer Pat Aulton. Bon wanted to try out some Dusty Springfield songs.

The Valentines were a bit like babes in the woods in Sin City, Sydney, but they quickly took to it all.

MARIA: "In his letters, he would say, Don't worry, I'll be faithful. What a liar he was!"

Drugs were a new dimension altogether.

VINCE: "We met this piano player called Bobby Gebert, who turned Bon and I onto our first joint. We didn't know it then either, but these guys were gay. We were so naive, we just thought they were in fancy dress. They had licorice papers, to roll joints—it was the whole thing. We were sitting there looking at each other, giggling like two little kids, saying, Has it affected you yet? Then we realized, we were just these two guys sitting in the corner at this party, we were stoned, and so we panicked and ran out of the place. We got back to the hotel and the other guys said, You guys have had drugs, you're out of the band—because we had a rule, no drugs—and so we said, yeah, well, okay . . ."

At the end of April, Maria paid Bon a visit in Sydney. Long-distance love affairs are inevitably hard to handle, and Bon and Maria's was starting to show the strain. But the couple spent a happy weekend together. As soon as Maria got home, however, the push and pull started all over again. The band had gone up to Brisbane. Bon spent all his time and money on long-distance phone calls. Maria was sick of Bon's absence—she knew there were other women—and she was talking about going back to Perth. Bon began to fear that Maria might have taken up with someone else herself. When the band returned to Sydney, Maria came up again. It was plain to both of them then that it wasn't going to work. They had been each other's first love, but they'd grown apart.

For the second time in just over a year, Bon saw Maria off on the train—but this time, there would be no reunion down the line. Maria would always occupy a special place in Bon's heart, and he remained in touch with her right up until he died. More immediately though, there was too much going on to waste time moping and any number of willing young women to help take the pain away.

The band finally got into the Festival studio in Sydney in late May and cut their next single, "Peculiar Hole in the Sky," another Easybeats song. This they did with a session player on drums, as Warwick Findlay had buckled under the financial pressure, having a wife to support, and had left the band to find a real job. The Valentines were over the moon about "Peculiar Hole in the Sky," and rightly so. It was a quantum leap for them, a good song done justice, cut in an almost modern studio with a capable producer, invested with all the appropriate psychedelic overtones. It was released in July. Go-Set, strangely, was not terribly impressed and it didn't sell.

When the band pleaded in an ad for the single, "Please buy a copy—we're starving," they were only marginally stretching the truth. They had by then moved back to Melbourne and recruited a new drummer in Doug Lavery, and though they were starting to get ahead playing the Ivan

Dayman circuit, Vince was still looking for a stronger connection.

They moved into a two-storey terraced house in seedy St. Kilda, in Dalgety Street, just off the notorious Fitzroy Street sleaze strip. Bon, now a legitimate bachelor again, had the attic bedroom, which he painted fire-engine red, where he reigned as gay blade supreme.

It was around this time he met Mary Wasylyk, who would become a lifelong friend. Born in 1950 of Ukrainian parents, Mary grew up in Melbourne's grimy western suburbs, and after school went into fashion design. She saw the Valentines for the first time at a Sunday afternoon show at the Bowl, a disco in Melbourne. "You used to have arguments, you know, who was better, the Valentines or the Zoot? I used to make these hippie beads, and the band all really liked them, so I got to know them, and I stayed friends with Bon ever since.

"They were just trying to copy the English bands, sort of like an extension of the Easybeats but not as good. I mean, looking at them, none of them seemed talented, really!"

It was at Dalgety Street that the Valentines started to run really wild. They became the premier party animals in a scene that aspired to complete psychedelic degeneracy. It was 1968. *Sergeant Pepper's* had changed everything. Hendrix and the Doors were having hits. Bon's brother Graeme, then 15, came over on vacation and had his life changed. "Women were everywhere, and ganja. Vince gave me my first smoke. They'd go off to a show, and come back with women, sit up all night and smoke, whatever. For someone like me to come straight out of Fremantle, I couldn't go back to that, so the only way out was to jump a ship." Graeme remained a merchant seaman for many years to come, and he would drop in on Bon whenever he was in port.

Vince sussed a new opening for the band back at AMBO. Headed by Sri Lankan-Australian Bill Joseph, the agency had been revitalized by its employment of one of the new breed, Michael Browning. Browning was running two discos, Berties and Sebastian's, and also managing Doug Parkinson in Focus, then the hottest new act in town. Vince figured that if he could parley an AMBO agent into managing the Valentines, too, the band might find favor in the same way Doug Parkinson seemed to.

The Valentines were well drilled, well established on the live circuit, and even though "Peculiar Hole in the Sky" had failed to set the world on fire, its potential, plus Vince's determination, was incentive enough for AMBO boss Bill Joseph himself to take on the band. Ron Tudor, who was then launching his own June Productions company (and would go on to form the Fable Label), also came on board, signing the Valentines to a deal whereby June would record the band, and then lease the tapes to Philips.

Everything was thus in place, finally, for the Valentines to launch a full-scale assault on Australian teenagers.

The Summer of Love took place officially in San Francisco, and nominally also in London, in what was Australia's winter of 1967. Its impact would be superficial in Australia. A local pop hit that could be described as psychedelic did not arrive until 1969, in the form of "The Real Thing." Acid rock, as such, hardly happened at all, at least not until a later mutation appeared.

The reason why Australia missed the first blooming of flower power was essentially because the guards had reclaimed control of the asylum. The new order that had pulled the rug out from under the music business establishment in the early to mid-sixties—independent record companies and young entrepreneurs as well as artists—had by then been absorbed by the mainstream. The big record companies, those that traditionally ran the music game, had had enough time to adjust to the new rules and now they wanted their ball back.

Radio was reluctant to play far-out new acts like Hendrix, feeling more comfortable with the Monkees. The black soul sounds of Tamla-Motown and Stax, so successful in America and Britain, were hardly heard in racist Australia.

1968 was not a vintage year for Australian pop. Not a single Australian record went to number one all year, whereas previous and later years saw many local chart-toppers. The impetus of 1965-66 had been completely dissipated.

The success of acts like the Ohio Express and the 1910 Fruitgum Company, following in the footsteps of the Monkees, certified bubblegum as the biggest commercial trend of the year. Bubblegum was music that was shamelessly commercial—simplistic and repetitive to the point of inanity. Ultimately disposable, and more than likely manufactured, it particularly impressed Australian record companies.

Australian musicians had only just come to terms with chirpy Beatles-ish harmonies, but now they were discouraged from going any further. In America and Britain, sales of albums overtook singles in 1968. But Australia didn't even have album charts until 1970. The hot new local acts were the Groove, who would go on to win the 1968 Battle of the Sounds, and Johnny Farnham. Both were confectionery.

At the end of 1968, an intense marketing campaign swung into action around the Valentines. In November, they made the unequivocal statement in *Go-Set* that they were a bubblegum group, "not afraid about being commercial." The band had buffed up its image—Bon was dusting down his tattoos with foundation, and straightening his hair with sticky tape—and they wore matching orange frilly shirts, flares and beads. Although they would suffer in comparison with prettier band the Zoot, who exploded onto Melbourne around the same time with their "Think Pink" campaign, they hit the media all over Australia with a season's greeting card proclaiming, "The slogan for this year is "BE MY VALENTINE IN '69.""

Bon filled out a profile in which—claiming to be 19 when he was actually now 22—he revealed:

Likes—My room (painted red), long blonde hair, sex, showers, swimming
Dislikes—People who hate Crater Critters (ex-Weeties pack), being disturbed whilst thinking, washing and ironing
Loves—Parents, my pet Crater Critter
Favorite Food—Ice cream
Drink—Sand Zombie
Actor—Vince
Actress—Julie Christie, Vanessa Redgrave
Groups—Beatles, Moody Blues
Singer, Male—John Lee Hooker, Otis Redding
Singer, Female—Supremes
Music—Scottish Pipe Band music, soul, worried jazz

In early December the Valentines put down a new single, "My Old Man's a Groovy Old Man." This was yet another product of the prolific songwriting partnership of the Easybeats' Harry Vanda and George Young; it found its way to the band via Ron Tudor. Tudor also proffered an obscure Pretty Things song, "Ebeneezer," for the flip-side.

June Music had an office conveniently located just a couple of doors down from the state-of-the-art Armstrong's Studios which *Go-Set* had trumpeted some months earlier: "People will no longer be able to blame a lack of equipment for poor Australian record production. Last week, Bill Armstrong's studio in Melbourne installed an 8-track Scully recording machine."

The skiffle-like "My Old Man" was as dynamic as it was vacuous—classic bubblegum.

After sessions for the single were completed, the Valentines hit the road again. Brisbane was something of a stronghold for the band; they spent the holiday there. Vince remembers a remarkable Christmas Day:

"We had this fan up there who was Chinese, and he invited us over for Christmas dinner. But what happened was, we took this mescaline. It was hilarious. Ted thought he was a hippopotamus, he just sat in the pool all day. Bon and I went to this lunch, it was meant to be a traditional Western Christmas—roast turkey and everything, you know. So we get there, and this guy comes to the door, and as soon as we walk in the room, where the parents are there to meet us, Bon just becomes a Chinaman, you know, he's got his arms folded and he's squinting with this stupid grin on his face, and he's bowing and going, Ah so, Ah so. These people didn't know what was going on. Anyway, they serve the food, and I suppose we must have thought this turkey was alive or something, because we just ended up getting out of there, we were virtually running down the road screaming. We started hitching, and of course no one would give us a lift, so we ended up walking all the way back to the motel, it was seven miles or something. We got there, and Ted's virtually turned into a prune, he's still in the pool, he still thinks he's a hippopotamus!"

Returning to Melbourne, the band had to find new digs; the lease on Dalgety Street was up. Bon, Wyn and Ted set up headquarters at a flat in South Yarra, on Toorak Road, at the center of something of a pop-idol enclave. Johnny Farnham was a neighbor on one side, Johnny Young the other. Vince moved in just around the corner.

In January Molly Meldrum interviewed not just Vince but the whole band for *Go-Set*. What image were the Valentines trying to project? he asked John Cooksey. "A very happy, sweet, but sexy commercial type image," Cooksey replied. "At the same time, we want to be able to entertain the disco crowds."

"My Old Man's a Groovy Old Man" was launched on February 14, 1969—Valentine's Day itself. It took off immediately, although almost inevitably it was overshadowed by the Zoot's contemporaneous first hit, "One Times, Two Times, Three Times, Four." But the Valentines were away nonetheless.

When they played the That's Life disco in Prahran that night, "the audience," Meldrum reported in *Go-Set*, "screamed in unison, We love the Valentines. As soon as they appeared the audience went completely berserk and started to storm the stage. The two lead singers, Vince and Bon, were dragged to the floor and Bon's pants and jacket were completely ripped off him."

Writing on March 1, Meldrum went on: "This has been a regular occurrence since that particular day. Last Saturday night the Valentines appeared at another Melbourne dance, Piccadilly, and drew a record attendance of over 2,000 teenagers. Cupids (the Valentines' symbol) were thrown out to the audience and in turn the audience threw back bubblegum. The Valentines didn't even get through their first number before the stage was stormed.

"Ripped clothes and accessories was repeated and when Doug, the drummer, got up to sing, he left the stage two minutes later sporting only a pair of red underpants. The group were supposed to appear for 45 minutes but their performance had to be cut down to 20 minutes because the audience became completely uncontrollable."

On March 10, the Valentines played a free concert before a crowd of 7,000 at the Alexandra Gardens, as part of Melbourne's annual Moomba festival. A "riot" ensued during which Vince was arrested on charges of assaulting police. Vince was certainly a provocateur—Bon was the passive one of the pair, content to hang back and just sing—but all Vince did was push an overzealous cop from the stage with his bare foot. He was fined $50, and put on a 12-month good behavior bond.

With a new drummer, Paddy Beach—Doug Lavery had left to join Axiom—the Valentines concentrated on gigging around Melbourne, working Beach in and consolidating their support. "My Old Man" eventually peaked on the national charts at number 23.

Paddy Beach (né Veitch) was recruited from a trio called Compulsion, a Maori Hendrix-clone act that Michael Browning had brought to Australia from New Zealand just before they fell apart. When Paddy, who was white, joined the Valentines, pint-sized roadie John Darcy came with him. Darcy, as he's known to all, remembers his first meeting with the band, at Toorak Road.

"I meet the guys, and they're checking me out, because of the size of me, you know, because they'd just started to get some of the bigger gear. They said, Do you reckon you'll be able to handle the gear? I said, I'm pretty fit, I've always done a bit of boxing, I go to the gym. So they said, Alright, we'll give it a go. Then Bon says, Hey, you feel like a fuck? Well, that sets me back a bit, but I say, Well, yeah, I could always go a fuck, and so he says, Well, just whip into the front room there, there's a young chick there, she'll give you a go, no worries. So I go into the front room and there's all these chicks there, stark naked, so I figure I'll go for it. So I'm laying on this bed, stark naked, there's this chick going down on me, and Bon comes in and says, How do you think you'll like the job? I go, Well, I suppose I can try and adapt."

The Valentines' image might have been squeaky clean, but their reputation was easily the worst of any band around. Dope smoking was also constant.

The band played a lot of cards and neighbor Johnny Farnham was a frequent visitor, but Farnham's manager Daryl Sambell wasn't at all keen on his charge being seen associating with such degenerates.

DARCY: "You'd wake up each morning, and look out the little eyepiece in the door, and by 9.30 there'd be maybe three or four young girls there, in the hallway at the top of the stairs. At maybe 10.30, it'd be, Oh, there's seven out there now. They were all like under 12. After lunch they'd start to get a bit older, you'd get the 14-year-olds starting to turn up. Of course, I'd be in and out, I'd have to duck up to the Toorak Village to get the papers, milk. I'd be stepping over girls. They'd be, Oh, can we come in, can we see the guys, can you get us their autographs? So I'd say, Look, I'll see what I can do for you. So you'd let some in for 15 minutes or so, hand out some autographs. And then later on you'd let the older ones in; they could cook the meals for you, and clean the flat, do the washing and ironing. Then of course there'd be a couple of older ones who'd supply a bit more than that, give you a bit of a work-out before you had to go off to a job. It was unbelievable. Every day of the week it was the same."

Even in their wildest dreams, the Valentines couldn't have imagined it would be as wild as this. Bon was in his element. He had a little trick he employed to sort out the goers from the prickteasers among the girls who came backstage. He would let off one of the smoke bombs the band exploded on stage as part of its act, and when the smoke cleared, he would be standing there naked. The girls who didn't run off screaming had to be goers. The band performed indecent acts on young girls in the back of the bus on fan club picnics, and then dropped them off back into their worried mothers' waiting arms, reassuring these women, as sweet and innocent as you like, that their daughters had been in good hands—as indeed they had—and then laughing at how Bon especially could put it over them with all his boyish charm.

The band went out on the road, touring through Canberra, Newcastle, Queensland and South Australia, but cracks were already appearing in the facade. Back in Melbourne in early August, they played a reception at That's Life to launch a new Coca-Cola commercial. "Most surprising thing though," the *Herald* reported, "was to hear the Valentines play a bit of rhythm in contrast to their labeled 'bubblegum' style. As bass guitarist John said, 'We weren't under any pressure tonight, so we decided to prove a point'—that they are versatile."

The very next night, the Valentines failed to take out the Battle of the Sounds, finishing second to the tied Doug Parkinson and Masters Apprentices; but the band was already set on a new path. Having met with commercial success, the Valentines, predictably, now wanted artistic credibility. Bubblegum, after all, was throwaway pap for little girls.

VINCE: "The scene was changing, it was starting to get serious, it was getting to the point where you had to be good."

The novelty of local bands was wearing off. It wasn't enough to merely ape your idols any more. Australia might have missed out on the Summer of Love, but in mid-1969, with Woodstock just around the corner, it was starting to catch up. New British and American bands that anticipated seventies rock, like Led Zeppelin and Santana, had an immediate and profound impact. A deep divide was drawn between dances and discos. The dance circuit catered to teenyboppers, with bubblegum bands; whilst discos, though still unlicensed, became the province of adult-oriented so-called "soul artists" like Max Merritt and Billy Thorpe, both on the comeback trail, and Doug Parkinson and the Levi Smith Clefs, who would take Australian rock into the seventies.

"Our aim," Vince told *Go-Set,* "will be to present to dance crowds a wild act with a heavy sexual slant and attempt to please disco audiences by playing original free-form music. Just as Doug Parkinson made the transition from discos to dances, we hope to do the reverse."

The Valentines made the transition that the Zoot, and even the superior Masters Apprentices, couldn't. They would soon become a staple on the disco scene in Melbourne and Sydney alike. Ultimately though, and ironically, the Valentines' musical coming-of-age also proved to be their undoing.

VINCE: "We found we had too many ideas for one band. We started to fall apart as well as become a better band."

As the single "Nick Nack Paddy Whack" was released, the band went out on the road with Russell Morris, Johnny Farnham, Ronnie Burns, the Zoot and the Masters Apprentices as part of the huge Operation Starlift tour. "Nick Nack Paddy Whack" proved to be something of an embarrassment. An adaptation of the children's nursery rhyme originally cut as a possible theme for a proposed afternoon TV show, it was never intended for release. But its failure to chart was proof positive that the bubblegum bubble had burst. Further encouragement to get serious came in the better response to the single's B-side, a song called "Getting Better," which marked Bon's first ever writing credit, shared with Wyn. It was a convincingly urgent call to arms.

Bon particularly wanted his due. What credibility the band did have was largely thanks to him—his voice was acknowledged as one of the best in the business—and with an increasing amount of confidence, not to mention experience, he was ready to assume more of the initiative.

Vince was naturally reluctant to relinquish leadership, but he knew which side his bread was buttered. At the same time, Bon was sensitive to Vince's feelings, and so he still looked to him for the nod. But certainly, the days of Vince's autocratic rule were over. Vince told *Go-Set:* "Admittedly, I'm more popular than Bon, but he's a far better singer than I'll ever be. In fact, I think he's the most underrated singer in Australia."

The Valentines were delighted when "real musicians" like Billy Thorpe and Wendy Saddington started showing up at their gigs. They were invited to Billy's pad in East Melbourne for spaghetti or a curry, and in doing so joined a quite exclusive little club. The Levi Smith Clefs came around and hung out at Toorak Road.

But still the Valentines clung to their original teenage female fan base, playing dances as much as discos, if for financial reasons as much as any other. They would work every week from Tuesday or Wednesday through to Sunday, building up on Friday to Saturday night, which often entailed three or four gigs. They would get around in the Ford Thames van that Darcy drove, lugging increasingly large amounts of equipment. The aesthetic progression rock was making was directly related to the advancements in its technology, its gear. Bon even wrote an essay for *Go-Set* at the time, admonishing bands who might be cheating their fans by settling for second-rate PA systems.

VINCE: "On a Saturday night, you'd do three shows: an early dance, a late dance, and then you'd do a club, a disco. Racing around all night, and you did it carrying all your own gear, so the thing was, you couldn't possibly do all that without some kind of stimulant."

DARCY: "On a Saturday night, you might start off, say, at the Ringwood Town Hall, do the first spot there, about 8:30, and of course, you'd only play for half an hour, and then you'd throw the gear in the van, and tear down to Dandenong. You might do the Dandenong Town Hall in the second spot, then whip the gear out again and race down to the Frankston Mechanics Hall and do the feature spot there. That would finish at about 11:30 or so. We'd stay straight for those gigs. Then the last gig would be back in the city, at one of the clubs there, Berties or Sebastian's, so on the way there, as soon as we'd loaded out of Frankston, we'd be tearing up the highway, and that's when the joints would start coming out, and we'd get stuck into the cookies. We used to make these hash cookies, it was a real good blast, and we found we could eat them without all the smoke giving the game away, you know. Wyn would come out of his room with this big cookie jar; they looked like butternut snaps!"

WYN: "We would undergo this transformation at midnight. We would literally change, we would take off our matching outfits and put on jeans. We'd stay straight up until then, if you like, then we'd let our hair down, and go to Berties and do what wasn't the mainstream music—Led Zeppelin, guitar solos, percussion, all that. And that's when Bon really came into his own."

DARCY: "We'd get so stoned we'd just be giggling and carrying on, but it was really harmless sort of stuff. Anyway, we'd end up back at Berties, and I'm sure people used to come there just to watch us set up. You'd be off your face, and they had this tiny little triangular stage there in the basement, at the bottom of this really narrow stairway, and you'd have to set up.

"The signal was, they used to flick the light on and off when you were meant to start. Of course, we were always late, so it got so it was like a strobe! They'd have to keep the joint open just so we could play."

VINCE: "That's when a lot of the best music came, you know."

DARCY: "We'd get home at maybe 3:30 in the morning, and we'd just get home and keep partying on. Barrie McAskill and the Levi Smith Clefs, any band that was around from interstate, they'd come back and party with you.

"It was like a little world of our own, we could sit up there nice and stoned and just watch the world go by outside. But we were pretty well known by then, the flat was, so anyone who drove by at four in the morning could have looked up and thought, Oh, the Valentines are having another party."

WYN: "Then you'd have to be up at 7:00 to go out to Channel 0 at Nunawading to do *Uptight*. There'd be some pretty sick-looking people wandering around, wanting to get their make-up done."

When John Cooksey announced his intention to leave the band in September, the Vallies decided not to replace him, but rather have Ted Ward switch from second guitar to bass. It was in order to rehearse this new line-up that the band took off on September 15 for a two-week sojourn at the Jan Juc Surf Lifesaving Club near Torquay, on the western Victorian coast. And it was here they came a real cropper.

"The pop world rocked last week," read Go-Set on October 4, "when the police raided the practice hideaway of top pop group, the Valentines, and found them in possession of the drug, marijuana."

It was the first en masse bust of a band in Australia, and it caused a scandal, although within the rock world it only enhanced their credibility.

It transpired that the band had been turned in by, to quote Go-Set, "a well-known member of one of our top pop groups," who "informed [on the Valentines] to save his own neck on a similar charge."

Unbeknown to the band, they had been under police surveillance for some weeks. The cops followed them down to Jan Juc, where they were dividing their time rehearsing, smoking, listening to Led Zeppelin and smoking. It was too cold even for Bon to go in the water.

Having watched the isolated clubhouse for five days, the cops simply knocked on the door with a search warrant on Saturday night, September 20. The band shat themselves. The cops found a pipe and a quantity of Moroccan powder.

With a court hearing scheduled for October—though they would not eventually appear until the following February—the band either boldly or foolishly spoke out against drug laws. "We believe it should be legalized," Vince told Go-Set. They even got onto the subject of police harassment. Bon had always been known as the joker in the band, but he was becoming more serious in his new, more frontal role, and on this occasion, came about as close as he ever would to making a directly political statement.

"They should realize that what we do is right for us," he protested. "We respect a lot of things about their job, but they shouldn't persecute whole groups of people just for being different." In another interview, he said, "The Australian government deserves a few ripples. They'll be the last to legalize homosexuality, and pot will be the same."

In the aftermath of the bust, the band instituted a no-smoking rule, but it was doomed to failure, and in fact, all it did was create divisions.

DARCY: "We made a pact, Okay, no more smoking, we've got to

straighten out, for the good of the band. Well, Bon, Paddy and myself just sort of ignored it. Vince went off on his own trip too, I think. Wyn and Ted went along with the letter of the law, and that went on for a few months before they realized what we were doing. They were pretty cut, actually."

In late October, the band went to Sydney for the first time since the Op-Pop days. Sydney had regained some initiative, because it had taken so readily to the new dawning in rock. Bands like the La De Das, Flying Circus, Jeff St John and Copperwine, Chain, Max Merritt and the Meteors and Levi Smith Clefs boasted firm followings in licensed discos like the Whiskey-A-Go-Go, Caesar's Palace, Here and Chequers, which catered as much to R&R'ing American servicemen as local hipsters. "Head" bands like Taman Shud and Tully were so far out they ran their own "stirs," free gigs for freaks.

VINCE: "Sydney and Melbourne were two totally different places then, in terms of the audience. Melbourne was a lot more teenybopper orientated, which we'd foolishly catered to because it was good for the ego. But it wasn't really doing us much good musically."

The band was happy to be back in Sydney, where they hadn't suffered so much from labeling. Playing a residency at Caesar's, as Tony Johnston later reported in the *Herald*, "They didn't wear their uniforms, because as Vince said, that age group aren't really worried about a group's image, they're just interested in the music." Bon described what the band was doing as "trying things, feeling around for a musical direction."

For two nights at Caesar's, they supported the Easybeats, who, on the verge of folding in England, had been lured back to play a final tour of Australia. Yet though this was the band that had given the Valentines so many pointers, the Vallies were somewhat perplexed, because whilst everyone else in rock was launching off into the smoky stratosphere, the Easybeats had come full circle and gotten back to basics, playing straight-ahead rock'n'roll.

Staying at a big house the promoter provided for them on the edge of the expansive Centennial Park in Sydney's trendy eastern suburbs, the band was hanging loose. Bon and Vince became friendly with a couple of girls who were waitresses at Caesar's, and so they spent much time at their Kings Cross flat, getting friendlier. They would drop acid and go tripping in Centennial Park. Bon was developing a taste for liquor too, becoming something of a bar fly.

The Caesar's gig was so successful that the band was booked back there for a fee reported "to be the second highest paid an Australian group," whatever that meant.

Although the rot was already setting in, the band's demise would be a drawn-out process, simply because of its common bond. Vince, who had just turned down a part in the Australian production of *Hair*, told *Go-Set*: "We probably have more personality conflicts within the group than anyone else—Bon and I have often come really close to punching the shit out of each other. But with all of us the group is the most important thing—it always comes first, before personal arguments, before chicks, before smoking, everything."

In December, the band was lured to make its triumphant return to Perth; and, as it happened, this homecoming would appropriately serve as a virtual last hurrah. The band always said they wouldn't go home until they could do it as stars, and certainly, they were welcomed back like prodigal sons. When they arrived at Perth airport, they had to run the gauntlet of a reported 4,000 screaming fans, to be sped away in waiting cars.

The band played a big New Year's Eve show for 6KY back in their old stamping grounds, the Supreme Court Gardens. Staying at Vince's parents' place in Applecross, they enjoyed the run of the Perth clubs.

On the five-hour return flight to Melbourne, they kept up the bratty rock star routine, outraging fellow passengers with their obnoxious behavior, all to the tune of the tape they'd just acquired of the second Led Zeppelin album, which they blasted at full volume from the back of the cabin.

When they finally appeared in court in Geelong, near Jan Juc, in February, the band pleaded guilty as charged. Counsel William Lennon argued, "The group have told me that under the influence of marijuana they become more perceptive to musical sounds," and that "long-haired pop stars weren't automatically louts and drug addicts, and that they had not encouraged other teenagers to follow their example." The band each received a $150 fine and a good-behavior bond.

With the dissolution of the Toorak Road flat, the Valentines' end drew nearer. Rumors were rife that they were breaking up. Even Bill Joseph had to ring *Go-Set* to find out what was going on.

DARCY: "We were like lost souls then. After having something going so strong for a while."

Only a sense of loyalty was holding the band together now. What would be their final single, "Juliette," was released in April. A dead ringer for "Dear Prudence," and written by the band collectively, it ran right into the so-called radio ban anyway, and barely scraped into the top 30.

The radio ban was a strange episode in Australian pop history, in which the big record companies demanded payment from radio stations for the right to play their product, on the basis that it was providing radio with programming; a demand at which radio naturally scoffed, claiming that it was providing record companies with essential, free promotion. The result was a stand-off, during which time no major label records, locally-produced or otherwise, were heard on the airwaves. What happened, of course, was that independent labels, who could see the opportunity in refusing to side with their major big brothers, stepped into the breach and filled radio's programming void for free, with a glut of local cover versions of American and English hits, plus even the occasional original Australian track. Yet though June Music boss Ron Tudor's new Fable Label would be a big winner out of the ban, the Valentines, whose records still came out on Philips, lost out.

The failure of "Juliette," for whatever reason, was the last straw. The Valentines were on the road in Newcastle when the bullet was bitten. Talking later to *Go-Set*, Vince said it was because their opinions conflicted so much. "None of us were really happy in the group any more, but we didn't say anything because we didn't want to hurt the others."

Bon wrote to Maria, to whom he was speaking again, from Newcastle on June 2:

> Got some news for you. Guess what? The Valentines are breaking up on the 1st August. It's been coming about for a while now and it came to a head last week when we found out that Vince was waiting for confirmation from a couple of jobs. Ted, Wyn and I decided we'd dig to split anyway and form a group of our own and run it the way we wanted to, so that was it . . . Vince is going to work for *Go-Set* and Paddy will get another group. We're going to add an electric piano and organ and a new drummer and go into hiding for a couple of months. Then we'll record an LP and a single and follow it up with a shit-hot group and make lots of money. The funny thing about it was that there were no arguments or hard feelings as everyone realized that a change was due.

The band returned to Melbourne and played its last show with a distinct lack of fanfare, at Werribee, a desolate, far-flung suburb known only for its sewage treatment plant.

DARCY: "The last job, it was a funny one, because no one . . . it didn't sort of hit home, that we were doing the last job. I was sort of blown out, What, we're doing the last job down at Werribee? It was like, it was a Sunday night, and so we were doing this job, and that was it. It was like, Shit, what are we going to do now?"

But if Bon had plans, they ended up just that, best-laid plans. He was made a better offer, one that held great promise.

Fraternity get back to nature, Aldgate, September 1971. Left to right: Mick Jurd,
John Freeman, "Uncle" John Ayers, Bon, Bruce Howe, Sam See, John Bisset.

6. FRATERNITY

Adelaide was probably the last place Bon would have expected to end up, but within six months of the Valentines' dissolution, he found himself there, living the whole communal hippie trip as a member of the band Fraternity.

Fraternity leader Bruce Howe asked Bon to come up to Sydney to join his band as soon as he heard the Valentines were breaking up. Bon leapt at the chance: Fraternity was the hottest new band in the land, even if they didn't yet have a true lead singer.

Fraternity had strong Adelaide connections from the start. The band had spun off from the hallowed Levi Smith Clefs, an Australian musical institution led by Adelaide legend Barrie McAskill. Bruce Howe himself was an Adelaide boy, as was drummer John Freeman. And Fraternity was already tied to Adelaide-based independent record company, Sweet Peach, as were the Levi Smith Clefs.

But relocating to Adelaide, removing themselves from the center of things, would in fact quell Fraternity's potential. Such was the naiveté and conceit that characterized the times, however, that Fraternity were convinced the world would come to them, and in the process establish Adelaide as an alternative music center—like an antipodean Nashville. It wouldn't quite work out that way.

Adelaide is a sleepy small town; not a city, many say, but a big country town, if a very sophisticated one. As Australia's first free settlement (all the other major cities have convict roots), the capital of South Australia has always regarded itself as a bastion of liberalism and the arts. The biannual Adelaide Festival remains Australia's premier arts event.

Adelaide also has an extremely significant rock'n'roll tradition. As the

Adelaide's Clefs in Melbourne, 1966, before Barrie McAskill took over the band and it became the Levi Smith Clefs. L-R: drummer Gil Matthews (who later joined Billy Thorpe and the Aztecs), singer McAskill, bassist Bruce Howe, guitarist Les Tanner (kneeling), and original leader, organist "Tweed" Harris.

city that spawned Cold Chisel, the Angels and the Little River Band in the seventies, it has proved a wellspring of talent. But Adelaide bands have always had to flee Adelaide to make it.

Fraternity flew in the face of convention when they were lured back to Adelaide by an offer of support from a wealthy patron of the arts. They were immediately elevated to superstar status there, and it was this that blinded them to reality.

But then, in the early seventies, reality was a concept seriously under siege.

Adelaide had produced a disproportionate share of top groups during the sixties as well, among them the Twilights, the Vibrants, the Masters Apprentices, the Groove and the Zoot.

In 1967, South Australia predicted the coming national sea change when Don Dunstan became state premier. Dunstan was a Labor Party man in a pastel-colored safari suit, who set a pace that even reformist Labor Prime Minister Gough Whitlam was hard pressed to equal in the 1970s. South Australia was the first Australian state to legalize homosexuality, to decriminalize pot, and to recognize equal rights for women.

When South Australian licensing laws were amended to allow late-night closing, rock'n'roll moved into pubs. The climate was thus perfect for a band that believed it could rewrite all the rules.

Bruce Howe had only ever reluctantly left Adelaide in the past. Growing up in the rough and tumble docklands of Port Adelaide, Howe became a professional musician almost as soon as he left high school in 1964. He joined an outfit called the Clefs, a rock'n'roll revue led by Englishman Tweed (né Winston) Harris. Gigs were plentiful; the scene was exploding.

When Scotsman Barrie McAskill joined the Clefs later in 1964, he was already something of a godfather of the Adelaide scene. With his band the Drifters, he had helped pioneer rock'n'roll in South Australia. The Clefs provided McAskill with a more contemporary vehicle, and gradually he took over the band from Tweed Harris. Moving to Melbourne in 1966, the Clefs established a reputation on the circuit there, cutting a couple of singles. But it wasn't long before the young Bruce Howe returned to Adelaide. Tweed Harris himself would also eventually leave the Clefs when the band became a game of musical chairs revolving around McAskill as he moved on to Sydney.

But by May 1969 Howe was back in the fold as the wild and sometimes outrageous McAskill assembled an all-new incarnation of what was now called the Levi Smith Clefs. The old one had left en masse to form Tully, one of the very first Australian "head" bands. This new version of the Clefs met with the greatest success. Its line-up was completed by guitarist Mick Jurd, keyboardist John Bisset, and drummer Tony Buettel. Jurd was a few years older than Bruce, a Sydneysider who had played since the early days of rock'n'roll; Bisset was a New Zealander who had come to Australia with a band called the Action; Buettel had been in Brisbane's seminal blues crusaders, the Bay City Union.

The Levi Smith Clefs were a disco band without peer, except perhaps for Max Merritt and the Meteors. They learnt their chops playing four sets a night, six nights a week, at the Whiskey. "They constantly draw huge crowds," read one newspaper report. "Many American negro R&R men who come to Sydney on leave speak highly of the Clefs' gutsy sound." It was a measure, however, of the lack of initiative of major Australian record companies that the Clefs' success as a live band didn't translate onto record. It took maverick new Adelaide-based independent label Sweet Peach to try to achieve that.

Sweet Peach was a forerunner of Australian indies like Havoc, Sparmac and Mushroom, which sprang up with a new wave of music in the early seventies. It was the result of a partnership between American emigrée Pam Coleman, who wanted to buy into the thriving music scene she saw in Australia, and expatriate English producer Jimmy Stewart, who had set Australia on its ear when he created the huge 1968 hit "Love Machine" out of an anonymous studio band called Pastoral Symphony. Sweet Peach's first album release was 1969's *In the Quiet Corners of My Mind* by Kevin Johnson, who is today best remembered for his redoubtable 1973 hit, "Rock'n'roll (I Gave You the Best Years of My Life)."

The Levi Smith Clefs visited Adelaide in June 1969 to play a season at the 20 Plus Club. Sweet Peach put them into the studio at that time; in a matter of mere hours they emerged with a finished album. At around the same time, Doug Ashdown, a folkie who had recorded for CBS during the sixties, was back in hometown Adelaide at a loose end. Joining forces with Jimmy Stewart, he set to work on an album for Sweet Peach, for which, taking a leaf out of Dylan's book, the Clefs were recruited "to provide some rhythm."

The Clefs' album, *Empty Monkey*, was released in March 1970, following a single, a lackluster reworking of Junior Walker's "Shotgun." Complete with a laminated, stiff-card gatefold sleeve and esoteric artwork, it looked for all the world like an American record. Appropriately, it was greeted with unbridled zeal. *Go-Set's* review opened with the line, "THIS IS THE BEST ROCK ALBUM EVER PRODUCED IN AUSTRALIA."

In retrospect, *Empty Monkey* is ponderous and overwrought, but at the time it was ground-breaking simply because it was an album, when so few Australian bands had actually cut albums. Even so, it wouldn't sell.

Meantime, MCA America had heard the Doug Ashdown album—a double-set no less (Australia's first) called *Age Of Mouse*—and expressed interest in releasing it. All this went to the Clefs' heads. Didn't backing Australia's answer to Dylan on a double-album make them the Australian equivalent of the Band? The Clefs became convinced they were leading Australian rock's charge into a new age of seriousness. So, like Tully before them, they split from Barrie McAskill (with Bruce Howe leading the mutiny), leaving him high and dry on the road in Melbourne. Christening themselves Fraternity, the new band returned to Sydney and set up house in a two-storey terrace in Jersey Road, Paddington, near Centennial Park. Sweet Peach put them straight into the studio to cut a single to capitalize on the radio ban.

With two tracks in the can—a Doug Ashdown original "Why Did It Have to Be Me?" and a cover of a Moody Blues album track, "Questions"—Fraternity signed on with the dominant Nova agency to look for work.

The Valentines' decision to break up had been announced by then, and so Bruce got in touch with Bon. Even before Bon could make it up

Early Fraternity days: Bon and Bruce Howe at Jersey Road, Paddington, August 1970.

to Sydney, Fraternity scored the resident spot at Jonathans, a disco on Broadway in south central Sydney (junior partner in the residency was a young band from the Sydney suburbs called Sherbet).

With Bruce and John Bisset sharing singing duties as they had on the single, the band played Doug Ashdown songs, songs by the Band, a few songs left over from the Clefs, and occasional standards like "Little Queenie." Other musicians would sit in, among them Maori vocalist extraordinaire Leo de Castro; "Uncle" John Ayers, a harmonica player who regularly sat in with Copperwine; and a singer by the name of Dennis Laughlin, who himself had recently left Sherbet and was then working for Nova. All the while Fraternity was promising the arrival of a great new singer.

Meantime, in Melbourne, as Barrie McAskill assembled yet another Clefs lineup, Bon played the last few Valentines shows. By the time he arrived in Sydney, he had sprouted a goblin-like beard. He slotted straight in. "The last time we saw Bon Scott was at a teenybopper concert in Melbourne, with the Valentines," wrote one Sydney paper. "We thought he was wasting his voice then. We know he was now. A distinctive, heavy voice . . . and the group is very, very professional."

Fraternity was hot. The band boasted that MCA in America, after hearing the single, now wanted an album from them. Sweet Peach started hustling studio time. The Sydney *Sunday Mirror* ran a full page pin-up of them, proclaiming them as "rapidly on the way to becoming Australia's greatest hard rock group."

Bon wrote to Maria on July 15:

> Well, everything up here is peaches and cream. If the writing is worse than usual it's because I'm sloshed. I've been sitting out on the patio in the beautiful warm sun writing for about two hours drinking brandy and coke. I've managed to become quite an alcoholic in two weeks. The disco we play in is licensed + we get spirits real cheap so . . . The group is gas. I'd go so far as to say world class. We'd shit over anything in Australia as over-all sound goes. We've had offers to go to Adelaide and Perth already but we're not going on the road until our LP is released. We start recording next week. It will be all original, most of the stuff written by Doug Ashdown who you may have heard of. We signed overseas contracts yesterday for America and we should be going in about three or four months. I'd love to go to the States and make it without ever appearing anywhere in Australia except Sydney and without any bullshit.

Sydney, with its licensed disco circuit, was booming, so much so that it momentarily overshadowed Melbourne. Copperwine had had a hit album. The Flying Circus was in line to win the Battle of the Sounds. Fraternity led a pack of newer bands, which included Chain (with Wendy Saddington on vocals), Blackfeather and Leo de Castro's King Harvest.

Woodstock's effect had been felt. The musical naiveté of the sixties had been outgrown. As far back as 1968, Australian musicians had begun searching for something—a sense of where the music had come from, so as to know where it might now go. When the radio ban was lifted after six months in October 1970, a new mood dawned. "It was an explosion of creativity, not all of it for the best, but everyone was having a go, trying to forge a new path," said Sam See, a founding member of Sherbet, who would go on to join the Flying Circus, and then later Fraternity, and then later still, rejoin the Circus.

SAM SEE: "I got to know Fraternity by being a late-night drinker at the Whiskey. The thing I really liked about them was that they were trying to approach an Australian sound. Later on it happened. They weren't really popular, but musicians, the hip cognoscenti liked them. We would have heated arguments at Jersey Road—Bruce and I used to argue at great length and great volume—where I'd say, Well, we blew you guys off stage tonight, in terms of the audience, and he'd say, Yeah, but we're doing something of our own."

"There were a lot of folk singers around then too, and so we all got into songs, words that meant something," said Peter Head, who had much in common with Fraternity as a member of Adelaide allies, Headband. "It was the first time anyone used Australian place names in songs. I remember having arguments with people who said you can't use Australian names in a song, they sound daggy, they've got to be American."

When Barrie McAskill and a new Levi Smith Clefs arrived back in Sydney to resume their Whiskey gig, Bruce Howe immediately swooped on them and poached drummer John Freeman, another old Adelaide boy, to replace Tony Buettel.

When Bon moved into Jersey Road, the first thing he did was paint his room fire-engine red again. The house was a regular meeting place. Sam See lived just around the corner. Virtuoso Blackfeather guitarist John Robinson often slept on the couch. Robinson had almost completed a song called "Seasons of Change" which Fraternity helped him finish, and so he gave it to them.

The turntable hit in the house was *In the Court of the Crimson King,* the recently-released debut album from English art-rock outfit King Crimson. Bon would sit cross-legged on the floor in front of the stereo, stoned, soaking it up. Other favorites included Deep Purple, Procol Harum, ("A Whiter Shade of Pale" had been a hugely influential record), Poco, the Band, Rod Stewart, and Van Morrison. Mick Jurd was the band's resident musicologist, and he named artists like Wes Montgomery, Barney Kessel and B.B. King as his heroes. The mood of the times was such that the more esoteric your taste, the more "progressive" you must be.

Fraternity were trying to get a start on recording the album the Americans apparently wanted. Bon wrote to Maria in September.

Being Saturday it's our last night for the week. We will be leaving Jonathans soon and going to greener pastures for more money. It's been gas working there because it helped the group improve over three months what would have normally taken six. We're doing about 70 per cent original songs now and by the time you see us we'll be doing about 150 per cent or something.

Wendy Saddington and Jeff St John (name dropping again) came down to hear us on Thursday night and sat in with us on a couple of songs. They reckon we would probably be the best in Australia. Coming from them it's a real compliment.

Our record called "Why Did It Have to Be Me," is released this week. Unfortunately it was recorded before I made it up here and I'm not singing on it. But it don't matter as long as it gets airplay for the group. It will be released in the States next week and with a lot of luck, well, who knows. We start the LP again soon as we have to have it out for Christmas and this time all the songs on it will be our own. I haven't contributed anything worthwhile yet but once again it don't matter. The only thing that counts is the group.

The single failed to do any business. By then though, the band was able to fob it off as a premature and already redundant artifact. They were only thinking about the album. But the single was never released in America, and the album they would eventually finish, after a few false starts, would be shelved even in Australia.

Livestock, as the album was called when Sweet Peach finally released it over a year later, was a mishmash. Often featuring Bon on recorder, songs like "Jupiter's Landscape," "Raglan's Folly," "You Have a God" and "It" were pompous, ponderous art rock; "Grand Canyon Suite" was would-be Aaron Copeland; only "Sommerville," "Cool Spot," and the title track still stand up as tight, sharp exercises in sophisticated songwriting and arrangement.

Even without this new vinyl the hype kept running hot. Fraternity appeared live on super-groovy new TV show *GTK*. New national magazine *Sound Blast* put Bon on the cover, wearing war-paint and an expression to match.

After playing a few shows late in September on the belated Australian tour by the 1910 Fruitgum Company, the band played the support spot on a tour by Jerry Lee Lewis. They "did some nice instrumental things," Greg Quill reported in *Go-Set*, "and Bon, all painted and cheeky, managed to make people laugh a little."

The Killer tour took Fraternity to Adelaide, where they supported Lewis at the Apollo Stadium and played a couple of gigs of their own at a disco called Headquarters. It was this visit which would alter the course of their career.

Anticipation surrounding Fraternity naturally ran high in Adelaide. It was further pumped up because Vince Lovegrove, ironically, had also landed in Adelaide, and was in a position to hype his old mate's new band vigorously.

In addition to his gig as *Go-Set*'s Adelaide correspondent, Vince was writing a music column for the *News*, and had managed to get a local TV show up and running on Channel 9. The show, which like his newspaper column was called *Move*, was essentially an expanded, weekly variation on *GTK*. Its premiere episode on October 17 featured Fraternity, "Australia's only group with a completely original repertoire."

"They came—they played—they CONQUERED!" Vince wrote in *Go-Set* of the Headquarters gig. Never had prodigal sons been made to feel more welcome. But if the band was progressing quite nicely, the course of its career was about to alter with the intervention of one Hamish Henry. Henry was the man behind the Grape Organization, a booking agency that promoted Headquarters, among other Adelaide gigs. But Hamish Henry was much, much more than the average rock entrepreneur.

Henry was a rich kid with a vision, a patron of the arts who had been swept up in the euphoria of the Age of Aquarius. Born into old Adelaide money, he held down a day job with the family business, State City Motors, and ran a successful North Adelaide art gallery as well as Grape. But what Henry really wanted—like Andy Warhol and John Sinclair—was a band he could cultivate himself. When he saw Fraternity at Headquarters he knew he'd found what he was looking for. He made them an offer: he'd set them up in Adelaide, house them, equip them, manage them, pay them a wage. It was, of course, an offer Fraternity couldn't refuse. They left Adelaide set to return there for good in January.

The band swung through Melbourne on the way back to Sydney, to play two nights at the Thumpin' Tum. Bon caught up with Darcy there. In Sydney at the start of December, he wrote to Maria, whom he'd missed in Melbourne.

> We went over real well at the Tum both nights although I must admit it looked like a Valentines' Fan Club outing. I was really knocked out at the old faces who hadn't forgotten me.
>
> Adelaide was too much. It was the best trip I have ever done anywhere ever. We were treated like Kings. We were given a Valiant station wagon to drive around in and a van and roadie for our gear. We didn't carry a single item the whole time we were there. We absolutely killed the crowds at Headquarters where we played and we even had four days' holiday at John (drummer) Freeman's beach house. Toooo much.

Saw my pal Vince. We did his TV show. It's really good and when it goes national he should be on top of the world again. I don't know if Graeme told you but we're going to Adelaide to live on Jan 4. I'll tell you all the reasons next time I see you as it's too detailed to write about.

On December 19, 1970 Vince broke the news in *Go-Set* that Fraternity were about to take the radical step of moving to Adelaide. The talk was still of going to America by the following June or July.

The band played the Odyssey festival outside Sydney, between Christmas and New Year, before heading for Adelaide where it would play the Myponga festival—a virtual homecoming.

Neither Odyssey nor Myponga was the first Australian outdoor rock festival—that distinction belongs to Ourimbah in 1969—but all three predated Sunbury, which first took place in 1972 yet is still the Oz rock festival most commonly mythologized.

Allowing six months for the idea of Woodstock to reach Australia, Ourimbah was nevertheless premature. True, its bill boasted the cream of Australia's progressive bands, but virtually none of them had a record out at the time. When Myponga took place a year later, it was a different story. 1971 can be considered a golden era for Australian rock'n'roll, a time when it came of age. By early 1971, with at least a couple of the major record companies now confident enough to get down among the grass roots, a new wave of credible, creative post–San Francisco Australian bands dominated the music scene. Having worked their way up on the live circuit, bands like Billy Thorpe's born-again Aztecs, Spectrum, Chain, Blackfeather and Daddy Cool—nearly all of them from Melbourne—populated the singles and newly-instituted albums charts alike, and filled houses all over the country.

The timing was apposite. Australia in general was on the eve of a social revolution. After more than 20 years' of conservative government by the Liberal Party, the Labor Party stormed to power in 1972, led by the great reformer Gough Whitlam.

With a bill boasting an exclusive appearance by Black Sabbath as well as the cream of Australia's progressive bands, Myponga—bankrolled, almost inevitably, by Hamish Henry—was the biggest thing to hit Adelaide since the Beatles attracted a record crowd of 300,000 to a civic reception there in 1964. "The age of historic high cultures is at an end," said Adrian Rawlins, the Meher Baba disciple who emceed Myponga. "[It is] an age when rhythm brings a new and real spiritual uplift to the young. The kids are responding to vibrations within themselves, rather than to conventional standards imposed from without." This sort of psychobabble went down a treat.

Even though Myponga received them rapturously, it would ultimately prove to be more like a death knell than a homecoming for Fraternity. The revolution in Australian music would not emanate from Adelaide, and Fraternity would be too far removed from the center of that revolution to benefit at all from it.

Sydney enjoyed a place in the sun around the turn of the decade, but that momentum dissipated just as quickly. Everybody just seemed to skip town. As the American presence decreased with the winding down of the Vietnam War, the disco circuit degenerated and became the province of showbands. Melbourne regained the initiative again and played host to 1971's extraordinary surge of creativity.

The act that epitomized the era was Billy Thorpe and the Aztecs. After Thorpe was declared bankrupt in 1967, he repaired to Melbourne to start over. By 1969 he had assembled a new incarnation of the Aztecs, featuring guitar hero Lobby Loyde, and had gained an ambitious manager in Michael Browning. Thus commenced an ascent which would see Thorpe reign unassailable as the king of Oz rock in the early seventies, and the Aztecs become a band which would change the face of Australian rock'n'roll.

Chain (now in its classic form with erstwhile Bay City Union singer Matt Taylor out front) and Leo de Castro set up shop in Melbourne. Ross Wilson also exerted his patriarchy—the break-up in 1969 of his Party Machine spawned not only Daddy Cool but also Spectrum.

The other legacy of the repressed late sixties was that there were not only musicians, but also entrepreneurs who were all the more determined to break through. The power structures were then being built that formed the basis of those which still exist today. Future Mushroom Records mogul Michael Gudinski emerged during this period. After serving an apprenticeship at Bill Joseph's AMBO agency, he corralled Joseph and fellow former AMBO agent Michael Browning to form Consolidated Rock when AMBO folded in 1970.

The generic guidelines for Australian rock were being set. Bands like Spectrum, Daddy Cool and Company Caine might have taken individualistic tangents, but together bands like the Aztecs, Chain, and Carson constituted a unified push. These bands were trying to connect with the roots of rock—the blues, basically—in which Australian music had so little tradition and for which reason it had always lacked body, not to mention soul. And even if the Aztecs' recordings have not stood the test of time—today they sound sludgy and bloated—their grinding, guttural base established the foundations for a monstrous mutation of the blues which was unique to Australia.

Billy Thorpe's sole ambition at that time, as many have testified, was simply to be the loudest band in the world, and with his trademark massive stacks of Strauss amplifiers, designed by Lobby Loyde (who had by then left the band), he came pretty close. Former Valentine Wyn Milson was then serving as Thorpe's sound mixer: "It was a rougher, boozier sort of thing. The start of headbanging. The audience didn't so much want to listen to the music as be flattened by it."

Fraternity had more than a little in common with both the blues and arty strains, but they were in no position to capitalize on it, stuck away in Adelaide, apparently reluctant to get out on the road, and tied to a record company whose reach was severely limited.

After playing Myponga, the band went into the studio to put down "Seasons of Change," the first single featuring Bon. On April 8, they played a support spot on the Adelaide leg of the Deep Purple/Free/Manfred Mann tour. At the end of April, as the single was released, they moved en masse to the farm up in the hills.

It was perhaps the first sign of things to come when "Seasons of Change" was beaten to the punch nationally by the version released by Blackfeather, whose John Robinson was, after all, the song's author. But their idyll in the Adelaide hills lulled Fraternity into a false sense of superiority, and as their version of "Seasons of Change" climbed the South Australian charts, they chose to ignore the signs.

7. UP IN THE HILLS TOO LONG

"Fraternity live like no other band in Australia," Vince Lovegrove wrote in *Go-Set,* "in a house in the hills 17 miles from Adelaide. Surrounded by seven acres of bushland, they're secluded from everything but nature. What a buzz!"

Fraternity had noted the Band's example—they had set up a communal base on a Woodstock farm called Big Pink—and Hemming's Farm, as Fraternity's Aldgate property was known, became their own Big Pink.

In May, "Uncle" John Ayers came to town with Copperwine and stayed behind. Bruce Howe asked him to join Fraternity and he moved straight onto Aldgate.

"Fraternity are into a trip of their own," Vince went on. "Sure they know they're good. Why else are they playing music professionally? But they've passed the ego scene years ago. They don't need ego trips, because they see too many good things in life, and they don't want to lose them."

This idea was farcical, of course. Fraternity was a strictly hierarchical and very volatile band. Bruce Howe was the boss—there were no two ways about that—and Mick Jurd was his senior partner. John Bisset, who wrote more material than any other member of the band, was a brilliant but troubled man; he and Mick Jurd did not get on. Both Bon and Uncle simply managed to go with the flow. Uncle was "upstairs" (Fraternity-speak for out of it), even by the standards of the day.

HAMISH HENRY: "Bon was just a gregarious, very nice guy. I used to swim with him; he was a very good swimmer. To Bruce and Mick and John Bisset, a singer was probably something of a necessary evil, and so Bon revolved around them, rather than vice versa. Bon was always late, for rehearsals or gigs or whatever, and Bruce and Mick probably did discuss sacking him, but they couldn't have done it. I think the band was appropriately named, because it was very much like a family, and Bon belonged to the family."

"Fraternity was a shitter for Bon, because all those other guys were educated, and he started to feel he was inferior," said Pat Pickett, who became friends with Bon after encountering Fraternity in Melbourne around this time. "They wouldn't let him write any lyrics. A lot of the early AC/DC stuff was written during those days."

JOHN FREEMAN: "Bon joined Fraternity to learn about music really, I think. Whatever else, he could sing, and he had what most singers would give their eyeteeth for—a distinctive voice. He joined Fraternity so he could learn about music, so he could go off and be a rock'n'roll star."

Bon and Bruce were like chalk and cheese, but they shared a bond, and Bon readily deferred to Bruce. With his portly stature and prematurely thinning hair, Bruce looked almost Buddha-like, and indeed, he had a sort of an aura about him, and a hold over the entire band. Bon and Bruce remained close even after Bon effectively deserted Fraternity. Bruce was perhaps the only man Bon ever really confided in, whose advice Bon always sought out and respected.

If Bon's own musical input was less than it might have been, he nevertheless felt privileged just to be working with musicians he held in awe. But they were by no means a band who worked hard. Fraternity played a couple of gigs a week at most, and in their three-year, two-album career produced barely a dozen original songs.

PETER HEAD: "Fraternity spent most of their time on magic mushrooms. Everybody smoked dope, everybody. Everybody took mushrooms. Plus, Fraternity were all heavy drinkers as well."

The days and nights at Aldgate passed in one long, slow, lazy, hazy stoned-immaculate flow. There was no call to do anything especially. If food was required, a big, brown, sloppy pseudomacro stew was concocted. "Hamburgers hurt," muttered Uncle. Every weekend, tribes of beautiful people from Adelaide would descend upon the place, tripping out, soaking up the good vibes generally, and fucking each other silly.

Bon was almost 25. He hadn't a care in the world. He acquired the nickname Ronnie Roadtest due to his willingness to try anything. Vince described him as "constantly in a dream world of his own . . . but he's having a ball."

In late May 1971 Fraternity went out on the road, first to Perth, then Queensland. The response in Perth was ecstatic—the band up-

"They wanted to be the Band" (Vince Lovegrove). Fraternity as a six-piece, winter 1971: Mick Jurd, John Freeman, "Uncle" John Ayers, Bruce Howe, Bon, John Bissett.

staged Chain, then riding high on the back of "Black and Blue"—but in Queensland it was mixed. A *Go-Set* review of a Brisbane gig described them as "loud, too loud sometimes." Sheer volume was part of Fraternity's arrogance.

At this time Queensland's infamous hillbilly dictator Joh Bjelke-Petersen was at the height of his powers, and Fraternity ran afoul of the law. Playing on the Gold Coast, the cops showed up and told them to turn down. Which they did, but with qualifications.

BRUCE HOWE: "Bon made this speech, on stage, about the Queensland cops, you know, and the promoter was standing there, just shaking his head. Bon was quite naive about political things. He was very street smart, he had this ability to assess people on the spot, their character, and generally his gut feelings were pretty good. But when it came to politics, that sort of knowledge, he was absolutely fucking hopeless. Of course, it went over really well with the crowd, because he'd stood up.

"The cops stopped the show; we had to get off. I said to Bon, you dickhead. Because I used to be like that with him, when he'd do things like that, when he'd be at his most naive. I said, I told you what it was like up here. We started to talk about politics. Bon didn't understand the technicalities. Like, listening to politicians talk on the TV, or reading about it in the paper, used to bore the shit out of him, but we might be just sitting on the bus, out of it, nobody else around, and Bon would say, Well, why is it? Why is that allowed to happen in Queensland, and yet if I said that in Adelaide nobody would give a fuck?"

UNCLE: "Bon was really perceptive in some ways. Blind in others. In some ways he had his feet firmly on the ground. He was so down to earth, there were some areas where Bon could see the wood for the trees where others couldn't. Yet there was that other side that was out to lunch."

Back in Adelaide, the band resumed its comfortable lifestyle around the winter fires. Talk around the rest of the country was that Fraternity had become complacent and spoiled in their private domain. They countered that they were preparing to go to America.

JOHN FREEMAN: "Hamish should have made us work a lot harder, we should have done much more work on the east coast. But we always thought we were above that."

At home, Fraternity could do no wrong. Routinely playing at least once a week at the Largs Pier Hotel, they established themselves as an Adelaide legend.

Melbourne is usually cited as the birthplace of pub rock, but while it may have been the cradle, it was in Adelaide that Australia's first real regular pub gigs sprang up—and the first of those was the Largs Pier. At the height of Melbourne's renaissance in 1971, its live circuit still consisted largely of dances and discos. Pubs wouldn't open up to rock'n'roll for a few years yet. Adelaide pubs, however, embraced this new trade.

The Largs was down by the beach at Semaphore, opposite the pier of the same name. After all the taboo-breaking of the sixties, kids were growing up a lot quicker, and nothing made them feel more grown-up than going into pubs. This meant that the crowds at the Largs ranged from 15-year-olds, who were able to get away with getting in, to sixties survivors—all determined to write themselves off to the tune of roaring rock'n'roll.

Bands that regularly went over to Adelaide—the Aztecs, Daddy Cool, Max Merritt and the Meteors, the La De Das—loved playing there. But Fraternity were the hometown heroes who had baptized the place, and they were the house band.

Fraternity changed with its audience. The Largs was as rough as guts and Bon felt right at home there. He would prop up the bar, a hard-up hero wallowing in Scotch and adulation. Occasionally he would catch some flak. After all, as a tall poppy he was asking to be cut down. Besides, he would flirt with all the wrong girls. Bad girls. Who had bad boyfriends. Brawling was commonplace. Regular audience members included future Cold Chisel singer Jimmy Barnes and his half-brother John Swann.

JIMMY BARNES: "We used to go into Adelaide, and we'd go in a gang to fight, you know. It was, hey, let's go into Adelaide—and wreck it!"

JOHN FREEMAN: "At that stage, because it was the only gig of its type, it used to draw a much wider audience than just the locals, and I think there might have been an element of the locals versus everybody else. The thing was, it was just so crowded—we used to play on this tiny stage in the corner—and so how 700 people could possibly spend four hours in an environment designed for four, without some sort of aggravation, well, it just couldn't happen."

SAM SEE: "Bon was always into a bit of a scrap. I was never partial to it. But he'd go out to the bar, have a drink with this guy, fight that guy . . ."

UNCLE: "I remember Bon and JB [John Bisset] at the Largs Pier once, both totally blind drunk, trying to find the biggest Maori in the room to fight him. He had to be at least nine foot six! I saw Bon jump off the stage a couple of times, because he saw it actually happening in the crowd. But I never saw him set on anybody, or set them up."

The Largs crowd had no truck with anything "poofy" or cerebral. As a result Fraternity's art-rock tendencies rapidly disappeared, replaced by a harder, rockier edge. Fraternity's claim that they single-handedly spawned pub rock is an overstatement, but given their evolving style and the seminal influence they exerted on Cold Chisel (the highpoint of the genre), there's more than a grain of truth in it.

BRUCE: "You had this young audience that would come and see you, and the more quad boxes and horns you stuck up, the louder you were, the more they liked it. They could tell what you were trying to do."

In August, Fraternity took out the national Battle of the Sounds. Sherbet were the only group to come near them, as *Go-Set* reported. But again, this only had the adverse effect of reinforcing Fraternity's belief that all was well.

The Battle no longer carried the prestige it once had—and the crowd at Melbourne's Festival Hall, where the final was held, was quite thin—but still it meant that Fraternity went home with much booty under their arms, including air fares overseas, and free studio time at Armstrong's.

"They won the Battle," remembered John Brewster, a friend of Bon's who was a roadie, "and there was all these prizes, so they divvied them up among everybody, and there was this stereo left over, after everyone had got their equal share. So they decided what they'd do was, whoever did the grossest deed, got it. So they're on their way back to Adelaide and Gus—they used to have this bus driver called Gus—all of a sudden, he pulls up the bus on the side of the road, and jumps out. He leaps the fence, grabs a sheep, humps it, and he goes, Howzat! He got the stereo. Bon told me that."

Sam See, home from Canada with the Flying Circus, was at the Battle of the Sounds show. Bruce asked him to join Fraternity. He leapt at the chance.

After the Battle victory, Adelaide's Channel Nine produced a special on Fraternity. The show portrayed the band at work and play up on the farm. Of course, there's no show without Punch, and so Bon had to put on a performance. Attempting a party trick riding one of the company trail bikes, he left the dirt road and came off into a briar patch. He emerged wearing a sheepish grin and many cuts and bruises.

Bon's trail bike stunts were legendary. He is variously said to have taken off on one from a party in the nude, and rode one up a flight of stairs into a crowded gig. On another occasion he impulsively rode over to Melbourne from Adelaide one weekend for a birthday party. Ill-prepared, wearing only a T-shirt, he got sun- and wind-burned by day; while by night he froze, sleeping in a ditch by the side of the road.

In September, Go-Set ran a cover story which proclaimed, "Fraternity: The Next Big Band?" The band journeyed to Sydney to play a short season at Chequers. A backstage scuffle ensured the season was even shorter—the band was sacked as a result. Fraternity's petulance had a way of turning on them. The question mark with which Go-Set had qualified its headline was prophetic.

Back in Adelaide, Bon moved off the farm and back down to town. Along with Bruce and John Bisset—and Bisset's wife Cheryl and son Brent, not to mention dog Clutch—they found a place on Norwood Parade, within spitting distance of the city.

BRUCE: "Me and Bon and John didn't take too kindly to the house in the hills. All these people would go up on the weekends, and just sit around and look at the trees and say how lovely everything was. Me and Bon, if there was a prospective fuck or a wild time in the offing, we'd go back down to town. The problem was getting from the hills down to town. So we shifted back down."

Bruce was running amok because his girlfriend Anne was in England.

Bon was raging as ever. At first Bon took up with a girl called Fi who was one of the Valentines' foremost Adelaide fans. She'd returned to Adelaide after Bon saw her in Melbourne, where she was working for, of all people, Mary Wasylyk (now Walton), who had opened a boutique on trendy Chapel Street in Prahran. Bon hadn't seen much of his old friend Mary since she got married, until he walked into the In Shop to see Fi. He was surprised and delighted to encounter Mary there too, and their friendship was renewed.

The relationship with Fi was short-lived; she was looking for a man who was husband material. Bon was many things, but he wasn't that. On the rebound, he met a woman called Clarissa, a dancer with the Adelaide Festival Theatre, but that too was a brief fling. Before long, he was having an affair with a married woman called Margaret Smith. With her doctor husband, the petite, attractive dark-haired Margaret was a regular visitor to the farm. Her marriage was crumbling, and though her relationship with Bon was doomed in the short term, she would reappear later in his life.

PETER HEAD: "She was a rock'n'roll groupie made good. As soon as I saw her, I thought, She belongs with Bon. She was that same sort of wild woman."

BRUCE: "Bon loved his girls, but he didn't give them a lot. Sex. And things. Like, he'd come home with a bunch of flowers, or he'd cook a meal. But he wouldn't talk intimately to them, or share secrets, about his past life, whatever. He could commit to the boys, because boys are boys, and so when you have to go off and fight another war, everyone pats you on the back. But when it came to women, a family, that was very scary to Bon."

There was something about Bon that set him apart. Maybe it was the tattoos he'd become so ashamed of, as if they were indelible watermarks of an uncool, cruel youth.

JOHN FREEMAN: "I don't think anybody ever saw the real Bon, I don't think Bon ever knew the real Bon, that was his trouble."

UNCLE: "He was always willing to look for it!"

FREEMAN: "That was running away from it. He had such charisma it was difficult for him not to be on stage 24 hours a day.

"You know, he could walk into a room at a party and sit down in the corner, and he would be instantly surrounded by a crowd of women, who would put down their lives for him. My mother said he could put his slippers under her bed anytime, and my mother's a very conservative old woman."

UNCLE: "My mum too. Bon had this thing about him, he really

touched people when he met them, in a way you thought he really cared about you. So many guys considered him their best mate."

FREEMAN: "Life was only ever a transitory thing to Bon. He would drop a trip without worrying if there was anything he had to do that day. I know him to have gone to the dentist, for major surgery, whilst he was tripping. I've never known anyone else that would do anything like that."

UNCLE: "Bon lived for the moment. Forward planning, I mean, I don't think that was a part of his life. But I can never remember Bon not trying his hardest. I remember him living for the show, being alive during the show, and everything else being an anticlimax."

In September, Bon met the woman who would become his wife, Irene Thornton. Irene had just returned from a year-long working holiday in England. She knew Vince's girlfriend Julie, and through her and Vince, met Bon. She decided, as so many women did, that she fancied him. The difference was, she snared him.

Born in Adelaide in 1950, Irene was a nice girl from suburban Prospect. That she had just returned from England made her very cool. That she was also strikingly attractive, quite tall, with long, straight blonde hair and a slender figure, and was very down to earth—she liked a drink, wouldn't say no to a smoke, and enjoyed a joke, dirty or otherwise—made her irresistible to Bon.

Irene went with Vince and Julie to a party up on the farm. It was then that she first encountered Bon. Looking for the toilet, she burst in on him in a bedroom, sucking some woman's toes. The next time they met, at the Largs one night, she was more impressed: "He was funny. Chatting away, you know, he just came out with comical things. We just hit it off."

It was a whirlwind, fairy-tale courtship. For their first date, Bon and Irene went to the drive-in, and both sat bolt upright all night. Such was the effect Irene had on Bon, he was uncharacteristically nervous in her presence. They would go out and hold hands, and Bon would plant a peck on her cheek as he sent her inside at her parents' place at the end of the night. Irene was a princess, just as Maria had been, but unlike Maria, she would extend her golden braids out from the ivory tower. Irene fell in love with Bon, and she loved him for what he was. She remembers a night they spent early on in their relationship poring over the recently released book of comic strips, *The Adventures of Barry MacKenzie*, both cracking up. "I suppose we just had the same sort of sense of humor," she said. Indeed, it's impossible to overestimate the value Bon placed on laughter, and this

Bon and Irene on their wedding day, January 24, 1972, just prior to leaving for England with Fraternity.

he shared with Irene.

Irene was amused by his banter, and his high jinks. One time, to shock Irene's teenage sister Faye, he took off all his clothes and bounded past her and a girlfriend watching TV like he was Skippy the Bush Kangaroo. Faye was mortified; Irene, like Bon, was reduced to tears.

Soon Irene was staying over at Norwood, and before long she moved in.

The headline on Vince's column read, THEY'VE FAITH IN ADELAIDE: TO RECORD IN SOUTH AUSTRALIA, but the fact of the matter was that Fraternity didn't trust anyone in Australia to produce them. If Adelaide studios were inferior, at least if they were at home Fraternity could produce themselves. But the battle was the same all over Australia.

SAM SEE: I don't think [the sound] was ever caught on record, as a lot of Australian acts at that time weren't. The bands were victimized by the studios."

BRUCE: "The live gigs were the greatest satisfaction. We could not get it down on record. But we had some great live gigs."

October saw two "new" Fraternity singles released. The band had by now left Sweet Peach, and so in retaliation the label exhumed a track left over from the *Livestock* album sessions. "The Race" was a lyrically complex Doug Ashdown song described by *Go-Set* as "not [a single] which will help the group." The other new slice of vinyl was "If You Got It," which the band cut itself in Adelaide, and put out independently on its own Raven label. A straight boogie, it climbed to number two on the South Australian charts.

The band was now talking about going to America by June or July of the following year, 1972. Meantime, it's not as if they put their heads down at all. It was summertime, and the living was easy.

UNCLE: "There was this one party, the Three-Day Party . . . I think we'd played these two gigs, the Largs Pier, and the Bridgeway, there was 2,000 people there, it was Christmas or New Year's Eve or something, and so everybody was invited up to our place for a party. It went for three days. There was barbecues, security guys, whole bars full of spirits, bonfires all round the lawn. I had children born in my bed and grandmothers die; I remember picking up my sheets with a broomstick and taking them out to the bonfire at the end of the three days, I wasn't going to sleep in them again. I haven't been to a three-day party since. Those days are gone."

Bon and Irene were getting on swimmingly. Bruce was a lot happier too, because Hamish had flown Anne out from England to be with him. That was the sort of thing Hamish did. He believed, and he put his money where his mouth was. When the band needed a new Hammond organ because this particular song called for that particular sound, he got it for them. He had the foresight to form a publishing company for the band, so that they owned their own songs, which few bands do even today.

"With hindsight, I've got a lot of respect for Hamish," said Peter Head, who was also managed by him. "We all used to rubbish him at the time, can him about being rich—we had no appreciation whatsoever of the value of money—but he was the one who made things possible."

As big fish in a small pond though, Fraternity were getting nowhere fast. Even Vince dared suggest they needed to "get off their arses and get some hard work done."

SAM SEE: "Even though there was a sense that Fraternity shows were special, we were still doing the same gigs week in, week out. In those days, the concept of making it had no reality at all."

By January, plans had changed again. The band was now going to go to England. This was yet another mistake—the wrong place to go, at the wrong time—but it was where Hamish had connections. In the past year, as he'd tried in vain to get both T Rex and Yes out to tour Australia, he'd at least made some contacts over there. The plan was to finally use the free recording time they'd won at Armstrong's, then play a tour of South Australia for the Arts Council, then leave.

Again, the band spent a mere few days in the studio, cutting the album which, in a fit of Australianness, would be called *Flaming Galah*. It contained only three all-new songs—"Welfare Boogie," "Hemming's Farm" and "Getting Off"—alongside rewritten and re-recorded versions of old material. Hamish set up a deal to release it through RCA.

The decision to leave was a bad one not only because the climate in England at that time wouldn't suit a band like Fraternity, but also because Australia itself was just about to bound into the future. Only weeks before Fraternity left, Billy Thorpe acquired the first remote mixing desk ever seen in this country. Of course, right then, Fraternity couldn't wait to get out of Australia.

HAMISH: "We had this supreme self-confidence, coupled with a certain naiveté, and so we couldn't see any barriers whatsoever."

Prompted by Hamish's offer to pay for wives—but not girlfriends—to go overseas with the band, Bon and Irene decided to get married. They'd known each other for only a few months.

IRENE: "Everyone seemed to be doing it at the time. Bon had asked me to go away with him; then he told me that Hamish would pay, and so there was a few weddings going on. But we were really wrapped up in each other."

Bon and Irene's wedding merged into a blur along with Bruce and Anne's, and John Freeman's. Uncle had taken up with Freeman's wife's sister Vicki and while they wouldn't actually tie the knot, Vicki would go to England anyway. John Bisset and Mick Jurd had both been married all along; only Sam See was unattached.

BRUCE: "I didn't like the idea of Bon getting married to Irene, I thought it was premature. They didn't really know each other that well. But she was a nice girl."

With the wedding scheduled for January 24, Bon's mother Isa came over from Perth. She wasn't terribly impressed by the whole business either.

Bon and Irene, however, were extremely pleased with themselves. Bon loved Irene as she loved him; but as much as that, he loved the idea of her: that is, the most wanted woman in Adelaide was his.

SAM SEE: "Bon and Irene, when they got married, I remember it being like, I was going to say, Paul and Linda—it was all a bit glam, you know."

Bon and Irene get married, Adelaide, January 24, 1972. Graeme Scott: "It was a surprise to me, because not long before, Ron was telling me, 'You don't ever want to get married!'"

A civil service was held in town, with Bruce and John Bisset as witnesses. The bride wore a cream crepe forties-style jacket and a long crepe skirt; the groom, a poo-brown suit with flared trousers and wide lapels. A reception was organized up on the farm afterwards. "It was like the best party I ever went to I think," Irene said.

All possible futures seemed golden.

At the very same time, at a site 50 kilometers north of Melbourne, the first Sunbury festival was taking place. Billy Thorpe and the Aztecs headlined. It was this performance that crowned Thorpe's ascent. The resultant double-live album, released later in the year, outsold every other Australian album released in 1972. Everybody who was anybody was at Sunbury that weekend—except Fraternity.

Any ideas of a honeymoon that either Bon or Irene may have harbored were waylaid in excited anticipation of going to England. Besides which, the band was due to hit the road on February 12, on a tour devised by the Arts Council to take a bit of urban rock culture to the bush.

Trucking through South Australia in a big black bus, Fraternity were their own merry pranksters. Bon, Ronnie Roadtest, was in fine form, even if he was away from his new bride—or maybe because of it. Bruce Howe remembers one incident in particular, at Port Lincoln.

BRUCE: "It was one of those really still, hot South Australian days, and Bon said, I'm going for a swim. So he put his bathers on, and we walked out on the jetty. All these people were there. At the end of the jetty, they had these scales, for hanging the sharks they used to catch—the big white pointers. The water was so still and so clear you could see everything, and you could see it was just a sea of great big huge stingers, jellyfish, you know, with tentacles ten feet long, all just beneath the surface. Bon looks around, sees he's got an audience, and so what does he do? He climbs right up to the top of the shark tower and dives in. He swims underwater out of the reach of these things, and climbs back up. Of course, everybody on the jetty sends up this big round of applause. That's the sort of thing he was capable of. I was amazed."

Back in Adelaide by early March, the band played two concerts as part of the Adelaide Festival of Arts program, another first for rock music in the State. Repeating a role created by Tully in Sydney, Fraternity accompanied singer Jeannie Lewis and the Melbourne Symphony Orchestra in a performance of Australian composer Peter Sculthorpe's "Love 2,000." It was a last gasp for the band's "classical" aspirations.

"Welfare Boogie" was released by RCA as a single later in March. It did nothing, except perhaps provide a glimpse of the sort of themes Bon would later explore more fully with AC/DC:

I've got me a problem, a real social problem
I can't find employment for more than a week
You might think I'm sleazy, but you know it ain't easy
Finding employment's a job for a freak.

The album followed in April. But the general attitude to Fraternity seemed to be that they'd frittered away their potential. By then though, the band was in England—not so much a band as a juggernaut, an entourage numbering 16 people and a bus (plus Clutch the dog of course!). As far as Australia was concerned, Fraternity would be heard from no more. All the unfulfilled promises would be forgotten; the name Fraternity would just fade away.

England in 1972 was teetering giddily on the stack-heels of glam rock. The glittering stars were T Rex, David Bowie, Gary Glitter, and the Sweet. Fraternity were a bunch of bearded wonders playing what was more than once described as "country-rock." It was all they could do to polish their RM Williams stockman's boots.

Fraternity's 18 months in England would do nothing but grind the band down—and finally out. The experience also took a heavy personal toll, as interpersonal relationships, including Bon and Irene's marriage, soured. For the first six months they were there, they did virtually nothing. They found a place to live—a big four-storey house in Finchley—and sat around waiting for something to happen.

Had they gone to America as they'd originally planned, they might have fared better; they would have fitted right in on the West coast. But from the moment Fraternity arrived in London, it was obvious it wasn't going to be the picnic they'd expected. The mountain of gear they'd hauled half way round the planet was already antiquated.

Hamish Henry set up shop with his partner, former DJ Tony Mac-Arthur, as the Mainstreet Gramophone Company. MacArthur was managing French crooner Charles Aznavour, and acting for Dutch art-rock band Focus. Hamish got Fraternity on the books with a powerful agency, MAM, but he had little to sell the band on. That they were almost the next big thing in Australia just wasn't enough.

With more than a dozen people living under the same roof in Finchley, it was inevitable friction would occur.

IRENE: "Being young, you have expectations. I was 21, Bon was 25. The thing in England didn't help matters, because it wasn't conducive to normal life—a lot of pressure, not enough money, no one really with any privacy. If you wanted to go out to the back yard to hang out the washing, you had to walk through someone's bedroom. It was pretty hard to live like that, coming from Australia, having to live on nothing in miserable conditions. I think everyone got to really hate England."

The girls all had to go out and look for work to support the boys. Bruce and Anne—Anne who was at once pregnant and bedridden with a broken leg—holed up in the attic, above it all. Everyone was feeling the strain. England was cold and gray; Fraternity were nobodies there, and they were broke. Sparks started to fly. The only consolation the band found in England was the price of hash. They smoked red Leb by the brick.

In November, they played their inaugural English gig at the Speakeasy. It was a non-event. Beyond that, all the band really had lined up was a short German tour. At least it got the boys out of the house.

John Freeman wrote home to the *News,* "We are now moving into top gear in a flat-out bid to gain the necessary exposure that is vital for a new group such as ours." That flat-out bid consisted of infrequent gigging—the most Hamish could hustle—playing supports with bands that were second division at best—Atomic Rooster, Sparks, the Pink Fairies, Mungo Jerry. The most impressive bill Fraternity shared was with Fairport Convention.

SAM SEE: "The basic scam was that the wives went out to work and the band loafed at home. Really, to be honest about it, not doing much of anything, just sort of goofing off, watching telly and playing cricket in the back yard. It was really a bummer. And so maybe it's idle minds, I don't know . . .

"It really was a very squalid house, full of people who weren't united by anything except the music. I mean, the different personalities in that band, I don't think I've ever played in a band that was so diverse. And so when the music dropped off, all these personality differences came out. There was all sorts of cross-pollinations, violence both physical and verbal, mostly verbal."

Bon didn't know what to do with himself. He became frustrated when he was denied the release of performance. His whole being was thrown into question, he feared.

HAMISH HENRY: "The essence of Bon was when he was on stage, his thumbs stuck in his jeans and his chest sticking out, strutting his stuff. That was all he ever wanted to do."

Bon was reduced to getting a day job, like the girls. He went to work in a factory where he knotted wigs. He got Sam a job there too. He and Irene were squabbling constantly. Bon could be distant, cold almost, certainly brusque, and Irene felt the brunt of his frustration. They both grew resentful. It was a vicious circle. Irene gave as good as she got. She and Bon both had sharp tongues, and when they were downcast, especially after a few drinks—which was most of the time—neither of them was prepared to give an inch. If one slipped, said the wrong thing, the other jumped on it. Or else Bon just clammed up.

But there were good times, however few and far between. Irene remembers fondly how Bon was perplexed by the English propensity for forming queues—he would brazenly jump them, for no other reason than to rock the boat. She also remembers how he went to see Little Richard, one of his oldest heroes, and came home mortified, since it was obvious that the Georgia Peach was gay. Bon, in his innocence, never would have thought . . . Alex Harvey, however, was a different matter. Already thirty-something in the early seventies, the godfather of Scottish rock'n'roll was then at his peak, and Bon became one of his biggest fans. His humor, his storytelling bent and his energetic showmanship had a profound effect on Bon.

Fraternity scored only the odd gig. They'd had the wind knocked out of their sails. Sam See remembers one of the last gigs he played with the band. "We were all in the bus, the juggernaut, rolling down to Bourne-mouth to support Status Quo. The only thing we knew about them then was 'Pictures Of Matchstick Men'; it would've been just before they broke again with *Piledriver*. This was probably the last sign of the Fraternity arrogance which I always loved. As usual, on the way to the gig, we're having a few drinks, we reckon we're gonna cream 'em. So we're sitting there in the bus, waiting for the hall to open, because we were egalitarian, we all used to help lug the gear in. No stardom for us—bullshit! Anyway, so we're sitting outside the Bournemouth Odeon, and these two Bentleys pull up, and these guys resplendent in Kings Road finery get out. We're there, you know, 'Look at these pooftas,' Bon's going, 'Yaarrrgh!' We're at this point extremely confident we're going to make a name for ourselves in Bournemouth. So we went on, we did quite well, didn't get an encore but did okay, and then Status Quo came on, and they'd changed out of their satin and bells into the familiar Status Quo jeans and T-shirts, and they were three times as loud as us and twice as polished. They were hot.

"We lurched back to London with our tails between our legs. It was probably one of those nights where someone had too much to drink and punched somebody else, I can't remember for sure. But something went wrong within the ego of the band, definitely. By the time winter rolled around, I'd had it."

Sam moved on to Canada to rejoin the Flying Circus, where they were enjoying a modicum of success. "It was really the end I think, because we could all see that the band had lost its fight."

During the winter, Billy Thorpe, in all his arrogance, blundered through London. Fraternity were glad to see a familiar face. Thorpe hit town expecting to lay 'em in the aisles. He left after blowing one gig, at the self-same Speakeasy, where he had the plug pulled on him, ostensibly for being too loud. Thorpe's convenient excuse was that the imminent second Sunbury festival wanted him back, for a record fee of $10,000 plus air fares. He was on the first plane he could get.

Some time early in the new year Fraternity changed their name to Fang, "to fit in with the current English trend," whatever they thought that was. To Hamish, this marked the real beginning of the end.

In April 1973, Fang played a couple of gigs with Geordie, the Newcastle upon Tyne band whose singer, Brian Johnson, would eventually replace Bon in AC/DC. Graeme visited England at that time, and remembers those shows. "They had the bus, and the thing was, if they'd support a band,

Fraternity, now renamed Fang, play their last-ever gig, an outdoor show at Windsor, just outside London, August 1973. L-R: Bon, John Freeman, Uncle.

they'd take the other band's equipment too, and they were booked to go with Geordie. I think we went to Torquay first, and then we packed up that night and went on to Plymouth. Brian used to carry his guitar player on his shoulders too, I think that's where Ron got the idea, because when he joined AC/DC there was no one around doing that sort of thing. Angus was the perfect guy to carry around. He was so small."

In May, the band played a short tour of the provinces with Kraut-rock doomsayers, Amon Duul. The headliners, the *Gloucestershire Echo* said, were "an enormous contrast to the raucous Australian band who started the concert [whose] unambitious but multi-decibel bedecked set sounded much like the rhythm and blues material that was churned out by a million would-be Rolling Stones in the early '60s."

Relations within the band and its extended family were deteriorating to the point that final implosion was imminent. Uncle hocked Vicki's Mixmaster to buy hash. The drinking became increasingly heavy, putting a surly spin on things.

GRAEME SCOTT: "It was the boredom I think. They were hardly doing any shows, making nothing, and there was a lot of arguments, wifely troubles as well as band troubles, not just Bon and Irene but a lot of them; nothing was going right, and so I think the drink really came into it then."

Bon was feeling desperate, and one day he again seriously tempted fate.

IRENE: "I was at work, and when I came home, he was crawling around like a gibbering idiot."

He'd eaten datura, a poisonous plant once believed to have hallucinogenic qualities. Most self-respecting heads wouldn't touch it.

BRUCE: "That's when the darker side emerged, and you really knew you were dealing with a person who didn't care if he lived or died. There was this fatalistic side to Bon which was always there. He was fatalistic because he took risks. He took risks with drugs, it's true, it's not a myth."

IRENE: "Impulsive is the best word. He liked being outrageous. When he was pissed, he could either be the life of the party, or else, you could see it happen, his eyes would glaze over, almost go black, like there was something there really crapping him off, and a nasty side would come out."

Irene was in a panic trying to find out what he'd done, what he'd taken. "I was trying to get him to drink a glass of water or something, but he was just so completely off his face, he couldn't even talk. Uncle was frantically telephoning the hospital trying to find an antidote. Eventually, we gave him some lemon juice, and he just threw up."

By the summer of 1973 the band had ceased paying rent. Vicki, who was subsequently diagnosed as schizophrenic, was behaving increasingly erratically. John Bisset insulted Mick Jurd's wife Carol one time too many, and that spelled the end of him. Bon and Irene were at each other's throats. Resentment was also growing towards Hamish, who the band perceived as living in the lap of luxury at their expense.

In August, the band played what would be its last ever gig, a two-bit festival at Windsor. Hamish bailed out. He'd had enough. He'd sunk a small fortune into Fraternity, and he could no longer see any prospect of a return. The dream was over.

HAMISH: "I think the real reason Fraternity failed in England was because they were just too loud!"

The band lingered in London, shell-shocked, just wondering what to do. Bon got a job in a nearby pub, behind the bar. Unsurprisingly, he was a natural. But his and Irene's days were numbered.

The band started limping back to Adelaide. Uncle was the first to arrive, in November. "We just didn't make it in England," he told Vince in the *News*. "It's good to be back. [The others] will be home soon."

Bon and Irene arrived after Christmas, and went their separate ways.

Irene stayed at her parents' place; Bon moved in with Bruce and Anne and their infant son, into a tiny house down near the Port. But hope springs eternal. Bruce especially was hopeful that Fraternity would rise again; and Bon, that he and Irene would get back together.

But you can't undo the damage done. And the damage ran deep.

Finally back in Adelaide, Fraternity were in suspension, licking their wounds. Bon felt loyalties strongly, but even he wasn't sure that Fraternity, as such, had a future.

He sat tight, or rather even while he fidgeted, he held his tongue. He had enough to worry about as it was, with his separation from Irene.

IRENE: "It just got to a stage where you're arguing about everything, and there's just all this bitterness. We were just arguing about anything and everything, stupid little things that you wouldn't normally . . ."

BRUCE: "The thing that went wrong with their relationship was that Irene just needed more intimacy, not sexual intimacy—communication, you know. I think she just felt like sometimes Bon just used to shut up shop."

Isa, never one to mince words, said: "They both liked getting their own way too much."

Bon was reeling. It was maybe just as well then that he had to go out and get a job. No one else was going to support him, and it might keep him out of trouble. So, like Bruce who was supporting his young family by working as a builder's laborer, Bon started a day job for the first time in almost ten years. He loaded trucks at the Wallaroo fertilizer plant. It was a monumental comedown, but it was what he had to do to stay afloat. Bon could be stoic about such things.

He got a bike, a big Triumph, to get around on. He was mucking around with Peter Head's Mount Lofty Rangers, a band, of sorts, which at least allowed him to keep his hand in. He would drop in to see Irene at the place she'd found for herself in Stepney, but all that did was upset them both.

Bon's stoicism didn't extend to matters of the heart. He would have willingly succumbed to the ways of the flesh, and damn the consequences. Had Irene let him, he would have happily climbed back into her bed, and ridden off the next morning. That was his whole philosophy—tomorrow would never come. Bon refused to accept the truth—the marriage was over—and his visits only served to hurt himself as much as Irene.

Irene showed the greater strength. For all the love she still felt for Bon—and knew that he felt for her—she knew their marriage wouldn't work. Cruel to be kind, to both herself and Bon, she had to cut him loose.

Bon couldn't accept it. And so it was that one night after he'd had a row with Irene he arrived, already drunk, at a Rangers rehearsal, then stormed off from there, even more drunk, and rode his bike at high speed into an oncoming car. He was almost killed.

Bon was in a coma for three days. Irene didn't leave his side. "I remember being there once, sitting there with my sister, looking at the screen, you know, the heartbeat monitor, and the line stopping, and yelling for a doctor. The doctor came and banged him on the chest. It started again."

When Bon came to, he asked Irene if he could come home. What could she do? No one else was going to look after him. He was released a few weeks later.

IRENE: "He was terribly sick, he looked like a thin, frail old man. He was hunched from the broken collarbone, his throat was cut—he had a horrible scar there—and his jaw was wired up. He was just virtually skin and bone. And he must have had some sort of internal problem too.

"The clearest memory I have of Bon is of him in a blue checked dressing gown, after his accident, with his teeth missing," said Peter Head's wife Mouse, "and I guess I remember it because he just looked so shocking. I mean, his face was scarred, and you know, it had an impact pretty much on us all, when it happened."

Isa came over from Perth, to tend Bon during the daytime when Irene was out at work.

Bon never fully recovered from the accident—he bore scars and suffered pain for the rest of his life—but he was quickly on the mend. He was nothing if not resilient. He'd taken beatings before, and he would take them again. He even managed to find something in it all to laugh about. He sent Darcy and Gabby in Melbourne a picture of himself taken not long after the event, leering toothlessly at the camera, bearing the caption, "I left my teeth behind on the road." He was laid up, but he was still able to roll himself a steady supply of joints. He drank—liquor—through a straw.

IRENE: "He made a bit of an effort then, but [the marriage] was already stuffed. But it was probably like the friendship was a lot better after it was all over, when the bullshit, the bitterness, was out of the way."

It wasn't long before Bon was back on his feet, if unsteadily. He was already anxious about his professional future.

IRENE: "We went to a concert, I can't remember who it was, it was an outdoor concert, and there were people there from the industry who just walked right past him, and he said something like, These arseholes used to be all over me.

"He thought he was just a has-been."

Lacking any other option, Bon joined in rehearsals with Bruce, Uncle, John Freeman and guitarist Mauri Berg, formerly of Headband. (In July, he went into the studio with Pete Head and Carey Gulley and recorded two songs, "Round and Round and Round" and "Covey Gully," which would eventually see the light of day in 1996.)

Mick Jurd, like John Bisset, had remained in England. But Bon wasn't entirely convinced. And when the *News* devoted a story to Fraternity's ostensible reformation, it started to smell suspiciously like the bad old days. The band came across as full of all the same old bullshit: "We've got a lot of plans, and we're in no hurry."

The last thing Bon wanted was a repeat performance of the last three wasted years. He knew he had to find a ticket out.

AC/DC's first photo session, July 7, 1974, outside Her Majesty's Theatre in Sydney. Left to right: Rob Bailey, Angus Young, Malcolm Young, Dave Evans, Peter Clack.

8. THE YOUNGS

Where the water sparkles on the harbor, in the wash of the Bridge and the Opera House, Sydney is one of the postcard prettiest cities in the world. But the daily reality for most Sydneysiders is a massive suburban sprawl. Crawling along Parramatta Road in a gritty carbon-monoxide haze, you are confronted by the bleak brick-veneer vista that is Sydney's dreaded western suburbs.

The west is commonly decried as a cultural wasteland. But that's the exclusive opinion of the snobbish arbiters of taste who believe that art doesn't exist outside institutions, and don't understand art that does. The first artistic language of suburbia is rock'n'roll, and Sydney's western suburbs have a long and impressive rock'n'roll tradition.

When William and Margaret Young and their six children emigrated to Australia from Glasgow, Scotland in 1963, it was here in the western suburbs that they landed and settled. George was 15 (born November 6, 1947); Malcolm was ten (January 6, 1953); Angus eight (March 31, 1955). The rock'n'roll scene was already thriving.

"Me dad couldn't get work up in Scotland," Angus later told *Sounds*, "he found it impossible to support a family of our size, so he decided to try his luck downunder."

Like others straight off the boat, the Youngs were ushered into a hostel—at Villawood—where they would stay until they found suitable accommodation for themselves. "It was like a prison camp," Malcolm later told *Spunky*, "all these old tin shacks."

The Young family was fairly musical in an amateurish sort of way, as George once put it. It was the boys' older sister, Margaret, who was largely responsible for turning the boys onto rock'n'roll; in fact, she was the one who gave AC/DC their name and put Angus in the school uniform. After the Second World War British seaports like Liverpool and Glasgow were on a direct shipping route to the United States. As rock'n'roll lore has it, Mersey-beat itself was inspired by the American music—R&B, blues and hillbilly records—which came ashore there. In Glasgow, Margaret was listening to Chuck Berry, Little Richard and Fats Domino even before they were stars.

Alex, the oldest Young boy, went into music professionally as a saxophonist in Emile Ford's Checkmates. He left home before the family emigrated, to join the Big Six, whose claim to fame was that they backed Tony Sheridan after the Beatles walked out on him. The Beatles connection was strengthened when Alex went on to join Grapefruit, a lesser light on the Beatles' own Apple label.

George Young was a promising schoolboy soccer player—an interest common among Scots, and one certainly shared by brother Malcolm—but he was keener still on music. Although the Youngs spent barely three weeks at Villawood before they moved into a place of their own down the road in Burwood, George managed in that time to hook up with the best part of a band. His cohorts numbered an Englishman and two Dutchmen: front-man Stevie Wright, who was lured away from surfsters Chris Langdon and the Langdells; guitarist Harry Vanda, formerly of Holland's premier instrumental combo the Starfighters; and bassist Dick Diamond.

Burwood, with its wide boulevards and solid, free-standing red-brick Federation homes, might almost have seemed posh to working-class Scots. Indeed, today it is becoming gentrified. But in the sixties, it was a rough and ready neighborhood of "new Australians," which would play host to violent meetings of rival gangs down at the station on Saturday nights. If the rough streets of Glasgow weren't indoctrination enough for the Young boys, this was a fine finishing school.

Burwood also boasted a thriving garage band scene. "Every new English kid that arrived brought all the latest things with him," remembers native Peter Noble, who played with Brits in a band called Clapham Junction.

George's nascent band found a drummer, Englishman Snowy Fleet, then resident at the East Hills Migrant Hostel. Fleet was a Liverpudlian and at 24 was much older and more experienced than his new bandmates. He had come out to Australia with his wife and child after walking away from a choice gig with the Mojos, who would go on to join Beatles manager Brian Epstein's stable and produce the classic 1964 hit "Everything's Alright." Snowy would name the band the Easybeats and initially manage it, too.

The Easybeats are generally acknowledged as the first truly original

Australian rock'n'roll band, but the irony is that its individual members were hardly Australian at all. Still, the band was immediately and passionately embraced in Australia as "our own." Their first proper gig was in late 1964 at an inner-Sydney joint called Beatle Village. From there, they leapt and bounded to the top of the charts.

The Easybeats looked good and sounded good. They dressed sharp, which gave them greater sex appeal than their closest Australian rivals, most of whom looked like civil servants. What's more, they could both play and write rock'n'roll. And Little Stevie was a livewire showman.

After signing a management deal with erstwhile north shore realtor Mike Vaughan, the band was introduced to Ted Albert, a friend of the high-flying Vaughan who was in music publishing. Albert, a budding producer with an ear for the future in beat music, was the middle of three sons of Sir Alexis Albert, whose father Jacques Albert had founded J Albert & Son, the oldest independent music publishing house in Australia. With interests in radio and film, too, Alberts was estimated in the 1990s to have a total worth of more than $45 million.

Jacques Albert had migrated to Australia from Switzerland in 1884 and set up shop as a music publisher. Immediate success with a single product called *The Boomerang Songbook* laid the foundations of the family fortune. Turnover was maintained as Alberts picked up Australian rights to an impressive array of song catalogues.

Ted Albert was 26 when Beatlemania hit in 1963, and he got caught up in it. He wanted a Beatles of his own. Initially, he had headhunted the already successful Billy Thorpe and the Aztecs to work with his newly-formed Alberts Productions. But when Mike Vaughan invited him down to have a look at the new group he was representing, Ted, in his own words, almost broke his neck getting a contract drawn up. The Easybeats, after all, did what no other Australian band did—they wrote their own material. To a publisher this is obviously important.

Ted immediately took the band into the old 2UW Radio Theatre (the family owned the station) to cut demos. A debut single, "For My Woman," was released in March 1965 through Parlophone, and while it wasn't a hit, it was encouragement enough to Ted to get any sort of reaction to original material. Two months later the Easybeats' second single, "She's So Fine," shot to number one, and dragged the forgotten first single into the top five as well. "Easyfever" took hold; only Normie Rowe could compete with the group for the title of premier Australian pop attraction.

The Easybeats went on to produce an incredible run of hits, and cut three albums before they left Australia in July 1966 for London, then the Mecca of the pop world.

With the rise of the Easybeats, Alberts Productions also established itself as a force in the fledgling Australian music industry. George Young would later praise the urbane Ted Albert as a man who, self-taught in the art of recording rock'n'roll, "knew as much about feel and balls in a track as anyone I've ever met . . . and had a very good ear for picking the right songs."

Ted applied his instincts to running Alberts, and was rewarded with a string of hits for Billy Thorpe and the Aztecs as well as the Easybeats. Dirtier, uglier R&B merchants like the Throb and the Missing Links fared less well commercially, but left a lasting impact.

When Ted followed the Easybeats overseas, Alberts wound down operations in Australia, at least temporarily. On the international scene, the Easybeats scored immediately, and massively, with the mod anthem "Friday On My Mind"—then spent the next three years falling apart in the search for a follow-up.

Manager Mike Vaughan was out of his depth overseas. It reached a point, in 1967, where the band was signed "exclusively" to several record companies around the world, which left them hamstrung. All this experience gave George the bitter wisdom he would later apply to AC/DC's career.

Artistically too, as George would later regret, the Easybeats strayed off the track, or were led astray. The band progressed through two very distinct cycles, in Australia and then overseas, both of which began and ended with rock'n'roll, but in between went very wayward. Initially, in Australia, flushed with their first success, the band indulged itself and tried to be clever. Whilst the resulting songs like "Wedding Ring" and "Sad and Lonely and Blue" were still hits, albeit minor ones, George at least claims to have derived much greater satisfaction out of the band's subsequent return to rock'n'roll with songs like "Women" and "Sorry."

By the time "Sorry" reached number one in Australia in November 1966, the Easybeats were ensconced in the studio in London with Who/Kinks producer Shel Talmy, cutting "Friday on My Mind." "Friday on My Mind" followed "Sorry" into the number one position in Australia a mere month later, and eventually, after a few false starts, made top ten in Britain and top 20 in America, not to mention hitting very big all across Europe, especially in Germany.

But "Friday on My Mind" would prove to be both a blessing and a curse, as big hits sometimes are for bands. Despite the layers of businessmen who siphoned off much of the Easybeats' earnings, it was certainly a meal ticket for Harry Vanda and George Young, at least, since they had written the song. It also made George aware of the value of the often overlooked European market.

Contrary to all the evidence which suggests it seldom works, record companies inevitably want a band to produce a clone follow-up to consolidate the success of a first hit. To an artist, this sort of pressure is like a red rag to a bull. George and Harry, who by now had taken complete creative control of the Easybeats, would do anything but repeat themselves, or anything close. So the band's singles that followed "Friday on My Mind" were all over the shop, a grab bag of psychedelic dabblings which only sporadically attained the vitality of their earlier work. It wasn't until late 1968 with "Good Times," a raging slab of rock'n'roll (successfully revived in Australia in 1988 by INXS and Jimmy Barnes), that George and Harry perhaps realized they'd been cutting off their nose to spite their face.

The lesson in all of this for George, which he would pass on in no uncertain terms to his eager little brothers, was that you must stay true to your roots.

"Good Times" came too late. By then, the public didn't know who or what the Easybeats were, and the band themselves no longer shared the sense of unity they had when they all lived out of each other's pockets. George and Harry had become estranged from the rest of the band, spending all their time together in the studio and refusing to tour at any length. Eventually they moved into their own four-track studio-flat in London.

The band was on its last legs—broke, and with drugs beginning to eat away at it. Stevie Wright began the downward spiral that would lead to the heroin addiction which would blight his life for many years.

The last album that bore the Easybeats' name, *Friends*, was barely that. A ragtag collection of demos recorded by Harry and George, with only Stevie otherwise appearing on a few of the tracks, it did, however, yield the Easybeats' last minor hit, the good-rocking "St Louis."

On the strength of that, the band managed to get it together sufficiently to tour Australia in the spring of 1969, when they were supported by the Valentines. It would be their last hurrah. At tour's end, Harry and George headed straight back to their London studio lair. Word was that the band had finally broken up.

Back in London, Harry and George picked up where they had left off. The next three years were like one long lost weekend as they worked at establishing themselves as an all-round production team, spotting talent, and writing and recording. They sold a few songs and produced a record or two, but nothing world-beating. Little wonder then that Ted Albert—who kept up an ongoing game of chess with George by telephone—was able to lure them back to Australia in 1973.

Spurred by success with a young pop singer-songwriter, Englishman Ted Mulry, Alberts was reborn in the new decade as a record label in its own right. Mulry's first single "Julie" was a minor hit. His second "Falling in Love Again," penned by none other than Harry and George, and released for Christmas 1970, was a smash.

The signing that consolidated Alberts' comeback was John Paul Young. Englishman Simon Napier-Bell, former manager of the Yardbirds, among other, more dubious, distinctions (he later managed Wham!) was then working at Alberts on a kind of exchange program. He was looking for a singer to match with another of Harry and George's demos which was lying around, a song called "Pasadena." Cut with John Paul Young, it hit just outside the top ten in April 1972.

At that point, Ted promised Harry and George the world, or at least that he would build them a studio, and that they could run it as they chose. Harry and George, in return, promised to get down to some serious work.

AC/DC has always been Malcolm Young's band—and it still is. Malcolm formed the band in the first place, and even as Angus has gradually assumed the role of front man, Malcolm was always the driving force—the primary writer, and the one to whom the last word in the band belonged. And while Angus has come to share much of the songwriting load with Malcolm, the pair's equal, if silent partner in the band has always been big brother George. Having already been around the block with the Easybeats, suffering shortcomings and rip-offs, George was embittered, and in many ways AC/DC would be his revenge. AC/DC would achieve what the Easybeats couldn't—control of their own destiny, and sustained success.

George was much more than merely AC/DC's coproducer—it was he who honed the band's sound and songs into a coherent, commercially viable entity. But George's brilliance was that he never tried to polish a turd. Where less incisive record producers would have tried to iron out AC/DC's rough edges and tart up the sound, all George ever aimed to do was harness that power, give it shape and direction.

As George's crowning achievement, AC/DC also marked the inauguration of a dynasty in Australian rock'n'roll, one whose influence is still pervasive. It is felt not just in the success of AC/DC, but also in the seminal influence AC/DC exert all over the world, and in the other work George and Harry have done as part of the Alberts Productions axis. In the mid-seventies, Alberts produced an unprecedented string of hits for artists like Stevie Wright (by then a solo artist), John Paul Young, and the Ted Mulry Gang. Perhaps more importantly still, George and Harry's production work for such bands as Rose Tattoo and the Angels virtually defined the unique Australian rock genre which grew out of the thriving pub circuit.

George Young lived at home in Burwood—when he wasn't on the road—right up until he went overseas in 1966. Growing up in his slip-stream, it was almost inevitable that Malcolm and Angus would follow him into rock'n'roll. Angus would later recall: "One day George was a 16-year-old kid sitting on his bed playing guitar, the next day he was worshipped by the whole country. I was going to school at the time—or rather, trying not to go to school—and I was very impressed. He was getting all the girls."

As Angus has testified, there was always a guitar around the Youngs' house. Nevertheless, as Malcolm told Glenn A. Baker, "We didn't get much encouragement. Dad was still asking George when he was going to get a proper job. The Easybeats weren't making much money in England by the end and I don't think the family liked the drug thing that was happening in rock by that time." But music was an irresistible force, and the two brothers picked up as much by osmosis as they did from old records by Muddy Waters, Ike and Tina Turner, Little Richard, Chuck Berry, the Who, the Stones or the Yardbirds.

Both Malcolm and Angus attended nearby Ashfield Boys High, a school notorious for its toughness. Malcolm told *Spunky*, "Because we were little guys, everyone kept pushing us around, and we had to fight or get beat up."

The boys' father insisted they get a trade no matter what, so when Malcolm left school at 15 he started work as an apprentice fitter. At the time, Sydney's inner west was buzzing with music. The powerful Nova agency, which had handled Fraternity, had its offices in Ashfield, and the specter of new local bands like Sherbet, Blackfeather and the Flying Circus loomed large. Malcolm jammed around in mates' bedrooms and garages.

In 1971, when he was working as a sewing machine maintenance man for Berlei, who make the bras, Malcolm met a band presumptuously called the Velvet Underground, who had just moved to nearby Regents Park. They were looking for a guitarist, and Malcolm got the gig.

The Velvet Underground had formed in Newcastle, a steel town on the New South Wales coast, in 1967. With a repertoire based around material by the Doors and Jefferson Airplane, they became top dogs on the local dance circuit. When front man Steve Phillipson threw in the towel, the band relocated to Sydney. Finding the guitarist they sought in Malcolm—they knew he was the brother of George Young, although Malcolm didn't play up the fact—they experimented with vocalists until they settled on Andy Imlah, who was poached off a nondescript local outfit called Elm Tree.

The band was picked up for representation by Dal Myles (now a newsreader on Sydney television), who constituted Nova's sole rival. Thus the Velvet Underground became popular on Sydney's suburban dance circuit, where they would often share the bill with another one of Myles' clients, erstwhile Alberts solo artist Ted Mulry, who was then using the aforementioned Elm Tree as a backing band. Like the Valentines, Elm Tree had started life with two lead vocalists—a young sheet-metal worker by the name of John Paul Young sharing the spotlight with Andy Imlah—but the band was left in the lurch after Imlah went off to join the Velvet Underground.

Malcolm already knew Ted Mulry through George, who'd met him at the 1970 Tokyo Song Festival where Mulry's "Falling in Love Again" was unveiled.

TED MULRY: "When I came back from Japan, it was around Christmas, and George was home for Christmas, and he said, What are you doing for Christmas? I said, I dunno, whatever; he said, Well, New Year's Eve, we're having a do at the folks' place, come around. So I said, Alright. And you can imagine! You go along with your guitar, and they're all musicians, and you have a few drinks . . . The funny thing was, I was the only non-Scot there, there wasn't even any other Englishmen, and you couldn't understand a word they were saying! But what a ball! We had a big singsong, and you'd get everything out, somebody had a squeeze-box, and there was a mouth organ, the bass would come out, guitars. It was great."

With the Velvet Underground gigging busily, Malcolm threw in his job and became a professional musician like the rest of the band. He would never work a day job again.

The young Angus was allowed to go out and see his brother play—and he would sit wide-eyed at the front of stage—as long as he was brought straight home. But the Velvet Underground were pretty well-behaved anyway. They would go back to Burwood after gigs to drink Ovaltine.

"We used to go round to pick Malcolm up," recalls Velvet Underground drummer Herm Kovac. "The first time, this little punk skinhead answered the door. It was Angus. I hid behind Les [the guitarist]; in those days you'd hear about the skinheads down at Burwood Station, Strathfield Station. Shaved head he had, big boots. He said, Eh, come in 'ere. So we follow him

Malcolm Young's first real band, the unapologetically named Velvet Underground, ca. 1972. L-R: Herm Kovac, Malcolm, Andy Imlah, Michael Szchefswick, and Les Hall. Both Kovac and Hall went on to play in the Ted Mulry Gang, AC/DC's Alberts labelmates.

into his room, he straps on his SG, jumps on the bed, and goes off on this exhibition, running over the dressing table, showing off, couldn't play any chords, just lead, and when he finishes he says, Whaddya reckon? You had to say, Pretty good, Angus. Every time you'd go there you'd have to go through this same ritual."

The Velvet Underground were writing a few songs of their own, but their set was still mainly covers—the Stones' "Can You Hear Me Knockin'?" and "Brown Sugar," and T Rex songs.

HERM KOVAC: "Malcolm never had guitar heroes. You know, when you're a teenager you have pin-ups on the wall. Malcolm and Angus never had any pictures on their bedroom wall. The one guitarist who was Malcolm's hero, who he did have a picture of on the wall, was the guy you'd least expect—Marc Bolan. Malcolm made us do about six T Rex songs. I said, I hate 'em, they all sound the same. But Malcolm loved Marc Bolan. Mind you, the picture he had of him was tiny!"

Ted Mulry had been the first to cut a version of George and Harry's "Pasadena," but Simon Napier-Bell was convinced there was a hit in it yet, and so he asked the Velvet Underground to do it. They demurred. They were a rock band, they protested, and "Pasadena" was pop schlock, even if it was one of Malcolm's brother's songs. The Velvet Underground in turn suggested that maybe "Mungy" Young, Elm Tree's other singer, would be well suited to the song. John Paul Young was thus launched on his own career.

With the dissolution of Elm Tree now complete, Ted Mulry, who was still producing hits as a solo artist, needed a new backing band, and so he became something of a double-act with the Velvet Underground. The Velvet Underground would open the show, and then play behind Ted for his set. But Malcolm was getting itchy fingers. He wanted to go off and get something of his own together. Late in 1972, then, the Velvet Underground folded. The rest of the band, plus Ted, transmuted into the Ted Mulry Gang.

HERM KOVAC: "When Malcolm left Velvet Underground, the reason he left was that Deep Purple had come out then, and he wanted to play all Deep Purple-type stuff. The rest of us weren't really into that. So he went and tried it, couldn't get any gigs, and then the early AC/DC played Beatles songs and all that, just to get work."

At around the same time Malcolm was starting to get something of his own together, George and Harry finally arrived back in Australia for good. But though they went back to work for Ted Albert, they did so with a guardedness that would become part of their trademark.

Chris Gilbey joined Alberts around the same time, at the start of 1973. Gilbey, a Londoner who had played in small-time bands in the sixties before moving to the other side of the desk, arrived in Australia via South Africa.

CHRIS GILBEY: "Ted had been giving George and Harry a retainer even when they were in England. They came back and I didn't meet them for quite some time. Ted would have these meetings with them. I was doing—I don't know what I was doing!—George and Harry were mysteriously making this record at EMI."

The record George and Harry were mysteriously making was the legendary Marcus Hook Roll Band album, *Tales of Old Granddaddy*, now a highly-prized collector's item. This project provided Malcolm and Angus with their blooding in the recording studio, and it was an experience that had a profound effect on Malcolm in particular.

The Marcus Hook Roll Band had its genesis during George and Harry's final days in England, when a friend called Wally Allen, then working as an engineer for EMI at Abbey Road, got them into the studio to cut a few tracks just for fun. George and Harry returned to Australia soon after, and it wasn't until EMI's American affiliate Capitol Records contacted them that they even remembered doing the sessions. Capitol was hot for a track called "Natural Man," and wanted more. "It was a free trip for Wally who wanted to see Bondi Beach," George told Glenn A. Baker, "so he scored a ticket and came.

"We went into EMI Sydney for a month and Wally supplied all the booze. We had Harry, myself and my kid brothers Malcolm and Angus. We all got rotten [drunk], except for Angus, who was too young.

"That was the first thing Malcolm and Angus did before AC/DC. We didn't take it very seriously, so we thought we'd include them to give them an idea of what recording was all about."

And indeed, Malcolm's eyes were opened by the experience. *Tales of Old Granddaddy* not only distanced George and Harry from the Easybeats, drawing them closer to forming Flash and the Pan—the mysterious duo persona with which they would later have Australian and European hits like "Walking in the Rain" and "Hey, St Peter"—it also betrayed seeds of the AC/DC style that was to come. One cut, "Quick Reaction," was pure riff-driven AC/DC.

Malcolm wasn't impressed by the fact that the recording process was so piecemeal, so separated, with everything overdubbed and multitracked. That wasn't the way real rock'n'roll operated. In his view, real rock'n'roll was played by a band, together, as a band. All this technology was obscuring the point of the exercise.

Disillusioned, Malcolm went home and threw his Deep Purple albums in the bin. They were phonies. Not like Chuck Berry, or the Rolling Stones, who were the real thing, who could do it for real, without hiding behind studio trickery. The band Malcolm was getting together would be a rock'n'roll band. It was going to be glam, to be sure, because sequins and makeup were de rigueur at the time, but it would still be rock'n'roll. The idea would prove visionary.

1973, after all, was not a great time for rock'n'roll. It was a mark of the immaturity of the business in Australia that the spirit of glory year 1971 was allowed to dissipate. Even Billy Thorpe, the movement's spearhead, couldn't maintain his momentum after that ill-fated trip to England in 1972.

By 1973, the scene was split down the middle. "Commercial" music had taken over the charts. Any new "progressive" bands had to rely on the live circuit to survive. With the arrival of American-style programming, radio had adopted rigidly conservative formats.

The two biggest Australian albums in 1973 both belonged to Brian Cadd, whose Americanisms segued smoothly onto radio playlists. Sherbet, who had won the last ever Battle of the Sounds, the year after Fraternity, were rapidly establishing themselves as teen heart-throbs.

A second wave of bands stormed Melbourne's "underground" ball-rooms, discos and pubs, and the scene was admittedly expanding. But beyond gigs in Adelaide and (to a lesser extent) Sydney, there was nowhere else to go.

Technology was improving, but the talent lagged behind. When Michael Gudinski formed Mushroom Records in 1973, it struggled initially because it lacked genuinely first-rate bands.

The best band of the day was Lobby Loyde's Coloured Balls, but—typically—they were marginalized and ultimately defeated. Loyde had built on the foundation he'd laid with the Aztecs, and taken it to a logical conclusion. The most profound legacy Billy Thorpe left to Australian rock'n'roll was probably his blithely confrontational attitude, and though the Coloured Balls inherited that tradition, volume for its own sake wasn't their weapon—they favored blazing dynamism, aggression and finesse. Echoes of this sound can be heard in Australian rock'n'roll to this day, but in 1973, complete with their tough, sharpie image, the Coloured Balls were resisted by the hippies who ran Melbourne music as much as by audiences.

In Sydney in 1973, the new rising band was teenybopper rocker outfit Hush. Sherbet dominated the national scene. It was enough to make Malcolm Young puke.

AC/DC, named by Margaret Young after a warning sign she noticed on her sewing machine, coalesced around the end of 1973, with a line-up comprising Malcolm, Angus, singer Dave Evans, bassist Larry Van Kriedt (a Dutchman, like Harry Vanda) and veteran drummer Colin Burgess (formerly of the Masters Apprentices).

15-year-old Angus had only just left school, which he'd hated. He had started work as a compositor (for porn magazine *Ribald*, or so he claims), and he wasn't automatically included in the band. Throughout his last year at school, Angus never had a guitar out of his hands. He would run home and run straight out again to go and jam with his mates. He wouldn't even change out of his school uniform; it was this image of him, wielding his axe, that inspired Margaret to suggest he take it on stage. Angus was putting together a band of his own called Tantrum when Malcolm asked him to fill the gap in AC/DC where keyboards wouldn't fit.

Dave Evans, whom Malcolm had met through the Velvet Underground, had obtained his position in the new band more because of the way he looked than the way he sang. He was not a good singer at all, in fact, but Malcolm wanted glitter—he himself dressed like a sort of space cowboy—and Evans had that in spades. As a performer, he was a shameless exhibitionist.

Still unnamed, the band played its debut show in the middle of the bill at a venue on Sydney's southern beaches, a converted cinema called The Last Picture Show. They played their first show as AC/DC at Chequers, in the city, on New Year's Eve 1973. No record exists of this show other than Angus's colorized recollection: "We had been together about two weeks. We had to get up and blast away. From the word go it went great. Everyone thought we were a pack of loonies—you know, who's been feeding them kids bananas?"

The band's repertoire at that time consisted of Rolling Stones, Beatles and Chuck Berry songs, maybe some Free, plus a few old blues numbers and a couple of tentative originals.

"I could never sit down with a record and copy it," said Angus later. "Malcolm had a better ear for analyzing and dissecting. I thought, he could pick it up and I can whip it off him . . . It's still the same way, I think!"

By April, the rhythm section consisted of Rob Bailey (bass) and Peter Clack (drums). Bailey and Clack had grown as a unit out of Flake, a band that first hit during the radio ban with a version of Trinity's version of the Band's version of Dylan's "Wheels on Fire." They passed an audition held at George's new place in well-heeled suburban Epping, and it was this settled line-up that would soon go into the studio to cut a debut single. Angus was wearing a Zorro suit, and the band was holding down a residency at the Hampton Court Hotel in Kings Cross as well as gigging around on the suburban dance circuit.

Harry and George, meantime, were ensconced at EMI with their old

Easybeats cohort Stevie Wright, who had been dredged out of the dual indignity of heroin addiction and the cast of *Jesus Christ Superstar*. Malcolm contributed guitar at these sessions too.

In June, what was probably the first ever press notice of AC/DC appeared in *Go-Set*. The news article stressed the band's youth, which it was putting to its advantage. "Most of the groups in Australia are getting on rather than getting it on," Malcolm sneered, "out of touch with the kids that go to suburban dances."

The piece also reveals as a lie that AC/DC were innocent of the sexual connotations of their name. Malcolm points out that it refers to electricity, "but if people want to think we're five camp guys, then that's okay by us."

Even Molly Meldrum, Australian music's foremost apologist, once described early 1974 as its "lowest ebb." But this was only the lull before the storm, a storm precipitated by the comeback of George, Harry and Stevie with the monumental "Evie," the first single off *Hard Road*, the album they'd finished recording.

CHRIS GILBEY: "Everybody had a sense of—it was post-hippie—we've decided we don't want to drop out, we're going to drop in and make it really work. Of course, the wonderful thing was that the Albert family had this tremendous cash base, so they could afford to play at being the record business in a way no other indy could."

In its full three-part form, "Evie" was over 14 minutes long, but even so it crashed through the radio barrier on its release in June, and went on to become one of the biggest Australian hits of the year.

If the Easybeats ever had a homecoming, it was the now legendary free show at the Sydney Opera House in June, which had Stevie fronting a band that included not only Harry and George, but also Malcolm. A crowd of 10,000 had to content itself with the sound from a PA system set up on the Opera House steps, since there was no room left in the theater itself. It was typical of the obstinately forward-thinking George that not a single Easybeats oldie was played that night.

AC/DC played that night too. *Go-Set* commented, "AC/DC opened the show and showed they're a force to be reckoned with. They play rock'n'roll intelligently, adding their own ideas to sure crowd-pleasers like 'Heartbreak Hotel,' 'No Particular Place to Go' and 'Shake, Rattle & Roll.'"

Praising Angus and Malcolm's dual guitar attack, whilst comparing Dave Evans to David Cassidy, the review concluded that the band "looked great and sounded great. Their material is part original and will undoubtedly prove popular as the band gets about a little more."

If family ties had given AC/DC a kick-start, George had to let them find their own way from there. Even if he was always looking over their shoulder. When the band was approached by Dennis Laughlin with a management offer, George gave the nod. Laughlin, of course, was the former Sherbet front man and Nova agent who, by 1974, was operating as a lone wolf on Sydney's southern beaches, running a gig in an old cinema in Cronulla called The Last Picture Show. He always had an eye for the main chance, and he certainly saw a chance in AC/DC. Laughlin grew up around Burwood too, though it was perhaps more important to George that he was a fellow Scot. Laughlin vowed that he would get the band out on the road—beyond Sydney—where a lucrative circuit awaited.

It was apparent by this time that Dave Evans had to be replaced. His onstage antics had become an embarrassment. "We used to kick him [Evans] off stage," Angus recalled, "and me and Malcolm would just jam on boogies and old Chuck Berry songs, and the band would go down better without him." Malcolm and Angus had contemplated getting rid of him for some time, but both John Paul Young and future Alberts two-hit-wonder William Shakespeare had declined their offer of the job.

The band was desperately looking out for a new front man when Dennis Laughlin scored them the support spot on the August tour by Lou Reed. Reed was then at the height of his junkie-faggot phase, and AC/DC, with their ambiguous moniker and coy debut single, "Can I Sit Next to You, Girl?," must have seemed perfectly suited to the bill. And hey, weren't they George Young's little brothers? It was in the blood, wasn't it?

As unremarkable as "Can I Sit Next to You, Girl?" was, it became a minor hit in Perth and Adelaide. As a result, Laughlin was able to arrange gigs there, as well as in Melbourne (then still very much the Australian pop capital), in addition to the Lou Reed shows.

After playing the last show of the tour with Reed in Adelaide, AC/DC played a couple of pub gigs of their own, and then went on to Perth for a six-week season at the city's top disco, Beethovens, as support act for famous transvestite Carlotta.

Bon saw the band in Adelaide. He was unaware of the strings that had been pulled behind his back. He had recovered sufficiently from his bike accident to be getting around, and was doing odd jobs for Vince, painting his office, putting up posters, driving visiting bands (among other things, Vince was helping a new young band called Orange become Cold Chisel).

In touch with George Young, Vince booked AC/DC into Adelaide.

VINCE: "George told me, We need a new singer, and I said, Well, what about Bon? George said, But I heard he had an accident. I said, He's alright now, and he wants to leave Fraternity, they're too serious for him. He said, 'Well, why don't you suggest it to Malcolm and Angus?' So I did, and they said, 'Your old mate? He's too old!' I said, 'He could rock your arse off.'

"I said to Bon, You want to go and check out this AC/DC. He said, Arrgh, they're just a gimmick band. Anyway, we went out to the Pooraka, went backstage, and I remember Angus said, So you reckon you can rock the arse off us? Bon said, You young kids? You bet! And they said, Well, let's see, and they arranged a rehearsal at Bruce's place."

ROB BAILEY: "Bon and Uncle turned up, and they were like regulars after that. Bon must have seen the opportunity, thought, This is for me, and set about to woo Angus and Malcolm. After gigs, Angus and Malcolm would disappear with Bon. Bon wasn't silly, he knew where to hit."

The popular myth that Bon had first been employed by AC/DC as their driver—a myth propagated by the band itself as much as anyone—must have had its origins here, as Bon played host to Malcolm and Angus, all of them getting around in the old Holden Bon had recently bought for $90.

"I knew their manager," Bon himself said later in the film *Let There Be Rock*. "I'd never seen the band before, I'd never even heard of AC/DC, and their manager said, Just stand here, and the band comes on in two minutes, and there's this little guy, in a school uniform, going crazy, and I laughed."

"I took the opportunity to explain to them how much better I was than the drongo they had singing for them," Bon said on another occasion. "So they gave me a chance to prove it, and there I was."

Angus, Malcolm and Laughlin went down to the cellar where an aggregation consisting of Bon, Bruce Howe, guitarist Mauri Berg, John Freeman and Uncle were half-arsedly rehearsing. These other guys, though, were unaware that what was going on was virtually an audition for Bon.

BRUCE HOWE: "Angus and Malcolm picked up guitars and started playing and I started playing bass, and I thought, Fuck me dead, these guys are just so together, with their rhythms, each other; they were almost telepathic. It was one of the best impromptu musical buzzes I'd had in ages."

Bon pulled out all the stops. Laughlin offered him the job on the spot. Bon said he'd think about it while the band was in Perth.

Bon was torn. He went down to the docks and, gazing out over the sea, mulled over everything—Irene, Fraternity, AC/DC. The easiest decision to make was that he didn't want to spend the rest of his life as a working stiff.

Next, he wanted out of Fraternity, despite the ties. And he wanted in with AC/DC. He knew it could work. It had worked for Alex Harvey, one of his heroes. The great Scottish rocker was already past thirty when he finally broke through, thanks to a new young backing band.

The hard part was Irene. Bon had never given up hope that his marriage might yet be resurrected, and he didn't want to abandon that possibility. But in the end, he knew he had to. As Irene put it: "I was ready to settle down. Bon still wanted to be famous."

BRUCE: "He wanted to do it, but he wanted to do it unencumbered by emotional baggage. Bon knew, because he'd done it before, you've got to be in a position where there's no wives, no children, you've just got to be able to get up and take the opportunities as they come."

After a few weeks in Perth, Dave Evans took to calling in sick. He was drinking a lot. Dennis Laughlin, who himself would occasionally fill in for Evans, rang Bon to reiterate the offer. Bon rang back later to say he'd do it. The band would be passing through Adelaide on their way back to Sydney anyway, so they could get together then. Evans was sent packing. He went on only to enjoy fifteen seconds of fame in 1976, fronting Rabbit on their immortal "Too Much Rock'n'roll." Bon got up with AC/DC for the first time at the Pooraka.

"The only rehearsal we had was just sitting around an hour before the gig, pulling out every rock'n'roll song we knew," Angus said. "When we finally got there Bon downed about two bottles of bourbon with dope, coke, speed, and says, Right, I'm ready, and he was too. He was fighting fit. There was this immediate transformation and he was running around with his wife's knickers on, yelling at the audience. It was a magic moment. He said it made him feel young again."

VINCE: "The next day, Bon came around to my office, and said, Whad-dya reckon? I said, Well, you know, I like them. I think they're great and I think they're going to be big. I asked him, Why? He said, Because I'm going to join them. I said, When are you leaving? He said, Today."

DENNIS LAUGHLIN: "I went round and picked Bon up at his place with Irene. And that was it, that was the end of the marriage too."

VINCE: "He just packed his bags. He came around with them in the car, he came around to say goodbye, and he wound down the window and said, Seeya later. And that was that."

AC/DC begins to coalesce: Melbourne, January/February, 1975. Left to right: Malcolm Young, Phil Rudd, a temporary bassist identified only as "Paul," Angus Young, and Bon.

Bon: "Fraternity worked on a different level to me. They were all on the same level and it was way above my head. They didn't have a chance in England. This group has just got it."

9. LANSDOWNE ROAD

Dennis Laughlin was paying AC/DC their wages in drugs and spare change. He wasn't going to last.

But then, the extraordinary thing about these early days of AC/DC is how so much happened so quickly. Bon joined the band at the end of September 1974. Within six weeks, they were without a manager, but in the studio recording an album. Within six months, with powerful new management and a new lineup, and now based in Melbourne, they would have both a debut single and a debut album in the top ten.

Dennis Laughlin and AC/DC parted company within a few weeks of Bon joining the band. Bon had expected to be based in Sydney, where the Youngs lived, but a management offer from powerful Melbourne player Michael Browning meant that the band would soon move south, although not before they cut the album with George and Harry in Sydney in November. By December, though, the band had set up base in Melbourne.

When Bon first arrived in Sydney in late September he stayed at Dennis Laughlin's flat in Cronulla. Bon knew Laughlin from when Fraternity used to play gigs at Jonathans, and he liked him.

Bon was mucking around with Malcolm and Angus, comparing musical notes. He was convinced AC/DC could be a world-beater. He was astonished by the musical acuity and empathy of Malcolm and Angus, despite their youth, and he was swept along by their single-mindedness. It was as though he'd been reborn. Any lingering pain from his injuries was overridden in the general rush of it all. And Bon gave something back to Malcolm and Angus in return.

GRAEME SCOTT: "I think Ron put a bit of life into it. I think it was what Malcolm and Angus were looking for."

"Bon was the biggest single influence on the band," Malcolm has admitted. "When Bon came in it pulled us all together. He had that real stick-it-to-'em attitude. We all had it in us, but it took Bon to bring it out."

"When I sang I always felt there was a certain amount of urgency to what I was doing," said Bon. "There was no vocal training in my background, just a lot of good whisky, and a long string of blues bands, or should I say 'booze' bands. I went through a period where I copied a lot of guys, and found when I was singing that I was starting to sound like them. But when I met up with Angus and the rest of the band, they told me to sound like myself, and I really had a free hand doing what I always wanted to do."

The band played its debut proper, with Bon singing, at the Brighton-le-Sands Masonic Hall. They had to get their shit together quickly because they were due to go out on the road in the second week of October. Laughlin had booked gigs in Melbourne, then over in Adelaide, then back in Melbourne again. Then they would return to Sydney to start recording.

LAUGHLIN: "The biggest problem I had with AC/DC in those early days, being a touring unit, and not having much money, was keeping everything together, keeping everyone happy. There's a few dope smokers in the band, right? Instead of giving everyone fifty bucks a week, it's like, alright, whatever you need, we'll get. Thirty bucks a week plus a bag of dope, a bottle of Scotch. Well, Angus was a pain in the arse, because he says, Fuck ya, I don't drink booze, or fuckin' take drugs. I'd give him a bag of fish'n'chips, a Kit Kat, a packet of Benson & Hedges and a bottle of Coke."

In Melbourne, the band played the suburban dance circuit, some of the new pubs, and the old discos. On October 16, for the first time, they played Michael Browning's Hard Rock Cafe on its gay night.

From Melbourne, the band headed to Adelaide, where Vince had booked them into the Largs Pier for three nights. Bon was extremely pleased with himself, being back in town with what he believed was the hottest band in the land. However, with the exception of Uncle, who got up one night to have a blow, Bon's old friends were dismissive, reckoning Bon was selling out to a simplistic three chords. It was the sort of condescension AC/DC faced continually, and would hold against Australia in later years. Bon's attitude was, Fuck 'em. He trusted only his own gut feelings, and they were good.

Adelaide would be the final showdown for Dennis Laughlin.

MICHAEL BROWNING: "They came down to Melbourne. They had a manager who was a sleazeball. I was just the guy running the club, and I really liked them. They came to collect their money at the end of the night, and told me they were going to Adelaide the following day. So I said, Well, seeya when you get back. Next thing, I got a phone call from Adelaide to say the guy had absconded with all their money or something, and that they were stranded."

LAUGHLIN: "I got the shits with them one night in Adelaide. Angus was complaining, Oh, Bon's got a bag of dope, a bottle of Scotch, and I ain't got nothin'." So I said, Fuck ya, I'm not workin' my arse off anymore, here's your books, you've gotta be in Melbourne by one o'clock tomorrow, I'm going home, seeya later."

BROWNING: "I sent them money so they could come back to Melbourne, so they could fulfil their commitments to everyone, including me. When they got to Melbourne, they came and saw me and we talked about management. I'd only seen them once then, and I just remember being totally knocked out. They had a new singer then too—Bon Scott—and my immediate reaction, I suppose, was a little skeptical, because my image of Bon Scott was as the singer in a teenybopper group, and AC/DC were more of a street rock'n'roll band. But it worked. Malcolm and Angus hated anything that was pretentious, or plastic, poofy, and Bon just exuded character."

If Bon had liked Dennis Laughlin, he was, however, quite prepared to defer to Malcolm and Angus. If Michael Browning was it, then fine.

Browning himself had been looking for an act to get involved with for the past six months—since May, when he had resigned from managing Billy Thorpe and the Aztecs after five years. "One tends to become a little complacent after such a long time," Browning explained to *Go-Set*, but more likely, he was disappointed that Thorpe had failed to give it a serious shot overseas.

George Young went to Melbourne to see Browning, and again was impressed with Browning's track record, and his ambitiousness. Browning and George shared a vision: George wanted to get AC/DC out of Australia as soon as possible. Browning wanted a band he could take overseas.

BROWNING: "My sole personal ambition to be the manager of an Australian band that broke internationally was a motivating factor in AC/DC's success. I mean, it was one thing for Alberts to say, We want to break this band internationally, but without someone to come along with the drive, and the game plan, well, it really wasn't going to happen."

Michael Browning was, indeed, one of the first Australians to seriously consider going overseas with a band. The first band he ever managed was Python Lee Jackson, which itself made a pioneering foray to England in 1968, only to turn up in America in the early seventies with an album called *In a Broken Dream*, which featured Rod Stewart on vocals. Browning went on, in the late sixties, to join Bill Joseph at AMBO, at which point he also took on management of Doug Parkinson. Doug Parkinson In Focus was probably the biggest band in Australia in 1969, having hits like "Dear Prudence" and "Hair." But if Parkinson was never going to go the distance, Browning picked up Billy Thorpe on the verge of his second coming.

By 1973, Thorpe was still a big draw, but his star was descending. Moreover, Consolidated Rock, the Melbourne booking agency Browning had formed with Michael Gudinski and Bill Joseph after the demise of AMBO, had itself folded. Gudinski had formed Premier Artists in its place—the agency that still has a stranglehold on live music in Melbourne today—and then went on to launch Mushroom Records, the definitive Australian label of the seventies and eighties.

Michael Browning was in need of a new initiative, too. The scene offered few immediate prospects, but with a more solid infrastructure now in place it was ready and waiting for a resurgence.

Over the Australia Day long weekend of 1974, Browning trooped out to Sunbury yet again with Billy Thorpe. The whole thing was becoming rather routine. Neither the Aztecs nor Sherbet nor the reformed Daddy Cool delivered anything worth getting excited about. But when a new Melbourne band by the name of Skyhooks took the stage and proceeded to tear it apart, people sat up.

Michael Gudinski jumped first and signed the Skyhooks to both management and recording contracts, and by the end of the year, they'd saved the floundering Mushroom's skin.

Between that and the new ABC pop program *Countdown*, launched at the end of the year and fronted by Molly Meldrum, the resurgence was finally on. Michael Browning saw AC/DC and he knew that they could not only be part of it—they could also transcend it.

BROWNING: "No doubt about it. Otherwise I wouldn't have undertaken it. I mean, I was married, and eventually I had kids and all the rest of it, we dragged them all around the world, and there was no way I was going to do that if the group didn't have the quality that people now recognize. They were definitely special. And still are."

AC/DC were not strictly speaking a product of the pub circuit. Nor were Billy Thorpe and the Aztecs, Chain, and the Coloured Balls, but AC/DC followed on from them in paving the way for pub rock.

It was a process of infusion. Sharing the same influences (Chuck Berry, blues, boogie, the Stones, a trace of metal), AC/DC played to the same audience Billy Thorpe had found—an audience that was young, male and left right out. An audience that liked its rock'n'roll hard, fast and tough. And loud.

In 1974, these suburban boys had nothing they could call their own. Their sisters had all the poofy pap *Countdown* could throw at them, like Skyhooks and Sherbet. Their older siblings were bonging on and getting into art rock and California soft rock. To these guys, all that stuff was hippie shit, and they hated hippies.

Heavy metal pioneers like Black Sabbath were already past it. The only new light was Status Quo. Or, if you were really hip, Alex Harvey or Lou Reed. No one had even heard of the New York Dolls. The local scene was an absolute desert. The sharpies (a rat-tailed Australian variant of skinheads) had had the Coloured Balls, but sharpies were dickheads, and the Coloured Balls were falling apart anyway.

It was into this yawning gulf that AC/DC stomped—too late, too ugly to be glam; too clever to be metal; too soon, too dumb to be punk.

They were at once a culmination and a fresh start for the push of what Anthony O'Grady, editor of new Sydney-based rock rag *RAM*, described as "high energy heavy metal boogie bands." AC/DC were distinguished, to begin with, by the telepathic guitar interplay between Malcolm and Angus, which determined their unique dynamic texture. Bon added color to movement with his street-smart edge, strangled vocals, gift for narrative, and mischievous sense of humor. George's sensibility and savvy helped pull it all together.

It was just what the suburban boys wanted.

BROWNING: "There were a lot of suburban dances, the sharpies used to go to them; there were certain dances that were just sharpies. The big groups of the time were Billy Thorpe and the Aztecs, and Lobby Loyde and the Coloured Balls. It was a scene, an atmosphere, I've never seen anything quite like it. AC/DC came in on the tail end of that. I'd stopped managing Billy Thorpe and the Aztecs, and there was this club called Berties, which had closed down, which I was also a part of. I'd been to London to the Hard Rock Cafe, and I thought, Oh, let's just deck it out and call it the Hard Rock Cafe. So I did that, and that's where AC/DC came in. They

became fairly regular performers at the Hard Rock Cafe."

George was of the old school that doesn't believe a band can even call themselves a band until they've played at least 200 gigs. The heavy roadwork AC/DC did was as important as anything in shaping them.

ANGUS: "When we started, as a band, I don't think there was anyone around really that was doing what we did. I think here [Australia] was really what geared it for us; when you first start here, a lot of the places you play all everybody wanted to hear was rock'n'roll, you know. The faster the better. For us, that was great, 'cos that's what we do best. And we were lucky, because of George and Harry, from their time in the Easybeats; they always said that the best time they ever had was just playing rock'n'roll songs, and you know, they said, That's what you guys are going to do."

Michael Browning proposed a scheme whereby his company Trans-Pacific Artists, which he ran in partnership with Bill Joseph, would absorb AC/DC's debts, set them up in a house in Melbourne, provide them with a crew and transport, and put them out to work, covering all their expenses, and paying them a wage. It was if nothing else an entrée to the Melbourne scene.

BROWNING: "Basically, they were broke. They needed an injection of capital, and an infrastructure placed around them, in order for them to continue."

George decided Browning's offer was a fair one.

Bon, like Malcolm and Angus, had already signed a recording-publishing contract with Alberts. Hamish Henry had been prepared to give Alberts his rights to Bon's publishing, but Bon said, Ask them for some money, you never made anything out of me before. So Hamish sold for $4,000. The recording deal Bon signed, calculating back from royalty statements, was for an equal share, as one of five members of the band, of 3.4 per cent of retail. Standard rate today is around 10 per cent; back then, it was around 5 per cent. Alberts has always been known for driving hard deals; no favoritism was extended just because Malcolm and Angus were family.

Before the band were dispatched to Melbourne, they went into the studio with George and Harry and cut what would emerge as their debut album, *High Voltage*. They were barely roadtested after only six weeks of gigs, but ready or not the market was crying out for them.

It is significant that the first single lifted off the album was a cover of the Big Joe Williams blues standard, "Baby, Please Don't Go." Widely covered during the sixties, the song had been in AC/DC's set almost since day one. Of the album's remaining seven tracks, at least one, "Soul Stripper," was credited only to Malcolm and Angus; another, "Love Song," sounds like a leftover from Bon's Fraternity days, even though the credit is shared. The remaining five tracks bear the Young/Scott/Young credit which would become so familiar. But to a great extent—and hardly unexpectedly—the album was half-baked. The story goes that the band already had a number of instrumental backing tracks arranged, and so Bon simply dipped into his notebooks full of rude poetry to find lyrics to fit. Drummer Peter Clack was asked to stand down during the sessions; the job was done by session-man Tony Kerrante.

Bon himself later conceded, "That album was recorded in a rush." "It was actually recorded in ten days," Angus said, "in between gigs, working through the night after we came off stage and then through the day. I suppose it was fun at the time but there was no thought put into it."

ROB BAILEY: "Malcolm and Angus would just jam out things, like 'She's Got Balls'—it was just two sequences—slap 'em together and away you go. If they worked, Bon stuck some words on them. He used to walk around with lyric books, and they were full of some of the funniest stuff you've ever read. You could sit down and read them and just laugh and laugh."

CHRIS GILBEY: "Because the band was called AC/DC I said to them, Look, we've got to call the album *High Voltage*. So that was the title."

CHRIS GILBEY: "Bon went away saying, What a great title, *High Voltage*, we've got to write a song called 'High Voltage.' Well, they wrote 'High Voltage,' but not until after the album was finished, so it was too late to include.

"Then I created some artwork—we were just making it up as we went—I came up with this concept, of an electricity substation with a dog pissing against it. It's so tame now, but back then we thought it was pretty revolutionary. EMI didn't want to put it out because of the cover either, they thought it was very much in bad taste. But it came out anyway."

After finishing the album, the band left Sydney for Melbourne, via Adelaide. They got to Melbourne at the start of December, and holed-up in the Octagon Hotel in Prahran, until Browning found them the permanent accommodation he'd promised. Bon immediately looked up old mates like Mary Walton, and Darcy and his wife Gabby.

AC/DC took off in Melbourne like a rocket. Boring old farts like Daddy Cool and the La De Das didn't know what had hit them when this snotty young support band blew them off stage.

BAILEY: "It was an exciting time, because we knew the impact we were having. The band sounded right there, we had a pack of very good songs, the act was great, the whole thing was just in your face."

AC/DC worked continually, anywhere and everywhere.

BROWNING: "It was a mixture of pub type crowds to teenybopper girls to gays. There used to be a big gay circuit in Melbourne. Bon used to camp it up, he'd wear his leather stuff, and they fitted into that scene quite well."

"I remember I first saw them when they were still kicking around Melbourne," said Joe Furey, who later became a friend of Bon's. "There must have been about a hundred people there, and there was this little guy rolling around the floor playing guitar, and the whole thing was exceptionally loud, it was about one o'clock in the morning, and everybody was sort of going, Oh, give us a break, it's late. That was one thing I always admired about them, Angus in particular, was that there was a guy who had his act, and whether there was a hundred people there at one o'clock in the morning or what, he was going to do it. It wasn't like, Hey, there's no one here tonight guys, let's cut the set a bit short. Years later I thought that was probably the difference between them making it and not."

If Bon felt any physical strain from his accident, he didn't let on.

DARCY: "He was in pain. Those early gigs with AC/DC really stuffed him up. Once you've broken something, it's never the same again. He had to be jumping around singing his heart out, you had to wonder, How's he going to hack the pace? People wouldn't see him to the side of the stage hitting his puffer."

Juke magazine, which sprang up in Melbourne after *Go-Set* folded, called AC/DC "new faces refusing to be restricted by an established music scene . . . brash and tough, unashamed to be working at a music style that many describe as the lowest common denominator of rock music, gut-level rock, punk rock."

The story went on to describe Bon, "an old face," as "charged by the unleashed drive in the group around him, as determined as the rest to have a good time on stage and off, as determined to shake Australian rock where it matters . . ."

Juke was taken aback by "these red-blooded young studs": "AC/DC quite obviously are not lax to take advantage of the favors in the offering from some of their more ardent female fans. The adjoining motel room was busy with extra bedding and bodies."

The party had started.

The band moved into a house in Lansdowne Road, East St Kilda. Malcolm and Angus had never lived away from home before, and so at the ages of 22 and 17 respectively, they were running amok, free to come and go as they pleased, to smoke and drink and swear and carry on. And fuck chicks.

ROB BAILEY: "That place was a bit of a madhouse. A really big, beautiful old house, it had a flat out the back, with what I'm sure were hookers living there. You'd wake up in the morning and there'd be bodies strewn all over the place, nothing left in the fridge . . ."

Bon divided his time between the house and Mary Walton's flat in Carlton. He and Mary had consummated their old friendship, since both their marriages had dissolved. But as much as Bon needed that retreat, he also joined in the fun and games down at Lansdowne Road. He wasn't going to be denied his second youth.

Over Christmas 1974, AC/DC was out on the road in South Australia.

BAILEY: "We had this Ansett Clipper bus, we'd put the PA in the back, but every trip we did, it would break down. It was supposed to be the logistical answer to all the problems we had, but it just became a bigger logistical problem."

Spending Christmas in desolate steel town Whyalla might not have been so bad for Malcolm and Angus, because everything was so new to them, and besides, they had each other. But Bon was hit by it. He thought of Irene, and where he found her he found Graeme, because Graeme had taken up with Irene's sister Faye, and they all lived together in Adelaide. And he thought of his folks in Perth, and his other brother Derek, who had a couple of kids by now.

So he had another drink, and rolled a joint. Bon had made his bed, he accepted that, and he knew these little pangs of longing would pass. The Youngs were his surrogate family now, and the music, to borrow Duke Ellington's phrase, was his mistress. And he could always count on the music's transcendence. The band was starting to find, and define (if not in so many words) its own identity—and self-discovery is an exhilarating process.

As part of that process, however, Malcolm and Angus decided the rhythm section had to go. Peter Clack just wasn't good enough, and Rob Bailey, while he played well, insisted on having his wife with him all the time. And that was a pain in the arse. Besides, he was too tall.

On returning to Melbourne in January, Bailey and Clack were separately summoned by Bill Joseph and given their marching orders. Russell Coleman, former sticks man with Stevie Wright, sat in for a few weeks before Phil Rudd joined. Rudd, nee Rudzevecuis, had been playing behind singer Angry Anderson in latter-day Melbourne boogie band Buster Brown. Erstwhile Coloured Ball Trevor Young (no relation) told him about AC/DC's vacancy, and he would become the band's secret weapon, a rhythm machine that created the space within which Angus and Malcolm could move around.

Finding a new bassist proved more difficult. One guy lasted all of a few days. "It's a pretty rare type of bloke who'll fit into our band," Bon told *RAM*. "He has to be under five feet six. And he has to be able to play bass pretty well too."

Meantime, the band would play as a four-piece, with Malcolm on bass.

Late in January, George flew down to Melbourne to discuss with Browning plans for the release of the single and the album, and to fill in on bass when the band appeared at Sunbury.

Sunbury was a big part of Browning's marketing strategy. He had seen the reach the festival could have, even though it was declining fast, and he wanted to use it as a launch pad in the same way Skyhooks had the year before. But this year the whole affair was a disaster, one that spelled the end of Sunbury, in fact. Deep Purple had been flown in as an exclusive international attraction; and, as Michael Browning put it, they just jerked everybody around, especially AC/DC. First Purple said they wouldn't play, so AC/DC had to be located in Melbourne and dragged out to the site to deputize for them. Then they changed their mind. Angus remembers being disgusted when AC/DC arrived backstage to find one of the two caravans reserved exclusively for Deep Purple, while all the Australian bands had to share the other one. Then, when Deep Purple finished their set they refused to let AC/DC follow them. In response, AC/DC simply took the stage as Deep Purple's crew was still pulling down gear. A full-scale brawl ensued, on stage, in front of 20,000 people.

BROWNING: "What really pissed me off on that occasion, and what really made it clear I had to get AC/DC out of Australia, was the fact that the local crew people actually sided with Deep Purple.

"It just really brought home how subservient Australians were to anyone from overseas. How if you really wanted to gain respect you had to go overseas."

The *High Voltage* album and "Baby, Please Don't Go" single were released simultaneously in February 1975, with the Hard Rock Cafe throwing a "Special AC/DC Performance, New Album, Adm. $1.00."

Rob Bailey was shocked to discover that his work on the album had not been credited. But then the packaging of *High Voltage* gave precious little away at all (and when it did, incorrectly attributed "Baby, Please Don't Go" to Big Bill Broonzy). The story that got around was that George played bass on the album, though that story is still disputed by Rob Bailey, who certainly has never seen any money from Alberts.

Critical consensus, such as it was, had it that *High Voltage* was, indeed, premature. That's when scribes weren't simply damning AC/DC as altogether rude, crude and uncalled for. But certainly the single, with its driving arrangement reminiscent of Golden Earring's 1973 smash "Radar Love," looked set to do business.

Mark Evans joined the band just after the record's launch. Evans, born in Melbourne in 1956, was working in the public service at the time, living with his mother in a council flat in Prahran and just mucking around on bass. There is no truth in the myth that Evans' introduction to AC/DC came when Bon stepped in to save him from copping a hiding off the bouncers at the Station Hotel. In fact, he was mates with one of AC/DC's roadies, who told him about them.

MARK EVANS: "I just went down and saw them—Malcolm was

playing bass then—and they gave me a copy of the album, I took it home, thought, Okay, that's fine, auditioned—straight in.

"That's all it was. I think it was more the look I had than anything else. I don't know how many times people would find out there was two brothers in the band, and they'd think it was Malcolm and me.

"At that stage, the band was on the bones of its arse. Like, I remember at one stage, Phil even running out of drumsticks, so we had to go and get pieces of dowel from the hardware store and fashion them into drumsticks."

But it wasn't long before Evans was convinced to quit the public service.

EVANS: "We had this roadie called Ralph, and he drove me home in the bus after I'd rehearsed with the band once, and he said, Oh yeah, things are looking pretty good, we hope to be in England this time next year. The whole arrangement for the band was to get out of Australia. And I remember thinking, Yeah, sure! But once I'd spent a month with them, I realized they were dead serious. One thing I will give them, they had an absolute solidity of purpose."

Still, it would be some time before Evans met Bon.

EVANS: "The audition was held in their house at Lansdowne Road. Bon wasn't there, I didn't actually meet Bon until the first gig. He was never at rehearsals. But I knew his name, I kept on hearing about Bon, and I knew, I'd seen the Valentines when I was a kid, at a concert, and I thought, That guy was called Bon, I wonder if they're the same one. I had this suspicion who he was."

The scene at Lansdowne Road was one of pure debauchery. AC/DC encouraged every kind of rock'n'roll excess Melbourne had to offer—and Bon, Ronnie Roadtest, would again come very close to going over the edge.

EVANS: "Bon's personality, and demeanor, would lend him to getting into areas where he would endanger himself. Just from, I'll try that! And just being lonely, I think, just being isolated."

Bon offset the deeper rapport he shared with Mary Walton with the pleasures of the flesh available down at Lansdowne Road.

EVANS: "A huge amount of women were hanging around, the only thing that kept [the band] going was the girls that would come around."

Trudy Worme was one of the teenage girls who was in love with Bon: "I used to visit the guys frequently at Lansdowne Road, tidying up for them and having a lot of laughs. And that's all it was, too—we were most definitely not into the groupie scene, although several other female visitors were! I used to bake these chocolate cakes, mainly for Angus, every time we called in—it was greatly appreciated as there was rarely any food in the house. My mum used to drop us off and pick us up on our Sunday afternoon visits. My mother had full trust in Bon and the other guys—she considered them a lot safer than 'real boys,' the ones our age from school who she thought had more than music on their minds. Angus was only a year older than us, but anyone who liked chocolate cake so much and didn't drink was okay in my mother's eyes."

It was the groupie scene that inspired "She's Got the Jack," though it's ironic that the song places the blame on a woman when it was the boys in the band (or so the self-proclaimed legend goes) who were always running off to the clinic. Bon was well aware of the inflammatory nature of the song. When he wrote to Mary in April after she'd gone to London, he admitted it "may get us castrated by Women's Lib," and the recorded version also predicted an outraged crowd reaction.

For all the party atmosphere, though, Malcolm and Angus were deeply suspicious of outsiders—other than chicks, of course. It was part of the clan mentality. Their approach was all or nothing: if you weren't with them, you were against them. As RAM editor Anthony O'Grady described it: "You'd say hi to them and they'd look at you sideways like, Whaddya sayin' hi to me for?" Bon was accepted as one of the family, a blood brother, and Mary remembers they were "very, very tight initially." Malcolm and Angus looked up to Bon as older, wiser and braver. Bon, for his part, was protective of Malcolm and Angus, but he felt more like a conspiratorial uncle than a father figure.

Mary remembers feeling a bit like mum and dad to them. "They were still just babies, and they're sort of so straight in a way too. Angus didn't drink, at least not until his eighteenth birthday, when he got totally blotto, and I don't think he's ever had another drink since.

"They were so family oriented. They would go and buy a roast, a leg of lamb, and they'd bring it around and ask me to cook it. Because they just missed that home life, I guess."

Angus once said "Bon gets the women with flats who cook him dinners." To which Bon replied, "I like to put my feet up. Not to mention other parts of my body. They say to me, Are you AC or DC?, and I say, Neither, I'm the lightnin' flash in the middle."

Bon's code in life was like his attitude to money: if you got it, spend it. Don't expect it to last, don't expect it, period. This was his bravado. He sometimes didn't even seem to fear for his own safety.

Mary was in no position to carp, but when Bon took up with a young girl called Judy King, well, her response was to book a ticket to London. Judy King was an innocent set on a path of self-defilement. Maybe Bon liked the idea of bringing home a beautiful bird, and just a chick at that, with a broken wing. But maybe the attraction was more basic, as Darcy put it: "I just think he did his balls over her, she was so young and fit and tight."

Bon may or may not have met Judy before she showed up at a gig AC/DC played down the coast at Jan Juc—she was, after all, the youngest daughter in the same King family that Vince Lovegrove had briefly boarded with in 1970. At that time, she was a promising prepubescent athlete, a sprinter. In 1975, at 17, she was an accident waiting to happen.

Within a couple of days of seeing AC/DC, Judy had hitchhiked to Melbourne. Bon was there, and so was her older sister, Christine, who was working in a massage parlor and maintaining a heroin habit. There were also a couple of other girls hanging around the band who would skip school to do afternoon shifts in a parlor in Richmond. Within weeks, Judy too was on the game, sucked into the vortex, complete with a heroin habit of her own. But if Judy was a working girl, she saved her best for Bon. That she was stoned all the time could be a bit of a drag, but she was caught in the classic vicious circle—she worked to make money to buy dope to make work bearable.

The affair flared up for the first time when Bon was hauled in by the cops to account for a stack of allegedly pornographic photographs. Phil, a shutterbug, had taken some shots of Bon and Judy rolling in the hay.

"One morning," Bon told *RAM*, "I was in bed—completely out of it—and the chick who was living with me at the time was trying to hitch to work—also completely out of it—well, she got picked up by the police and she's so gone she can't speak. [The police were familiar with the house.] So they drive her back and run through the place . . . and what happens but they bust me for pornography!"

Bon was pushing his luck.

"Baby, Please Don't Go" was starting to sell.

AC/DC enjoyed the support of radio and *Countdown*. Ever since "Evie" had been broken by 2SM the previous year, radio's faith in rock'n'roll had been somewhat restored (if only briefly: the arrival of FM later in the seventies saw it turn back to "classic rock").

Countdown rose in tandem with the music's renaissance. Coinciding

Bassist Mark Evans joined AC/DC in March 1975, completing the band's classic lineup.
L-R: Malcolm, Bon, Angus, Phil Rudd, Evans

with the arrival of color television in Australia, *Countdown* quickly became
"all-powerful," as Chris Gilbey put it: "the driving force behind making a
hit single." At its peak, the show had a fair whack of the country's population watching it. "It was a tough call," said Gilbey, "because it was very
much Melbourne, very much Molly."

Molly Meldrum and Bon knew each other from way back, of course,
though their relationship was always awkward. Molly had been a Zoot,
not a Valentines groupie. Much later, in 1978, Bon said to *RAM*, "If you
don't show your arse to Molly Meldrum all the time here, you're fucked."
But when Molly first saw AC/DC, at one of the Starlight gay discos, he
was knocked out, as many people were. And, of course, *Countdown* too

got value out of AC/DC.

But as much as AC/DC were becoming part of the Melbourne scene, they would always be interlopers. That they were for the most part native-born Scots, who would soon enough virtually renounce Australia altogether, was the least of it. Nor was it the fact that they were by rights a Sydney band that made them so unusual, because Sherbet, Hush and the Ted Mulry Gang were also Sydney bands. (Melbourne's status as pop capital was because of *Countdown,* its live circuit, and Michael Gudinski's growing power. But it was one of the ironies of *Countdown's* early days that apart from Skyhooks much of its talent was effectively bussed in from Sydney, including also Marcia Hines, Jon English, William Shakespeare and John Paul Young.)

In any case AC/DC were like a cat among the pigeons on *Countdown*—rough and ready, for real. Sherbet were clearly little more than froth and bubble, and while Skyhooks were always likely to be "outrageous," they were also playing down to their audience. But what really distinguished AC/DC was the sense they gave that they were just passing through, that all this was just a stepping stone to bigger and greater things. It was obvious even then that such favorites of the moment as Sherbet and Skyhooks would never surpass their *Countdown* heights. But AC/DC had something more.

Back in Sydney, Alberts was well pleased with itself. Cabal-like even in its hometown, it had penetrated Melbourne and its mafia. Alberts enjoyed an incredible reign during 1975-76, when you would sit down to watch *Countdown* every Sunday night (along with virtually every other household in Australia), as the show lurched forward, coughing and spluttering and glittering—and if you didn't love it, you most certainly loved to hate it.

After "Evie" put George and Harry back on the map, they followed up this success at the end of 1974 with William Shakespeare, a sort of cross between Gary Glitter and Pee Wee Herman, who scored two consecutive number ones with "My Little Angel" and "Can't Stop Myself from Loving You."

AC/DC, with their long-term potential, would become Alberts' flagship act, but Alberts had other fish to fry, too—and these were bigger in the short term. Between AC/DC, John Paul Young and the Ted Mulry Gang, AC/DC was the only act not to score a number one before 1975 was out.

CHRIS GILBEY: "It was an incredibly exciting period. Alberts was so small, it wasn't like a big record company. We were just making up the rules as we went along. And everything we put out became a hit."

John Paul Young's disco-pop sound was as different from AC/DC as anything could be. George and Harry wrote and produced his material,

Pin-up idols, 1969.

ABOVE: The Valentines in their last incarnation, Autumn 1970, not long before breaking up. Left to right: Ted Ward, Bon (wearing his 'Super Screw' T-shirt), Paddy Beach, Wyn Milson, Vince Lovegrove.
BELOW: Fraternity, by now rechristened Fang, on the road in their own magic bus; England, April 1973. Hamish Henry (centre) wearing shades and a moustache.

Bon, 'Wild Man of Fraternity', gracing the cover of short-lived Australian rock rag *Sound Blast*; November 1970.

ABOVE LEFT: On stage, Melbourne Festival Hall, New Year's Day, 1975.
ABOVE RIGHT: The same day: after a quick change into the kilt, Bon introduces 'Young Talent Time' graduate Debbie Byrne. Bon: 'She wanted me to be her "boogie man" and it just happened that I had a bit of costumery (like me balls). Said I ruined her image.'
BELOW: On 'Countdown', 1975. Bon's appearance in a schoolgirl's uniform prompted howls of outrage.

ABOVE: With Irene at Fraternity's Finchley house in London, 1972, before the rot set in. The house degenerated into a squat.
BELOW: Bon at Bondi on the bike he rented over the summer of 1977/78.

ABOVE LEFT: With Silver at her flat in London, circa 1977.
ABOVE RIGHT: With Mary and Peter Renshaw in Melbourne, after a few drinks; Christmas 1979.
BELOW LEFT: With Anna Baba
BELOW RIGHT: At Angus and Ellen Young's wedding; London, February 1980.

ABOVE: The block of flats in Overhill Road, Dulwich, where Bon died.
BELOW LEFT: Isa at home with 'the boys' after Bon's funeral.
BELOW RIGHT: The oft-stolen plaque marking Bon's grave at Fremantle Cemetery. After the first such theft in early 1988, Isa told the *West Australian*: 'We know there are plenty of visitors as we sometimes find fresh flowers. And we often have to remove empty beer and whiskey bottles, but there has never been any damage until now. How can anyone do a thing like that?'

Mary: 'This photo was sent to Graeme by a fan after Bonnie died, and then Graeme gave it to me. I just think it really captures Bon.'

which only confirmed their range. "Yesterday's Hero" hit number one in April; "Squeak," as Molly Meldrum dubbed John Paul Young, would go on to produce a string of hits. Chugalug boogie merchants Ted Mulry Gang, produced by Ted Albert himself, had been on the road even longer than AC/DC—often with AC/DC—when in November, their second single, "Jump in My Car," went to number one.

This was good, George thought. He liked to work, just as much as he liked to drink; both of which he did with a peculiarly Scottish zeal. The studio at Alberts was finally finished, complete with a 16-track mixing desk shipped over from England. George and Harry spent every waking hour there.

Appearing on TV show *Countdown* changed AC/DC's audience. The mixed crowd the band had attracted to its live gigs was driven away by the onrush of screaming teenyboppers. Not all the little girls, after all, could swallow the smarmy Skyhooks or Sherbet, or Abba, the Bay City Rollers or Peter Frampton. There were plenty of tough chicks to whom AC/DC's rough and ready image appealed immensely. "They were everything the Bay City Rollers didn't stand for," said *RAM*. "Maybe it was the way [Angus Young] jumped and rolled around stage like a demented epileptic while not missing a note of his guitar duties. Maybe it was the way Bon Scott leered and licked his lips while his eyes roamed hungrily up and down little girls' dresses."

MARK EVANS: "They could see, I guess, there wasn't any bullshit involved, like high heels and make-up."

Teen fandom is totally partisan, of course, but only to the same degree that it is transient. The difference between AC/DC and Sherbet or Skyhooks was that AC/DC had the vision for longevity. Skyhooks may have been the first Australian band to write hit pop songs that had overtly Australian flavored lyrics, but AC/DC went beyond the literal. They had a deep-seated originality that has stood the test of time.

AC/DC would outlive teen pinupdom because when the little girls abandoned them—as the little girls are wont to do—the boys came back. This to the band was a transient phase, as Australia itself was—a stepping stone to greater things.

At the end of March, as both the single and album entered the charts, and AC/DC were playing a good eight gigs a week in Melbourne and elsewhere, Bon's relationship with Judy King came to an ugly climax.

Smack was never far from the surface of the seventies rock scene.

Most people still came on like hippies, but the heady days of communal tripping were over. The me-decade demanded a more self-centered high. Harder drugs came in: at the up end of the spectrum, cocaine and speed; at the down end, heroin. No less an icon of cool than Keith Richards was a brazen junkie.

Bon's drinking had been on the increase ever since he joined Fraternity in 1970. As AC/DC progressed, Bon consumed more of everything. His drinking could be on and off—he was a binge drinker really—but the grog was a persistent presence. And smoking pot was a habit he never kicked, never saw the need.

But if there's ever been a suspicion Bon was more deeply involved with narcotics than it seemed, the fact is that he never really got into heroin. Certainly though, he dabbled in it, as Judy King went down on it. On at least one occasion, in Melbourne in early 1975, he almost died of an overdose. But that, it seems, was enough to warn him off it, even though heroin would surround him and touch him as a codependent for the rest of his life.

Until the Vietnam War, heroin had been only a minor presence in Australia, mainly in Sydney's Chinatown. In the early seventies, though, the drug spread out of Kings Cross. Supply reached Melbourne, where it flowed through massage parlors and hamburger joints on Fitzroy Street, St Kilda.

Judy King was working in the parlor and spending every penny she earned on smack. One night, Bon found her and Christine out of it as usual. But rather than just being on the nod, they were in high spirits, mischievous as sisters can be. They began goading Bon, trying to entice him to have a taste. Of course, if there was one thing Bon couldn't resist it was a dare, even if it went against his better judgement. He rolled up his sleeve.

The girls tapped out a measure of brown rocks into a spoon. Adding water and a dash of lemon juice over a match, the heated mixture dissolved. Judy drew it into a syringe through a filter from a cigarette. Bon took off his studded belt to use as a tourniquet. Judy found a vein, which wasn't difficult on Bon's sinewy arm, and shot him up.

Bon felt the warm, sickly sweet rush—and then . . . nothing. He slumped in his seat. He had no tolerance, and he was small-framed, too. He turned a hideous blue-gray color. But he was still breathing. Judy was hysterical. Stoned as she was, Christine thought quickly enough to shoot Bon up with some speed in an attempt to negate the heroin. She moved in a panicked sort of slow motion, fumbling with the syringe, having difficulty finding the vein without any tension left in Bon's body. When she did, he let out a whimper, but that was all. It wasn't enough. An ambulance would have to be called. The girls did so. As they waited, a scared Judy paced the room as Christine gave Bon mouth-to-mouth and massaged his heart.

When you overdose on heroin, it is a near-death experience, but it has no romantic qualities. There's no light, or St Peter waiting at the gates, just a falling into a deep gray void. Your life does not flash before your eyes. You are not privileged with the opportunity to repent for your sins.

Bon sat bolt upright into consciousness when the ambulance officer revived him. He felt like he had been set rigid in cement, alive, looking out, but hit so hard upside the head he didn't know where he was. Certainly, he had no immediate past. Then he remembered, and that was the worst part, when he looked up and saw the scene: Judy in tears and Christine relieved, the ambulance men packing up their gear and shaking their heads. He remembered everything, and he felt so bad.

Later in life, Bon resented forgetting. After his body and mind had taken so much for so long, his memory, both short- and long-term, was eroded. Remembering may be bad, but not being able to remember was worse. When he was younger, though the pain was sharper, his body was also stronger, more resilient. The spirit, spunkier.

Bon didn't blame Judy. But if this was a case of his non-judgmental attitude getting the better of him, he was about to have the illusion literally beaten out of him.

In a report in Melbourne's notorious *Truth* newspaper, under the headline, POP STAR, BRUNETTE AND A BED: THEN HER DAD TURNED UP!, Bon told Dave Dawson: "The girl's father had warned me once before not to sleep with her. But she is 17 and capable of making up her own mind. I had returned from Sydney the night before and she was there waiting for me. We were making love when our roadie Ralph knocked on my bedroom door and said someone wanted to see me urgently. I told him to come back in two hours because I was busy. Eventually I went to the door and was sprung by the girl's father. I was wearing only shorts. He said, I can see you've got your fighting shorts on. He took out his false teeth and said, Come outside.

"I followed him outside where he had two of his mates aged in their 30s. He said, Where's my daughter? I said, She will have gone by now. You are always bashing her up. Suddenly, he started punching me in the head and body. He knocked me into a rose bush and dragged me through it. Then his two mates came over and dragged him away. They could see that because I was just 5' 5" I didn't have a chance.

"That was the worst beating I have ever had. My manager Mike Browning took me to a dentist who couldn't stop laughing when I explained how my dental plate was smashed and my teeth were knocked out. It wasn't so funny for me because the dental bill will be at least $500.

"The girl's father has never given her any love and he certainly showed me none.

"After he bashed me he said, If she is not home by night I will send another ten blokes around to bash you. I'm certainly not going out of my way to see her again."

Eerily, Bon had almost predicted this incident in the lyrics of Fraternity's "Annabelle."

> Annabelle's got problems,
> The doctors can't repair . . .
> When her daddy gets here,
> He'll come knockin' on my door,
> The next thing I replace
> Bear-skin rug on the living room floor.

Bon was in disgrace.

In April, AC/DC played two momentous shows in Melbourne as "Baby, Please Don't Go" peaked at number ten nationally. The *High Voltage* album also reached the charts, where it stayed for an unprecedented 25 weeks. Overseas, Michael Browning's sister Coral was sniffing around.

Coral, who'd met the band in Melbourne earlier in the year, was based in London, where she was well positioned in the music business, working for the management company that handled Bob Marley, Peter Tosh and Gil Scott-Heron. She was very enthusiastic about her brother's new charges.

AC/DC's staple Hard Rock gigs in Melbourne remained. On Sunday, April 13, the band played a "Heavy metal rock nite" with the Coloured Balls; the next Saturday, with Richard Clapton. The very next day, they played bottom of a big bill on a Freedom from Hunger show at Myer Music Bowl. The following week, they supported the Skyhooks at Festival Hall.

It was a freezing cold Melbourne Sunday, but in spite of that, 2,500 still showed up at the Music Bowl. They paid $3.50 or $2.50 to see the Moir Sisters, Ayers Rock, AC/DC, Jim Keays, the La De Das and Jeff St John with Wendy Saddington. AC/DC, as one newspaper report read, "got the best audience response . . . As they walked off the stage at the end of their set, nearly half the audience decided to leave as well."

"Sure surprised us," Angus said in *RAM*. "Everyone always told us we were shit compared to real bands like Ayers Rock."

Perhaps as a gesture of appreciation, AC/DC were presented after the show with supergroupie Ruby Lips. A good time was had by all, so much so that Bon later eulogized Ruby Lips in *Let There Be Rock*'s "Go Down."

But not even success opened AC/DC up. Quite the opposite, in fact. *Countdown* was an opportunity for bands to get together—when they were all busy working by themselves they seldom saw each other—but AC/DC didn't fraternize with other bands. Malcolm and Angus always regarded themselves as separate, if not superior, to other bands. Bon would often go off on his own and meet other people, but when he was with the band, even Bon hesitated to break formation.

MARK EVANS: "We hated everyone as a matter of policy, the same way we hated hippies. No other band existed, except for maybe the Alex Harvey Band. Little Richard. Chuck Berry. Elvis. But no one admitted it. We just didn't even talk to other bands.

"Bon could get on with anyone, but Angus and Malcolm had this incredible tunnel vision where no one else counted. It must have had an effect on Bon too. There were times, I'm certain, when Bon would have gone home and said, Fuck this, I'm not putting up with it anymore."

Being so antisocial was against Bon's natural inclination, after all. He had acquired the nickname Bon the Likeable, after Simon the Likeable, a character on *Get Smart* whose secret weapon was that he was impossible to dislike.

MARK EVANS: "My mother was in love with him. He'd come around for dinner and say, Can I do the dishes?"

AC/DC's aloofness and arrogance was partly due to well-placed self-belief—a quality any artist needs to become great. But it was also a mask for something more troubling—an insularity that bordered on paranoia. It was an understandable defensiveness at the resentment, if not contempt, so often directed at AC/DC; but it was also a shield for insecurities. Maybe due to their sheltered upbringing, maybe just because of their lack of education, Malcolm and Angus were not blessed with many social skills. They were not articulate and were wary of other people. The family had always provided for them, and they saw little need to step outside it now. Bon had to skate around such obstacles.

The band played with Skyhooks at Festival Hall. "Needless to say what happened," said Bon cockily in a letter to Mary (AC/DC especially hated Skyhooks). Opening band Split Enz were booed off stage. "Only the little fellows of AC/DC really pulled it off," reported the *Sun*.

Bon wrote further to Mary:

> I've been in the badbooks with everybody lately & I'm really such a nice person. I just don't understand . . .
> Off to Sydney on the weekend for a couple of weeks. Life is so boring in Melbourne, still no word on Europe but it shouldn't be too long. I reckon before Xmas or we'll all go fuckin' mad. We just keep copping the same shit week in and out. We feel like packin' it in and going to Sydney and spend all our time putting down songs in Alberts. The rest of the country's fucked. Don't I sound like a bloody whinger. Grrr!!!

The band had started dropping into Alberts on their Sydney visits. They were eager to start recording again, now that they had a proper line-up and even had a few song ideas. AC/DC never rehearsed, as such, but Malcolm and Angus would sometimes sit around together with acoustic guitars. Bon had his notebooks, and he was scribbling away—if scribbling's the right term because his handwriting was extremely neat.

Bon wrote to Irene:

> Times is tough at the moment cause Caruso 'ere 'as lost 'is vocal sound, know wat I mean. Worked so hard this last few weeks, it's just said, Fuck you lot I'm havin' a rest. Had to cancel a week's work but because we're in Sydney we can spend all our time in Alberts recording our next smash . . .
> I miss ya sometimes 'Rene. Strange that comin' from me but it's true. It's probably the weather.

Bon was obviously still feeling a little sorry for himself. There can't have been much money around either, as Bon concludes the letter with a PS to Graeme: "If you can still manage the other $50 I'd love ya f'rever. It's no fun waiting round to be a millionaire!!!"

During the May school holidays, AC/DC played a special "Schoolkids Week" of daytime gigs at the Hard Rock. It must have seemed a lot like déjà vu for Bon, being back under siege at the club that had previously been Berties.

MARK EVANS: "Because it used to be so packed downstairs, we used to get changed in Michael's office, which was right by the front door, go out on the street, unscrew the air-conditioning ducts and we'd go in through there; they'd close them up after us."

On the Queen's Birthday holiday in June, in anticipation of the release of a new single, "High Voltage Rock'n'roll," AC/DC played, for the first time, their own headline show at the Melbourne Festival Hall. Stevie Wright and John Paul Young supported. The concert was filmed, and it was this footage, with judicious doctoring, that would effectively argue the band's case in England.

CHRIS GILBEY: "We did a video, this was before videos were the norm. I was pushing Ted, We've got to do videos. I wanted a video of AC/DC, and I wanted it to be something really sensational. Anyway, we shot it, it was live, they used four cameras, which was unheard of then, it was quite a big budget. And then we added applause at the beginning and end, which we took off the George Harrison *Concert for Bangladesh* album, to make it seem like it was live."

The gig itself marked AC/DC's conquering of Melbourne. It had taken just over six months.

Bon wrote to Irene:

HV (LP) has made a gold album (last week) so it caused a slight celebration. I'm going to give it to mum. So I told her to make a space on her mantelpiece. She told me to write some clean songs for the next one but. Wait till you hear a couple of 'em. The band is nothing like it was when you heard it last. Got a couple of better players, better equipment, and songs, just better all round. So watch out.

With Melbourne in the bag, and the lease up on Lansdowne Road, Sydney was beckoning. Bon wrote to Mary:

I think we'll be living in Sydney soon and try to get the band as big up there as we are down 'ere. We all prefer Sydney to Melbourne but we wish we could drop in and see you over there instead. This country's driving us sane.

10. SYDNEY

"The Lifesaver was an ungilded palace of rock'n'rolling, easy-going degeneracy," Anthony O'Grady wrote in *RAM* of the venue which in the second half of the seventies was "the most prestigious place in Sydney for top and soon-to-be top Australian bands."

"And if no one could exactly remember the details the next day—like exactly how or why they ended up in bed with Mandrax Margaret, Amphetamine Annie or Tom, Dick or Harry from the band, well, no blame on either side for the oblivion of the night before. In fact, the bed-hop after the bop caused the place to be nicknamed the Wifeswapper."

Sydney's scene at the time was very different to Melbourne's. In the early eighties, as its pub circuit flourished, Sydney superseded Melbourne as the center of rock'n'roll in Australia, but in 1975 rock'n'roll was only just taking root in Sydney.

Initially, while the Youngs went back to Burwood, the rest of the band and crew stayed at the Squire Inn at Bondi Junction. Everyone was happy, not least of all because they were in the studio, recording the new album. Coral Browning was on the case in England. Bon was happy just to be away from Melbourne, free to lick his wounds. Of course, it didn't help that directly across the road from the Squire Inn stood the Lifesaver (this was before both buildings was demolished to make way for a shopping center and car park).

The Bondi Lifesaver is as much a part of Australian rock lore as the Largs Pier, Sunbury or the TF Much Ballroom. Though it had faded by 1979, in 1975 it was a hotbed, its glory years just beginning.

"It was the sort of place where you'd be there three nights a week, even if there wasn't always bands on," said Helen Carter, a longtime regular. "It was a bar-restaurant, with music, which meant that you would get there at six, and didn't leave until two."

With his room across the road, Bon made a virtual office out of the Lifesaver, where the band also played on occasion. He was able to enjoy his celebrity, because Sydney was now for AC/DC what it had earlier been for the Valentines—less hysterical, less aggravating than Melbourne. Obviously Bon hadn't learned his lesson about jailbait, though, because he took up with the 16-year-old Helen Carter. But then, the gorgeous young Helen wasn't a fraction of the trouble Judy King had been.

Helen, who grew up in Bondi, had been going to pubs since she was 13 or 14, and she was a smart kid. She would later form the postpunk agit-rock band Do-Re-Mi, who scored in 1985 with the feminist anthem "Man Overboard."

HELEN CARTER: "I saw AC/DC at the Lifesaver—I must have seen them a couple of times—and I just decided one night, I wanted to meet Bon, I wanted to talk to him about what was going on. I guess I thought that sex would be part of it, but I can't say honestly that I didn't think I wouldn't like to sleep with him. So I just walked up one night, and it was quite late, I had to go, so he said, Well, I'll ring you tomorrow. I thought, Sure . . .

"Anyway, he rings up, and I was at work, so he came and visited me where I worked, at a jeans shop, and he took me out for lunch, so you know, he was courteous I suppose. He always had that, a gentlemanly manner.

"He said, Come up to the gig tonight. So I went up and I saw the gig, and I don't remember exactly what happened, but I know that night we ended up going back to the hotel and I stayed there. And I stayed there quite a lot; and when they went to the Sebel, I stayed there a lot too.

"When they were staying in this Bondi Junction place, they were all in one room. Bon had the double bed because he was the oldest. Everyone else had single beds. But we would sleep together, with everybody else in the room. That kind of irked me a bit, because it was something I felt slightly embarrassed about, but he understood that, and certainly never forced me to do anything I didn't want to.

"He was incredibly gentle. He realized I'd never seen any of this stuff before—not that it was so outrageous, there was a lot of drinking, but there wasn't any drugs.

"The boys in the band—the singer in a lot of bands is frequently apart, you're not actually involved in the equipment or anything like that. Bon very much kept to himself. It was almost as if there was an invisible wall. The boys in the band pretty much did their own thing. But he loved them.

154

"He was a really hilarious person too; he was really very funny. Cheeky. He would do all sorts of things just to amuse himself and me. He had a very stable view. And he was meticulous, the way he dressed and groomed. Very plain—sleeveless shirt, a pair of jeans—but always perfectly laundered. Belt, studs . . . that was it, that was the uniform. And he always washed his hair. Dried it properly. He was very proud of his hair. He wasn't just the archetypal grub rock'n'roller."

Bon and Helen hung out. They went dancing, Helen lurching on her clogs, at Ruffles disco, which was on the roof of the Squire. And they went to the Lifesaver, across the road. Sometimes AC/DC played there; other times it was bands like Dragon, Buffalo, Cold Chisel or the Ted Mulry Gang.

HELEN: "The stuff that used to go on in that backstage room at the Lifesaver! The room was minute, and they always had the most unbelievable groupies, the loyalty was unbelievable. Not so much a lot of girls, but regular. One in particular, I just couldn't believe what she would do. People would have sex with this girl, in the dressing room. This was a normal thing. Not just blow-jobs either, but penetration, actual fucking.

"You'd just be standing there trying to hold a normal conversation, and Bon would turn his back and say, Don't look. The girl would just lift her dress and they'd start doing it. You'd think it couldn't have been any fun for anybody.

"I guess for Bon, that was part of the reason why he tried to set an example. Although, God, you couldn't have got a worse role model for drinking. I saw him drunk a lot, but he never lost control. He was actually a big sooky drunk, like some people get, just subdued, you know. Not at all violent. He would rather have a nice soft relationship. He wasn't a wild man lovemaker or anything; to a certain degree that wasn't the only thing on his mind either, despite his songs, which are all just sex or rock'n'roll.

"He loved women, he used to love the attention of women, he loved to have lots of them around. I can say this now and it's probably crap because I look at that sort of behavior and think, Well . . . but you see, the difference was, he didn't treat anybody like shit. Even then, when I was 16 and pretty naive myself, if there was any of that we-just-fuck-'em-and-dump 'em attitude, I would have thought, Oh, that's not very nice. But there was none of that.

"Bon would say, Look, if I seem a bit strange sometimes, don't get upset, talk to me about it later. It was obvious even then he was aware there was some kind of public persona that he had to uphold as soon as he stepped outside his hotel room. But in private, he used to say things like . . . You know, he always used to wear those sleeveless vests, and he'd stand in front of the mirror in the hotel room flexing his muscles. I'd be just sort of sitting there looking at him. He'd say, Do you think it looks good? You know, he was as vain as any other man I've ever known. And I'd say, Sure. He said, You know, I buy them two sizes too small so it makes my muscles look bigger. He was really crucially and sometimes a bit embarrassedly aware of what was expected of him, or what he thought was part of the performance, even though he was very sincere about it.

"What I'm saying is, he was a professional."

AC/DC started to make an impression in Sydney, attracting much the same sort of disenchanted kids they had done in Melbourne. Hurstville Rock, a no-alcohol dance held every Saturday night in the local Civic Hall, became a stronghold gig. One witness recalls, "When AC/DC played it was always huge. You could stand in the middle of the dance floor, and it would be bouncing up and down.

"There used to be this thing between the Westie rockers, who'd come because they liked AC/DC, and everybody else, because we thought AC/DC belonged to us. The audience was mainly surfies, you know. Thongs, jeans, Hawaiian shirts. All these underage people would sneak in, there was no grog allowed but there was always plenty going round. And joints—that was where I got stoned for the first time. People would just pass joints around! You'd get drunk, stoned and you'd chat up girls. AC/DC were great."

Tireless roadwork was drilling the band into a lean, mean rock'n'roll machine. Malcolm told *RAM* (before he virtually stopped talking to the press altogether): "We used to worry about playing what was on the album—we used to play spot on—note for note off the album. But the people weren't getting off on it. Then George said, Don't play the songs, play to the people."

Bon was also taking his role as songwriter more seriously.

HELEN: "The thing about Bon was that he really did think a lot about what he was doing. He took it very seriously. He was a very meticulous person. So as a writer, he wouldn't just blurt stuff out. It would be very thought out.

"Bon would leave his lyric notebooks lying around, and I was fascinated by the way he would always write in capital letters. He'd have everything really neatly written out.

"And I think he found writing not an easy thing. Angus and Malcolm used to write a lot of music; they'd just sit down and jam and come up with stuff. So there was a constant flow of material being put to Bon, to write, and I think in some ways that was quite a pressure for him."

The band spent every spare moment during July at Alberts, mostly through the night. To Malcolm and Angus it was just like being back home. George was there, running the show with Harry, his redoubtable partner. Also there, as general trouble-shooter, was Sammy Horsburgh, the former Easybeats tour manager who married Margaret Young.

MARK EVANS: "It had a real family atmosphere. The Youngs are real Scottish working class, really good strong family, you know, staunch. Very hard though. Every time I'd go round there—and we used to play a lot of cards, after gigs, we used to play poker—there's seven brothers, and every time one or two or three or four of them would be punching the shit out of each other. Every time, without fail, someone would be having a brawl!"

The old Boomerang House on King Street in central Sydney, where Alberts studio was then located, was owned by the Alberts family. It had housed radio station 2UW, which the family also owned. Alberts Music was also there, though the studio wasn't built until 1975. That was Studio One; other studios were added over the next few years.

With a bare brick wall adjoining it, Studio One looked more like a squat than anything at the cutting edge of technology. And it wasn't that, either.

EVANS: "It was very small—we used to record in the side room, had two Marshall stacks and bass-rig, pointing towards the wall and miked up, and in what used to be the kitchen, drums in there—everything put down at once, generally the fire was in the first couple of takes."

What Alberts had that money can't buy was a vibe, an ambience. In recording studios, the vibe is something that goes down on tape—that's why it's so important. Alberts had a vibe merely because of the presence of George and Harry, astute manipulators of studio psychopolitics who consistently drew the best out of performers. Their other great strength, as Chris Gilbey put it, was that "they were tremendously good song men." In other words, they had ears for a hit.

TED MULRY: "You didn't go into Alberts saying, Let's record this song. You were going in there to come up with another hit. And that was everybody's attitude, the buzz going round. You went in to come out with a hit."

"George produces our material not just because he's our brother," Angus said. "He thinks we're good. If we were shithouse he wouldn't do it. But it's nice and easy-going in Alberts' own studio. When you get in there you feel relaxed and at ease."

Bon told *Juke*, "He's like a brother, no, a father to the group. He helps us with our writing. He doesn't tell us what to do, he just shows us how to get more out of the things we start."

AC/DC were much better prepared for recording their second album—tighter and more confident; they even had a few rough ideas to go in with.

Five more new songs were cut during July ("High Voltage" and "The Jack" were already in the can). Alongside a re-recorded "Can I Sit Next to You, Girl," and a version of Chuck Berry's "School Days," they turned out "Long Way to the Top," "Rock'n'roll Singer," "Live Wire," "TNT" and "Rocker," which complete the album's track listing. None of it seems ill-considered.

EVANS: "Malcolm and Angus would come up with riffs and all that, and then we'd go into the studio. Malcolm and George would sit down at the piano and work it out. Malcolm and Angus would have the barest bones of a song, the riff and different bits, and George would hammer it into a tune.

"Bon would be in and out when the band was recording backing tracks. Once the backing track was done, he would literally be locked in the kitchen there at Alberts, and come out with a finished song."

Angus once said, "[George would] take our meanest song and try it out on keyboards with arrangements like 10cc or even Mantovani. If it was passed, the structure was proven, then we took it away and dirtied it up."

AC/DC would record backing tracks live in the studio—sound spilling everywhere because the band played so loud—and then vocals and guitar solos were overdubbed. George and Harry were careful to give the group its head, but at the same time, they knew when to stop.

MICHAEL BROWNING: "Yeah, and then just embellish it a bit. George and Harry's most important criterion was rhythm, the whole thing had to just feel right. If you listen to those records today, they feel good."

CHRIS GILBEY: "The great thing George and Harry taught me, as a producer, was that if you've got a good rhythm track, you've got the beginnings of a record. If you don't, you've got nothing."

TED MULRY: "When AC/DC were recording, you'd walk into a session, and Angus would be on top of the quad boxes, in the studio. He couldn't just sit there, he'd be running around jumping up and down like it was a live performance."

BROWNING: "Malcolm used to come up with a lot of titles. He'd sort of come up with a title like "TNT," and then he'd play some chords to fit that title, and a lot of the songs were just developed that way. Bon would go away and write a song about TNT, or this or that."

In his notebooks, Bon had lyric ideas to put to music. Locked in the

Angus, Malcolm, and George Young in the studio, Alberts, Sydney, March 25, 1976, during the sessions for *Dirty Deeds Done Dirt Cheap*. Angus: "George would take our meanest song and try it out on keyboards with arrangements like Mantovani. If it was passed, the structure was proven, we took it away and dirtied it up."

kitchen, he ran lines through his head one last time, mouthing them out, getting it right. As a singer, Bon was a screecher (there are those who believe his voice was never the same after the accident that did so much damage to his neck and jaw), but like Sinatra or Dylan, his greatness was in his phrasing. And it was the interplay between his phrasing and his words, in their economy, that proved just how seriously he took songwriting.

HELEN: "Looking through his lyric books, you would see different versions of things. The sort of lyrics they were, you think, Oh, any old dickhead could write that. But it's not true. Even the simplest of lyrics, his timing and meter, he spent a lot of time on."

Bon told *Countdown*: "Things fall into place. Sometimes. You gotta keep your eyes and ears open for lines and words and stuff . . . ideas, just pictures, you know."

TNT was the album that really introduced AC/DC as a band. It still contained a few naff tracks, but its forcefulness was undeniable. If it was as impatient as it was bold, even that was impressive. 1975 needed rock'n'roll like this. And certainly, the album's one-two opening punch is as powerful as any ever recorded, with Bon virtually encapsulating his entire life in "Long Way to the Top" and "Rock'n'roll Singer."

"'Long Way to the Top' started as a guitar jam in A," Angus later explained. "It was just that little jam and George thought it cooked. And then Bon had the scribble which turned into the lyrics."

Completing side one, "The Jack" overplayed its card-table metaphor, while "Live Wire" was as good a piece of braggadocio as AC/DC produced. "TNT," the album's title track which opens side two, was on a par with "High Voltage"—fair but disposable. Next to "Can I Sit Next to You, Girl" and "School Days," "Rocker" was hilariously frenetic.

With the new album in the can, sales of *High Voltage* were still strong, boosted by the release of the new single with the same title. The band appeared on *Countdown,* with Bon doing his Tarzan routine wearing nothing but a lap-lap.

GILBEY: "At that time, we'd done what we thought were phenomenal units, about 70,000 on it, and that was unheard of, and then the single "High Voltage" took the album up to 120-125,000, and we thought, My God!

"We didn't think AC/DC would become a world-wide phenomenon the way they have. We were all just occupied, tight-focus, on making the act survive. It was just, get a record away. Keep having hits. Try and keep moving. And then it was, Hey, let's get outside the country and see if we can sell it overseas. That was the next step."

Chris Gilbey was possibly thinking this way when everyone else was thinking about England because he himself had already taken a knock-back on AC/DC overseas. When he went to MIDEM in January 1975, representing Alberts generally, he found more people interested in bubblegum pop star William Shakespeare! George, in turn, didn't mind that Gilbey was concentrating on Australia, because Michael Browning was chipping away in England. Browning had sent Coral a copy of the video AC/DC had shot at their Melbourne Festival Hall Queen's Birthday concert, and she was hawking it around London.

To promote a free show at Sydney's Victoria Park in early September, which on the back of the "High Voltage" single would serve as a Sydney launch for AC/DC, Chris Gilbey devised the "Your mother won't like them" advertising campaign for radio station 2SM. It worked a treat. The single peaked at number six nationally.

GILBEY: "It was like, instant attitude. Nowadays, everything is premeditated. Back then, we didn't have to philosophize, and come up with a psychological profile of the consumer, to figure out why it was we wanted to sell a bad-boy image in order to have those kids that were alienated from their parents love this group. We just thought, Hey, this is exciting, this is cool. Either you had it or you didn't have it. Rose Tattoo, either you have it or you don't."

It was another cold Sunday afternoon when AC/DC played at Victoria Park with Stevie Wright and Ross ("I am Pegasus") Ryan. The show was unremarkable—as usual, the band blew everyone away—save for the fact that it saw Angus climb astride Bon's shoulders for the first time.

Bon had obviously climbed back in the saddle because, as Angus said, "That notorious leader of thieves and vagabonds, Bon Scott, to celebrate the success of the show in Sydney, went out and got a new tattoo and pierced his nipples for earrings. The other boys celebrated in other ways."

The band was right on target.

In September, AC/DC went back down to Melbourne to renew their expired agreement with Michael Browning—a five-year management contract was signed—and to get it together for an extensive national tour to promote the pre-Christmas release of the new album. As it turned out, the album wouldn't eventually be released till February, but this is rock'n'roll, after all.

Bites were being registered overseas. Bon wrote to Mary, "A&M is wrapped in the band as is John Peel the DJ. Reckons we're the band England needs and we agree." He also wrote to Irene, "I'm not doing too bad on the booze thing these days and am getting drunk quite regularly. But I'm a peaceful drunk now. Have I still got any friends in Adelaide?"

Starting in Perth, the tour would take the band all over Australia before winding up in Sydney on Christmas Eve. Before heading to Perth, the band played a few shows in Melbourne.

Booked to play a week of free lunchtime gigs in the Miss Myer department of the big Myers store in the city, the band had barely started their first set on the first day when they were overrun by hysterical girls (reports vary from 600 to 5,000). The shop and its fixtures were turned upside down; strangely, a shoplifting frenzy was not reported. The rest of the week was promptly cancelled.

MARK EVANS: "It was just bedlam. It was probably the only time I thought one of us was going to get hurt. It was really scary."

The band had to run for their lives. Bon, however, even as he fled, still managed to sneak a peek over the saloon doors of the changing rooms.

A Premier Artists worksheet for the band for the second week of September saw them playing six gigs, plus recording an episode of *Countdown*, between the Wednesday and Saturday, for total earnings of $3,610, which included a $160 performance fee from *Countdown*. Certainly, it made their old $60 per week pay packet seem inadequate.

At an average of $600 per gig, AC/DC played the South Side Six on Wednesday and the Matthew Flinders Hotel on Thursday, both suburban beer-barns, where the band played one set between 10 p.m. and 11:30. At the Matthew Flinders, a scuffle in front of the stage involving Angus cost drummer Phil Rudd a broken thumb, necessitating an immediate stand-in. On the Friday, with old drummer Colin Burgess on Rudd's stool, the band played a free show at the Eastlands Shopping Center in Ringwood, between 6:00 and 7:00, and then later they appeared at the International Hotel. At 6:00 on Saturday night, the band recorded an appearance on *Countdown,* then played the Tarmac Hotel between 10:00 and 11:30 and then the Hard Rock Cafe between 1:30 and 3:00. On Sunday, the band flew to Perth.

Bon visited his mum and dad in Perth. Chick and Isa were very impressed by the boys. It was the first time they'd all met each other, and they were such nice boys, Isa thought.

The band worked their way back to Melbourne playing through South Australia, visiting even the towns of the dreaded Iron Triangle again.

Right on the back of recording *TNT*, the band was in blistering form, but it didn't always get the reaction it might have liked.

"We had been on a tour with AC/DC which led to our first record-ing ... our big break," Angels singer Doc Neeson recalled. "And because we were a covers band and they were an original band, we were getting encores and they were getting booed. People knew our songs and thought that they were a dirty heavy metal band." AC/DC, nonetheless, went home and told George about this hot new band called the Keystone Angels and, as the Angels, they would serve Alberts well.

MARK EVANS: "The band itself wasn't hyped, it was good, a good band; but the mechanics of the thing, it was hyped-up, there's no question about that. I don't know any successful band that isn't. But if it had have been left to the reaction from live gigs alone, we would have been strug-gling."

The fact that Angus was pushed as the focal point didn't bother Bon. Armed with an axe and a fag and dressed in his school uniform, Angus provided an image so readily identifiable, it became a symbol for the band. In fact, Bon was almost relieved that some of the heat was off him on stage. Jealousies simply weren't possible anyway. The power structure within the band was set, and if you didn't like it ... Nobody apart from Malcolm and Angus was indispensable, it seems, including Bon. And though Bon was granted special dispensations, he almost went too far on occasion. Like when he OD'd. But even then, the Youngs couldn't think of sacking him. Blood was thicker than water, after all.

Bon was elusive, and though he could be annoying on a day-to-day level, he always came through in the end. He was always running late, and he might often be the worse for wear, but he never once failed to show, and he always gave everything he had.

Back at the Freeway Gardens Motel in Melbourne, where the band now based itself, Bon was still likely to wander off by himself. But more often than not he was hanging out with Pat Pickett. Pickett had been living in provincial Geelong, employed at the local meatworks, when he heard about AC/DC. He immediately made a beeline for Melbourne. He joined the band's crew in a nebulous role—similar to that he had enjoyed with Fraternity—as Bon's consort, his partner in crime. Bon's frame of mind was pure reckless abandon.

MARK EVANS: "We were always looking after him, looking out for him, and we were only kids ourselves. You'd say, Hey, where's Bon? I remember carrying Bon home and putting him into bed. But he had this thing about him where you wanted to take care of him.

"You could see his charm kicking in. You could also see Bon Scott the singer of AC/DC kicking in when the press was around, you know."

The Freeway Gardens, a shabby motel at the mouth of the Tullamarine Freeway in North Melbourne—devoid of any sort of garden—was a haven for many bands, including the Ted Mulry Gang.

HERM KOVAC: "Bon used to carry around this little shaving kit. That was his whole baggage. It contained a toothbrush, toothpaste, one pair of jocks and one pair of socks. That was it. He'd wear his jeans till he might wash them at the hotel, and so he'd just get around in his jocks till they were dry. But otherwise, he'd have a pair of jocks and socks on the go, and he'd wash them each night in the sink, hanging them up in the bathroom, and get the fresh pair out of the little bag. He'd rotate them. He traveled very lightly."

MARK EVANS: "He would do anything. I remember one time he made this bet. It was the middle of winter in Melbourne and he said he'd dive into the swimming pool. Someone took him on for five dollars. A stupid bet. He said, Make it ten. So we went up to the third floor, the balcony, and he just dove straight in. Got out, Where's my ten bucks? He'd do these things that were just over the top."

Mark didn't know Bon had a history of high diving.

The debauchery of Lansdowne Road continued unabated at the Freeway Gardens. The band, after all, was even bigger now. And so, it seems, were some of the fans. It was at the Freeway Gardens that Bon met Rosie, subject of the all-time great paean to large ladies, "Whole Lotta Rosie." The band held in very high esteem anything that was what they called "depraved," "evil" or "filthy." Put Pat Pickett and Bon together and the conversation would take a seriously funny downward turn. Scatology was a favored topic, but that was just the beginning. The band ran an ongoing competition—the prize being booze which they would all hoe into—to see who could pull off the most disgusting, depraved, filthy act.

Bon's bedding of Rosie was a big winner in these stakes, but as the lyrics to the song suggest, he derived a lot more pleasure from the experience—"Whole Lotta Rosie" is actually very affectionate—than the band might have imagined.

Rosie was a Tasmanian mountain woman who had started showing up at gigs. An open challenge was thus issued.

PAT PICKETT: "We were sharing a room at the Freeway Gardens, and I woke up one morning and looked over at Bon's bed and I thought, Jeez, he's done it! There was this huge pile of blubber lying there, but I could see underneath it, this tiny little arm with tattoos on it was sticking out!"

EVANS: "The one myth about the band which was actually pretty true was the amount of females we used to get hold of. It was ridiculous. I used to be fairly lucky, but I was nothing on Bon. He had four days in a row where he got what we called a trifecta, three different girls each day for four days in a row. The man was a genius, I don't know how he did it. He had a huge . . ."

Penis is the word that might complete that sentence. At least several reports suggest that Bon was extremely well hung. He liked to show it off too, dressing all to one side in jeans that were inevitably almost sprayed on.

EVANS: "This other myth, the image the band had as this heavy drinking, you know, brawling bunch, it couldn't be further from the truth. We never got thrown out of one hotel.

"Bon didn't get into any more trouble than your usual bloke on the road. The whole thing was this huge image. There were a couple of instances, a couple. I remember once at the Matthew Flinders, Angus, because he used to spin around on the dance floor, a couple of guys started kicking into him. I remember Pat, Phil and myself jumping off the stage, and getting into that. Phil actually broke his thumb, and so we had to get another drummer for a while, when we were in Perth, we had to get Colin Burgess back.

"But Bon, you could hit him over the head with a baseball bat, and he'd just say, Hey, what are you doing? But if you hit someone he was with with a baseball bat, you couldn't hide anywhere. Ladies particularly. Guys, he might say, You asked for it. If one of the guys in the band got into trouble, Bon would tell them the next day, You were an idiot last night. But if it was someone you were with who obviously couldn't take care of themselves, my God!"

Pat Pickett remembers a time when Bon was at a pub with Irene, who moved to Melbourne, and a guy was hassling them, perhaps just because Bon was Bon. The guy was a well known hard man. Bon ignored him, until he went too far. As they were leaving the pub, the guy pulled Irene's pony-tail. Bon had a breaking point, and he had just reached it. He took the guy outside and gave him what witnesses remember as a fist-beating to within an inch of his life.

EVANS: "He was really a pretty mild mannered sort of guy. I mean, I never saw him lose his temper. He had this equilibrium, and he was very, very polite, a real gentleman. Once I saw him get the shits, and it was the strangest thing . . .

"The band appeared on the *TV Week* 1975 King Of Pop awards show . . . We played live, and Bon had a terrible time, everything went wrong for him; the mike lead got caught in his shoes, everything. When we got off stage, we went downstairs, and we had to break the lock on the door to get into the bar. There were just all these stacks of *TV Week* there, with [Sherbet singer] Daryl Braithwaite on the cover, the King of Pop. Bon was just standing there staring at them, and he said, Have a fuckin' look at this! And then he started just laughing, maniacally, he said, I don't believe this, and he started ripping up all the magazines. And then, from that point on that night, he was the most uncouth, awful, rude person I've ever seen. To the point where he took this turkey off the table and was drinking champagne out of it. He just had this turkey under his arm, drinking out of it, offering it to everyone. Something snapped, that one time."

The band headed out to play rural Victoria, and then ran through Sydney, before returning to Melbourne at the start of November to play a special Melbourne Cup Day show at Festival Hall. Hush supported.

Michael Browning, meantime, was in London. Atlantic Records had gone crazy for AC/DC. A deal would be struck. The album would be released, and the band would go over, sometime in the new year.

All November was spent on the road. The bus was in service when distances weren't too great, and speed not of the essence. After Cup Day, the band spent a week in Adelaide, then toured through the deep north of Queensland. Back in Sydney, they played at the opulent State Theatre on November 30. The first two weeks of December were spent in and out of Sydney, swinging through Canberra, before making a quick dash to Brisbane to play a Festival Hall show on the 14th.

It was a hectic time, and Bon was obviously feeling the strain. He wrote to Irene:

> What a cunt of a night. Just got back from Canberra a day early and no one is expecting us up until tomorrow. Got no booze, no dope and no body except my own to play with. Shit. And to top it off I left my black book in the bus, which broke down in Canberra . . .
>
> I reckon we'd have to be the hottest band in the country at the moment. Not bad for a 29-year-old 3rd-time-round has-been.
>
> I don't care if I never get a divorce cause I'm not planning on marrying again unless she's a millionaire and I think my chances of finding one are scarce. But when I pull out my photy album I like saying, And this is my wife. They all fancy you and tell me what taste in spunk I've got . . .
>
> I'm going through a fucking funny period at the moment. Hope you don't mind a heart balm letter. Don't wanna settle with anybody because I'm always on the road and won't be here long and on the other hand there's twenty to thirty chicks a day I can have the choice of fucking but I can't stand that either. Mixed up. I like to be touring all the time just to keep my mind off personal happenings. Become a drunkard again and I can't go through a day without a smoke of hippie stuff. I just wanna get a lot of money soon so I can at least change a few little things about myself (more booze and dope). Not really. I just wanna be famous I guess. Just so when people talk about you it's good things they say. That's all I want. But right now I'm just lonely.

After Brisbane, AC/DC worked their way down the coast to reach Sydney by Christmas Eve, to play a big shebang at the Royal Showgrounds. Bon spent Christmas with the Youngs, then flew to Adelaide to spend some time with Irene and Graeme, and his girlfriend Faye. "My wife and her boyfriend, that is," he wrote to Maria, from whom he had received an unexpected Christmas card. "Graeme wants to marry my sister-in-law. I'm saying noth-

166

ing." Bon also dealt with some legal matters in Adelaide pertaining to his bike accident. He was still paying off bills.

The band played in Adelaide on New Year's Day. Again, as Molly Meldrum reported in his column in *Truth,* "The street punk kids of Australian rock and roll, AC/DC, were the cause of a minor riot." The band had the power cut on them and Bon, inevitably, incited a storming of the stage in protest. "Power or no power, they were not going to be deterred," Molly went on. "Because, would you believe, Bon Scott appeared in the middle of the crowd, on someone's shoulders, playing bagpipes!"

Bon wrote further to Maria:

> I'm out on the road again but this time between Melbourne and Adelaide on the coast route. It'll be the third town tonight and there's twenty-one more to go. We've had a week off between Xmas/NY but now it's back to work. Got a couple of weeks off after this tour to record and tie up all the loose ends before leaving for England.
>
> All this touring has worn me out. But it's selling a lot of records and I'm seeing a lot of the country and people that you don't realize exist, so it can't be too bad.
>
> I'm finally making money, Maria. About $500 a week and it's all in the bank . . . I just hope I'm not still stupid cause now I can make a good start at doing something good. Don't know what though. I haven't finished rocking yet and that's all I want to do right now.

With the Atlantic deal now finalized, the rumor was that AC/DC would support labelmates ZZ Top on a British tour to coincide with the release of their first album; then maybe even do something with the Stones, who were also on Atlantic. Either way, the band's departure was now certain. It was just a matter of exactly when.

Bon had dreamed as a boy of leading a pipe band, marching beside it swinging the baton, feeling the sounds flow through him, feeling responsible and proud, the agent of so much joy as the drone and flutter reverberated in the air all around him. Now the dream was coming true.

A performance through the middle of Melbourne, on the back of a flat-top truck, was arranged by *Countdown* so they could shoot a video of "Long Way to the Top," AC/DC's new single. Three professional pipers accompanied the band.

This was different to what Bon had originally envisaged, but it was better. Bon was singing his own song. It was rock'n'roll—and it was the pipes.

Traffic stopped as the boys drove slowly through the city and fans ran alongside to catch a glimpse of their idols. Stomping along the length of the moving truck's tray-top (just like Elvis), Bon looked up to see the buildings of Melbourne passing above him under a blue sky and looked down at the adoring faces, and sensed everyhow the power of the music. It infused all his senses, his own body was as if wired, responding involuntarily. Bon was swimming with the power. This was what he lived for.

"Long Way to the Top" has become an anthem. Certainly, it was AC/DC's best single to date. Bon was best when he was working to his own brief, rather than writing to order—he expressed himself more honestly, more evocatively.

In "Long Way to the Top," it's as if Bon acknowledges he's living on borrowed time, and luckily at that. But even then, or perhaps for that very reason, the song remains celebratory.

At the end of January, "Long Way to the Top" peaked at number five. Three singles, three hits, and each outperforming the last—it's a record any act would envy.

When the album was released, sent out to the media wrapped in a pair of ladies knickers, it sold 11,000 in the first week, and shot to the number two spot, kept out only by Bob Dylan's *Desire*, which had just displaced Abba.

It was decided then that the band should go back into Alberts to cut another album, not knowing how long it might be before they got another opportunity to record. "In those days," said Michael Browning, "you didn't take two years between records. It was nothing to record two or three in a year."

The band's rapidly rising star was acknowledged when they arrived in Sydney in February and checked into the Sebel Town House, the five-star hotel still chosen by visiting rock royalty.

HELEN CARTER: "I was with Bon the day he got a $500 royalty check. They were staying at the Sebel, so obviously by then they were making a bit of money, but this was the first royalty check he'd got which was substantial, and he was just like, Look at this! His face lit up, he was just really happy at being paid for something he loved doing.

"He was of the old school, where rock'n'roll was everything. To him, it was still rebellion. I mean, it wasn't like he was a guy who was saying, Oh, I've been doing gigs for years now, how come I haven't got any money? That didn't come into it. He was an innocent, I suppose.

"By that stage, everywhere you went there'd be women hanging around, in the hotel foyer, outside the venue, or the dressing room. So Bon would say, Here's the key to the hotel room, I'll be up in half an hour; because he had to deal with not just women but fans. And he really felt he had an obligation to hang around and talk to them."

The band cut *Dirty Deeds Done Dirt Cheap* during February. So quickly after *TNT*, they had virtually nothing up their sleeves.

MARK EVANS: "Angus came up with the title. I remember when I heard it, I thought it sounded familiar, and ten years later I worked it out—it's some cartoon character, off *Beanie and Cecil*, the villain, Captain Pugwash, he used to say that."

HELEN: "Bon would play demos of music he had to write to. He'd just sit around the hotel room and have it going in the background, formulating ideas. He always had a cassette player, and at the time, his favorite song was "Love To Love You, Baby", by Donna Summer. Which shows another side to him, musically."

Bon still sought a lot outside the band.

HELEN: "Angus is pretty straightforward. Bon was almost an intellectual in comparison. The only way he could gauge anything, or write about anything, was to talk about other stuff, and we did a lot of talking. It wasn't like we went back to his room, had sex for 12 hours and that was that. To be quite honest, I don't think, say, talking to the road crew or whatever would have been terribly stimulating to him."

But of course, Bon could mix it with anyone. And if women weren't present, at least not ladies—as distinct from those with whom your secret was safe—then Bon could be a very bad boy. Bon's mythic persona was further fuelled by the subsequent publication of a feature story in the Australian edition of *Rolling Stone,* which opened on Bon vomiting after a show, the victim, apparently, of a "bad bottle of Scotch," whatever that means. In reality, his drinking was fair to middling. Anthony O'Grady witnessed the same episode, as the band played a few final gigs in Sydney whilst recording the album, and he reported in *RAM*: "[Bon] sometimes gets the same look that battle-scarred alley fighters have—a look of indifferent bloodlust. Kick 'em in the teeth and they'll just spit blood and get up again."

At the same time, O'Grady remembers that at the end of that night, back at Burwood, Bon and he were ushered outside to wait in the car when George wanted to "talk business" with his brothers, and Bon happily acquiesced, proceeding to simply pass out in the back seat.

HELEN: "I know that when you get a bit successful, because the pressure and everything else increases, you do drink too much. Especially if you've just done a fantastic show or something, you come off stage and you want to . . . But it didn't rule his life. It was part of his life, but it wasn't the major feature. The major feature was purely and simply getting up on stage and doing it, he just loved that.

"He used to gargle with Coonawarra red [wine] and honey, every morning. This is giving away trade secrets. But that was the secret to his great voice."

Dirty Deeds was rushed; but then, everything was a rush for AC/DC at that time. With the UK release of the *High Voltage* album (which was in fact a compilation of tracks from the Australian albums *High Voltage* and *TNT)* now scheduled for May, and a UK tour supporting Paul Kossoff's Back Street Crawler locked in for April, the flight to London was finally booked—for April Fool's Day.

When they finished recording it, *Dirty Deeds* was put into cold storage. It had turned out as an equally inconsistent echo of its predecessor. The title track was more sloganeering; "Big Balls" is pure vaudeville double entendre; and "There's Gonna Be Some Rockin'" and "RIP (Rock in Peace)" are pretty much the same song, both mindless chugalug boogies. "Squealer" was an inferior sequel to "Rocker."

The remaining four tracks save the album. "Problem Child" fittingly became a staple of the band's live set, a crunching, threatening flurry. "Ain't No Fun (Waiting Around To Be a Millionaire)" is a boogie elevated by a superior lyric and greater extension on the band's part.

But it was the album's closing two tracks, "Ride On" and "Jailbreak," that were its killers, a double-punch equal to that which opened *TNT*. "Ride On," despite borrowing the chords from ZZ Top's "Jesus Just Left Chicago," is a statement of Bon's tomorrow-never-comes credo whose poignancy has acquired a rueful dimension since his death. It segues abruptly but perfectly into "Jailbreak," a virtual manifesto for AC/DC—relentlessly thudding release.

In March, as the track "TNT" was released as a single, the band flew to Melbourne to attend a gold record reception and formal farewell party. Three plaques each for *High Voltage* and *TNT* were presented. The band regrouped in Sydney to play one final show at the Lifesaver before they left (it was at this show that Angus stripped for the first time, flashing his bare behind, a routine that features in AC/DC's shows to this day). The night before flying out, a celebration was thrown at Burwood for Angus's nineteenth birthday.

HELEN: "It was a very quiet affair, just a couple of pizzas and a Billy Connolly record. Bon was excited, but skeptical about it [going overseas]. You know, being 30, not that that's old, but in terms of starting a career, internationally, in an industry in which at that stage, if you were an Australian band, you may as well not have existed."

As "TNT" climbed the Australian charts, eventually peaking at number eleven, Michael Browning played down the band's departure. He'd been through it all before. "I've seen too many Australian groups say, Oh yeah, we're going over to England and we'll be big, and when it doesn't happen straight away, no one in Australia wants to know about them anymore," he told *RAM*. "AC/DC are an Australian group and we don't want to spoil anything we've built up here." Maybe he was just trying to cover his arse.

The band couldn't have cared less. As Angus told *Record Mirror & Disc* shortly after arriving in England, "Success there [in Australia] means nothing. We left on a peak rather than overstaying our welcome, and set out to plunder and pillage."

Spencer Jones, whose own band the Beasts of Bourbon would later cover "Ride On," remembers seeing that last show they played. "It changed my life. There was this girl there, and she got up on stage and started to do a strip. She was quite a big girl, and she was just dancing around without any clothes on. So Bon picked her up. He just put one hand around her neck, and one on her crotch, and he just raised her above his head and stood there with her aloft like that. It was the most macho, sexist pose imaginable, but Bon could get away with things like that.

"And while all this was going on, Angus was up on someone's shoulders, and he was trying to get to the bar, this long bar they had at the Lifesaver. The place was packed, you couldn't move, but somehow they punched their way through, the people sort of parted like the Dead Sea. Angus hopped off at the bar and he did the duck-walk. Meanwhile, Bon's just standing there with this girl on his shoulders. It was incredible. And then when Bon let her down, the roadies came on to help her, but they didn't just throw her back into the audience, she was ushered backstage."

HELEN: "No one else could get away with that stuff. I think that was what Bon actually loved about doing what he was doing, he really could, if he wanted, do anything he wanted. And he loved that. He loved that freedom."

Shortly after the band's arrival in the UK. Bon's shades conceal a fresh black eye . . .

11. ENGLAND

It was a hot summer in England in 1976—a long, hot summer. It was the eve of the Queen's 1977 Silver Jubilee, and the country was gearing up for a prolonged, jewel-encrusted celebration of royal irrelevance. It was simultaneously on the verge of a revolution.

To chic, would-be subversives, all the Jubilee did was provide a target for pot shots. Following their December 1976 debut single "Anarchy in the UK," the Sex Pistols' incendiary rewriting of "God Save the Queen' caused the sensation it was designed to. In doing so, the Pistols sparked the world-wide cultural sea change called punk rock.

Bon had left Scotland with his family to come and live in Australia in 1952, the year Queen Elizabeth ascended to the throne. Now he was returning to Britain in time for her jubilee. He couldn't have cared less. He didn't care much for punk rock either.

Punk rock, British-style, liked to think it was a political movement, but it was first and foremost an aesthetic one. It was an aesthetic decision inspired negatively, by an unspeakable hatred for hippies and for practically all the music that then prevailed.

Its anger was well-directed; punk was a necessary and overdue flushing out of the stagnant waters rock'n'roll had become. Rock had never been in a worse state than it was in the mid-seventies; it was almost exclusively the corporate domain of boring old farts, to use the preferred punk term.

Punk ultimately changed the face of rock'n'roll, and more beyond. But like glam, punk was nothing so much as a return to rock'n'roll classicism: the traditional values of teen rebellion and hit-single songwriting. It was getting back to basics because rock'n'roll—if it could be dignified with the name—had lost touch with its underclass roots. It's just that punk was packaged in apocalyptic urban-guerrilla garb.

When AC/DC arrived in London in April 1976, the storm was still brewing. The scene was still very sluggish. One of the first UK gigs that AC/DC played, later that month, was at the Nashville Rooms in Kensington, where the Sex Pistols had played their first-ever legitimate gig on the venue's "new bands" night only weeks before.

"We got people like the Sex Pistols," Angus recalls. "The Johnny Rottens would show up, cop a look—in fact, the guy looked like a clone of Bon the first time I saw him!"

"It's hard to believe now, but AC/DC were sort of caught up in that punk thing," said Richard Griffiths, AC/DC's first agent in England, who booked that Nashville Rooms gig. "This was the very early days of punk. The Sex Pistols were playing, the Damned were playing, and AC/DC were playing. There was another band playing, called Eddie and the Hot Rods, who I was also agent for. So there were two things happening at the same time, and they got slightly intermeshed."

Punk was largely a media-driven phenomenon. The British music press, which wielded even more power than *Countdown* did in Australia, latched onto punk and propagated it as the new anti-fashion. But if AC/DC couldn't count on press support—because they failed to conform to the punk stereotypes—it wasn't the end of the world. They'd never been critics' darlings anyway. When they got to Britain, their strategy was simply to do exactly what they'd done in Australia: build it up from the grass roots on the live circuit.

It was precisely because of the climate that gave rise to punk that AC/DC also found an audience—and so quickly—in Britain. There were plenty of kids just as fed up with all the boring old farts as the punks were—as AC/DC were—but who couldn't get into punk because it was so theoretical and confrontational that it was itself alienating. AC/DC had a lot in common with punk—an almost back-to-mono sensibility, a keenness to upset the applecart, and a hatred of hippies—but they were much more accessible because they had orthodox R&B roots.

MICHAEL BROWNING: "Building it up in the pubs wasn't that difficult because there was good word of mouth for it. It was just purely down to the kids that liked that kind of music, and they really got off on it."

"We went over to establish ourselves as a road band first of all," Bon later told *RAM*, "and then work for a hit single. Sherbet, a few years ago, got the hit single but they couldn't get anyone to concerts. Then they couldn't get another hit and they couldn't work at all. We didn't want that."

Angus concurred. "I think all the good bands are essentially live bands, the great ones, the ones that last, your Stones, Who, whatever. Your only gauge for AC/DC is if we play someplace and people come back to see us the next time we play there. You can't trust the hype side of it."

AC/DC's initial British schedule was arranged long before the band left Australia. First up, they would embark on an April and May tour of Britain supporting Atlantic labelmates Back Street Crawler, the band fronted by former Free guitarist Paul Kossoff.

Then, in June, they would tour the country all over again as part of a roadshow put together in conjunction with *Sounds* magazine. Coral Browning, with her good connections, had convinced *Sounds* that such a package—boasting a hard rock disco and films, as well as AC/DC, all for the meager admission price of 50 pence—would serve both the magazine and the band well.

Of the big three music papers, *Sounds* was the new kid on the block (it had been launched in 1970), and consequently it was out to challenge the traditional supremacy of the *New Musical Express* and *Melody Maker*. The *NME* was the market leader, with its fickle, elitist and intellectual championship of punk. *Sounds* took a more down-to-earth approach. It threw itself behind punk too, but not to the exclusion, or denigration, of the heavy metal bands it already championed.

Not surprisingly, then, AC/DC was *Sounds*' dream band. When the magazine compiled its "New Order Top 20" at the end of 1976 (in contrast to the "Boring Old Farts Top 20" led by the Stones, Led Zeppelin and Rod Stewart), AC/DC topped the list, ahead of Eddie and the Hot Rods, the Sex Pistols, the Damned, Iggy Pop (and the Stooges), Ted Nugent, Ritchie Blackmore's Rainbow, Motorhead, Judas Priest and in equal tenth position, the Ramones and the Dictators.

AC/DC's first UK single, released as soon as the band arrived in April, was "Long Way to the Top." It would be followed in May by the *High Voltage* compilation album.

The deal the band had with Atlantic Records was far from generous—a one-album trial, with an option for Atlantic beyond that—but since they had been the only interested party, Michael Browning was pleased to sign anything. And the band was chuffed just to be labelmates with the likes of Led Zeppelin.

Atlantic is one of the most celebrated labels in rock'n'roll history. Formed in New York in 1947 by Ahmet Ertegun, the son of a Turkish diplomat, it was one of rock'n'roll's midwives, making its name with classic R&B. The label survived by adapting to changing trends. By the early seventies, its roster boasted two of the biggest white rock acts in the world—Led Zeppelin and the Rolling Stones. With England further providing it with successful acts like art rockers Yes and Emerson, Lake and Palmer, Atlantic stepped up its English presence, opening a London office. The label's first direct British signing was the Heavy Metal Kids in 1974, followed by Back Street Crawler.

Atlantic UK Managing Director Phil Carson was sold on AC/DC from the moment Coral Browning walked into his office in 1975. He asked label manager Dave Dee what he thought, and he was just as keen. Dee thought AC/DC sounded like a cross between Zeppelin and Slade. Maybe they would succeed for Atlantic where the Heavy Metal Kids, a similarly street urchin–style outfit, had failed.

RICHARD GRIFFITHS: "I was at the Virgin Agency in London in 1975, and Michael Browning came in with one of those things—which actually I've only ever seen in Australia—it was like a suitcase, and you pulled it up and there was a screen, a machine, and it played a video. And it played a video of a live concert, in Melbourne, it would have been on the *High Voltage* record, and they were just amazing."

Griffiths left Virgin to form his own agency called Headline Artists, taking with him his own charge, Paul Kossoff, and, among others, AC/DC. It was only natural, then, that the two acts would tour together.

GRIFFITHS: "Then, the way I've always told it was that in between AC/DC leaving Australia and arriving in London, Paul died."

Paul Kossoff had maintained a heroin habit for the latter days of Free. He kicked it in 1974, but related ill health caught up with him by 1976. Bon said in an open letter to *RAM* back home, "That cunt Paul Kossoff fucked up our first tour (wait till Angus gets hold of him)."

BROWNING: "We were suddenly stuck in England with no work. We had to adopt the stance of doing what any English group would do, and that was just play around all the little pubs and clubs."

Coral Browning had an office at Atlantic. Often, a record company appoints a liaison officer to an act, and even though Coral wasn't officially on the Atlantic payroll, she served as that and more. She coordinated the band's publicity, and was its mother hen as well.

Although "Long Way to the Top" didn't dent the charts, it made a reasonably favorable impression. It was Hit Pick of the Week on Radio Luxembourg; and at least late night Radio One DJ, John Peel—the oldest hipster in the world, the man who discovered T Rex—would give it a spin. That was a good start. *Record Mirror & Disc*'s James Hamilton commented, "These Aussie youngsters boogie Stones/Elton John-style [huh?] with bagpipe noises yes!' Writing in *Melody Maker*, Caroline Coon was equivocal: "Up there with the likes of Kiss and Angel . . . mind-boggling," she began, but concluded cryptically, "Getting ripped off? Keep laughing."

Michael Browning and Phil Carson kept chipping away at America. Atlantic over there was not entirely convinced.

The band stayed briefly at a house in the West End, just around the corner from Coral Browning's place, before moving to more permanent digs in Barnes. Michael Browning had calculated it would cost around 600 quid a week just to keep the band; this was a bill footed by Alberts, albeit in the form of moneys advanced against royalties. The members of the band received the quite generous wage of 50 quid a week.

But they were champing at the bit just to play. To pass time, Mark and Malcolm would go down the local—the Bridge Hotel—to shoot pool. Bon went out on an extended pub and club crawl to check out the competition. Of course, give Bon an idle moment . . . He decided to pay a visit to the pub in Finchley where he used to work during Fraternity's last days in London. He came home with a dislocated jaw.

MARK EVANS: "He walked in and, he said, he'd only been in the place ten or fifteen seconds—he went on his own—and he got hit in the face with a pint mug! And this is like three or four years since he'd been in the place!'

No decent explanation was ever offered for the incident. When Bon wrote later to Pat Pickett, all he said was, "It wasn't even my fight. I didn't see what hit me."

The band had a photo session to do, so Bon donned a pair of wraparound shades to obscure the welts. It was excuse enough though to finally finish work on his teeth. Eight hundred quid spent in Harley Street bought him a new set of dentures.

GRIFFITHS: "I dug [AC/DC] up a gig at the Red Cow in Hammersmith. This show was probably the greatest show I've ever seen in my life. There was no advertising. They came on, they were doing two sets, and to start with there were probably ten people in the pub. They did one set and they did the whole number, Angus on Bon's shoulders, everything, I'd never seen anything like it. Then the place emptied. About half an hour later, they came out to do the second set, and the place was packed. Everyone had run off and said, You have got to see this band. It was packed, it was incredible; I'll never, ever forget it."

EVANS: "It was a real battle in London first off, I really had doubts that it was going to work. The Red Cow was, well, it wasn't a regular gig; it had bands on but there was no vibe out on it. People would say, You're playing where? But the reaction was pretty instantaneous. Browning and Coral were excellent at beating stuff up."

Among the Australians at the Red Cow that night was Silver (née Margaret) Smith, with whom Bon had had a brief affair in 1971. She had left her husband in Adelaide at about the same time Fraternity returned from England, and set off around the world, ending up in London. "I'd been away for a couple of years then, so seeing the name AC/DC meant nothing to me. I hated the Red Cow, but I had a friend drop in and say, Why don't you come and see this band, they're great; and it was free to get in, so I went down. The place was packed, everybody was really getting off on it, so I weaseled my way to the front, and I got there, and it was Bon! So I went and said hello afterwards. He didn't go home that night, it was all on again."

Bon was still officially living with the band in Barnes, but he started spending time at Silver's flat in ritzy Kensington.

From the Red Cow, the band graduated to the Nashville. Coral managed to woo a couple of important journalists down to see the show—Caroline Coon and the *NME*'s Phil NcNeill.

Under the headline I WALLABY YOUR MAN, the *NME* ran Phil McNeill's assessment. "In the middle of the great British Punk Rock Explosion, a quintet of similarly ruthless Ozzies has just swaggered like a cat among London's surly, self-consciously paranoid pigeons . . . and with a sense of what sells rather than what's cool, they could well clean up." Faint praise indeed. The taste-makers at the *NME* decreed that AC/DC were unfashionable.

Even though punk was in one sense very traditional, in another sense, it was almost avant-garde—and this was where AC/DC and punk most distinctly digressed. If, as is often suggested, the Rolling Stones' great worth was as an advertisement for the blues/R&B artists they ripped off, then the same could be said of punk and the Velvet Underground, the Stooges and the New York Dolls. Today, these three bands are acknowledged as seminal forces in rock's history; but at a time in 1976 when they were still regarded with contempt—if they were recognized at all—punk discovered them and absorbed their ground-breaking influences. With its do-it-yourself ethic, punk turned to its advantage a rudimentary or minimalist, even inept, technique. AC/DC, who wore their proficiency and strictly orthodox blues-based roots so obviously on their sleeves, seemed old-fashioned next to something so apparently modern. Besides, they had long hair and tattoos. Punk was rude and crude, but it was never gauche. But it was precisely because AC/DC bridged the gap between the old and the new, the traditional and the iconoclastic, that they would be so successful.

By now, Back Street Crawler had found a new guitarist, and a handful of gigs were arranged for May, to pay tribute to Kossoff if nothing else. AC/DC would still support. A showcase was held at the Marquee, the famed London club where bands like the Stones, the Who, the Yardbirds, Led Zeppelin and Yes had all paid their dues.

Sounds magazine's Phil Sutcliffe reviewed the show and was so taken by the resurrected Back Street Crawler—who subsequently imploded— that he feared, "the mere wildly exciting excellence of AC/DC could be forgotten. It shouldn't be. They are heavy, will be huge." Sutcliffe would go on to be one of the band's most stalwart critical supporters.

The album was released on May 14. The British version of *High Voltage* was actually mostly the Australian *TNT* album, minus two tracks ("School Days" and "Rocker"), and in their place "Little Lover" and "She's Got Balls" from the original Australian *High Voltage* album.

The *NME* did not deign to review the album, but *Sounds'* Geoff Barton awarded it four stars out of five. He called it "a tonic in the midst of the all-too serious, poker-faced groups of today." *Melody Maker*'s Mike Oldfield, on the other hand, commented, "It's the same old boogie . . . Still, there's hope. The lyrics have a brashness and lack of sophistication that's always useful in the heavy brand of rock."

In late May/early June, as "Jailbreak" was released as a single in Australia—it would reach number five—AC/DC were playing occasional pub and club gigs in England. Alberts crowed that the band had passed the million dollar sales mark, with *TNT* still shifting 3-4,000 units weekly. The release of *Dirty Deeds* was delayed for that reason.

On June 11, the band embarked on the 20-date tour for *Sounds*, which had been prophetically dubbed "Lock up your daughters." The band got around in a Transit van, which most of the time was driven by Phil, a full-scale car buff and petrolhead who wasn't really comfortable unless he was behind the wheel. Long-time Australian roadies Ralph and Herc traveled in another van with the gear.

MICHAEL BROWNING: "That was incredibly significant in terms of raising the profile of the group. I mean, we were on the front cover of

Sounds—for a group that was totally unknown, that had just come from Australia, that was a pretty good score."

The shows were like a revue. After a DJ had regaled the crowd with tracks by Led Zeppelin, Kiss, the Pretty Things, Black Oak Arkansas, Alex Harvey, the Who, Free, Status Quo and Alice Cooper, and some Stones filmclips had been screened, AC/DC played a 50-minute set.

MARK EVANS: "That was playing some weird places, it was really breaking the ice. We were booked into some weird little clubs. One place was called the Club 76, I'm sure because it could only hold 76 people! Another place we played in Wales, called Mumbles, in Swansea—five people turned up."

The dates in Scotland, though, were treated as a homecoming by the band and audience alike. Said Bon, "You can imagine what that was like . . . hoots, with an "H", mon!"

The *Ardrossan Herald* commented, "One fault with Scott's voice is whereas it might be undistinguished most of the time, it does, at others, sound rather like Alex Harvey. This may prove unpopular with Glasgow crowds who might feel that he is imitating their idol."

But Glasgow was obviously flattered. A *Sounds* review of the gig was glowing. "The audience even at this early stage," it began, "have nearly demolished the staid City Hall. Bon, halfheartedly and mischievously, asks us all to sit down, 'or else the management will turn off the power.' Nobody attempts to find their seat."

This minor act of civil disobedience was reported back home as a "riot." "As in Australia," the *RAM* news item went, "the group are attracting a young, volatile working class audience."

While Malcolm and Angus spent a couple of days off visiting long-lost relatives in Glasgow, Bon hired a car with Phil to go sightseeing. Scotland was his birthplace, after all, and so he thought he might try to find some of his roots. The pair made a circuit of Loch Lomond. But the highlight of the trip, as Bon wrote to old mate Pat Pickett, was coming across two bears shagging in the woods. Phil, the camera buff, filmed the occasion for posterity.

The tour wrapped up in London at the Lyceum on July 7, two days before Bon's birthday. Save for the fact that lighting engineer Herc had an accident at the soundcheck, falling from the rigging (and having to be sent home as a result), the show was highly successful. MC'd by John Peel, it featured a competition for the "Schoolgirl we'd most like to . . ." The winner was one Jayne Haynes from Harrow, Middlesex, who went home with the first prize of an Epiphone Caballero folk guitar, plus a bonus, bassist Mark Evans—much to Bon's chagrin, mock or otherwise. "She was beautiful . . ." he rued, "really sexy. Garters, suspenders. I was really lusting for her myself . . . we all were. But Mark won out. He's just too handsome for me to compete."

Against all his own forecasts, Bon had made it to the Big 3-0. The band threw him a party, which was missing only one vital ingredient—the birthday boy himself. Bon, as was his wont, had gone AWOL.

One of the few birthday cards he got from Australia was from Mary Walton. He replied, "Thank you for remembering my B. Day. Not many did. I wrote myself off for about three days and even managed to miss my own party."

Bon told Anthony O'Grady, who interviewed him over the phone a few days later, "Y'know what I did last night? I fucked my birthday in . . . started at 11.50 and finished at 12:15 . . . It's the first birthday I've done that."

The band sat around the table at the Russell Hotel waiting for the guest of honor, getting drunk. All except Angus, of course. Bon never did show that night, and he wouldn't do so for a couple of days to come. The band could only surmise he was off with Silver. At that stage, he still hadn't actually moved in with her.

MARK EVANS: "The basic thing about the band—it was very insular. There was no real camaraderie, and so being on the road, it could get lonely. And Bon, being a very outgoing person, and older, I don't think there was enough within the band to satisfy his social needs.

"Bon very much needed that space away from the band. So he could do what he wanted to do without having to worry about what we were going to say. Because we used to call him an old hippie. I mean, Bon used to wear his leather jacket and all that, but he was always wearing a kaftan and sandals underneath."

For one thing, Bon was a self-confessed pothead. This was a hippie crime which Angus barely tolerated. But Bon would still go off, to be with Silver. He also became friendly with Coral Browning, who like Silver was nearer his own age.

Bon and Silver had lost time to make up for. They say you can never go back, but in this instance, Bon was picking up where he'd left off. The cynical view was that Bon and Silver's relationship was mutually beneficial, in that Silver provided Bon with an entree to the London scene, and he provided her with a ready-made rock'n'roll star. While this may be true, the fact remains that Bon fell passionately in love with Silver.

SILVER: "He never made any friends of his own, which is sad. Like, he had friends in Australia; but in London, because of the pressure of everything, he never really got a chance to do that. But then, he had a ready-made assortment of my friends . . ."

When Silver had first arrived in London a year earlier, she lived in a house with, among others, a guy who worked for Rolling Stones' Ron Wood, as his percy. A percy is a personal assistant, a common appendage to most big rock stars—a minder and a gofer, who is often little more than a drug supplier. Silver met Ron Wood and became friendly with him. She met a few other bands on the scene too, like Thin Lizzy and UFO. If it's not exactly fair to say Silver was on the game at the time, certainly she was supported by sugar daddies.

SILVER: "They weren't older so much as guys with money. There was a few rich men hovering, I wasn't short of rich men, I traveled around on the strength of that. I just happened to be at the right place at the right time."

Silver lived comfortably in a flat of her own in the West End. She was a bit of an old hippie, an intelligent woman, a reader, who introduced Bon to books, and no shrinking violet. Like Bon, she enjoyed a smoke; where they differed was that while she didn't really drink, she had a growing taste for heroin.

MARK EVANS: "Everyone was very wary of her. Malcolm would have sussed she was involved with drugs. And once again, that was the band mentality, if Malcolm decided . . . And Angus, he was very possessive of people, he was funny. Like, when we were living in Barnes, I ended up matey with a few of the guys down the pub, the local garbagemen actually, and you know, it took Angus a while to warm to the idea of that."

Malcolm and Angus would have felt threatened by anyone who wasn't on their own payroll, let alone a strong woman.

SILVER: "I think part of it is that they feel inadequate. They're suspicious of anyone that might be in the least bit intellectual. Although they were always very good to me; my personal relationship with them was good."

They were also two-faced.

SILVER: "I think it was just that they were young boys that got very successful very quickly, and so they were like fish out of water. They didn't have time to enjoy themselves, I mean, that lifestyle, there was just so much happening. In all the years I've been around, I've never known a band that worked like that band worked."

To Bon, Silver was his refuge.

By the time Bon returned from his few dirty days off celebrating his birthday, the band was due back on deck.

RICHARD GRIFFITHS: "We then started booking them around London. I made sure Jack Barry, who booked the Marquee, saw them, and they were incredible. Jack said—it's a famous quote, but I don't remember it exactly—"The most exciting band I've seen play at the Marquee since Led Zeppelin." So we then sat down and worked out a strategy with Jack to basically break AC/DC out of the Marquee.

"This was the summer of '76, a very exciting time in London, incredibly hot summer, and we worked out that they'd do this residency at the Marquee, every Monday night, and then they would get a great slot on the Reading Festival. And somehow, during all this, we went to Sweden too."

MICHAEL BROWNING: We were just totally unfashionable, and so it was hard work, persevering, trying not to worry about the criticism."

The band recorded a 20-minute segment for Mike Mansfield's *Superpop* TV program, which also featured T Rex, and then headed off to Sweden.

GRIFFITHS: "They went off to Sweden for some time, because Tomas Johansen, the promoter there, represented Abba, and he couldn't get Abba into Australia, so we did this sort of exchange. He took AC/DC to Sweden, and Abba went to Australia!"

MARK EVANS: "We played what they call folk parks, which were like these outdoor barbecue areas with swings and all that, like recreation areas. It was weird because there was a lot of young kids there, but they had blackjack tables and beer, and they were selling beer to 14- and 15-year-olds.

"But it was enough for the hype to start, and we took hold very quickly in those places."

Bon was under instructions to keep the Australian media informed, and so in another open letter, this time to the Melbourne *Herald*'s Debbie Sharpe, he wrote:

They love rock'n'roll bands because all the Scandinavian bands are real cabaret. People dance to jigs and polkas, and the bands play Swedish beer drinking (oom-pah-pah) folk songs. The beaches and swimming pools have topless bathing (and I'm a great swimmer!).

AC/DC, however, kept their heads down, unimpressed by travelling to new places, seeing new things, meeting new people.

EVANS: "It was business as usual. There was never any excitement about anything at all. What was happening to us was taken for granted. Like, there was no difference to us in going from Australia and playing the Red Cow in England, to six months later headlining the Hammersmith Odeon. Having this meteoric rise didn't faze anyone at all, it was what was meant to happen. It was this tunnel vision that Malcolm and Angus had: this is what is going to happen.

"You could be driving through Switzerland, through the Alps, the most magnificent scenery you've ever seen, and Angus would have his nose buried in a comic. There was nothing that could surprise us, it was just work. The attitude was just, We don't give a fuck, what time do we go on?

"If someone interesting came backstage and wanted to party, Bon would be the one who'd go off with them."

But if there was an element of joylessness to life with AC/DC, the hour or so spent on stage every night made up for it. Most bands say that going on the road is an excruciatingly tedious exercise, only ever relieved or justified by the actual time on stage itself. The other 23 hours in the day are wasted. You spend a lot of time sitting around waiting: you wait to board vehicles, and then you travel; and then when you get where you're going, you sit around and wait till showtime.

EVANS: "That was the good thing about the band, whatever happened off stage—and there was always a lot of shit going down—as soon as we got on stage, it was just easy. Angus and I could have a screaming match five minutes before we went on, but then we'd go on, and it was, Bang! I'm biased, you know, but I think that line-up of the band—we just had this ultimate confidence, we had no sense of insecurity whatsoever; we would have played with anyone, we just didn't believe we could be beaten."

Richard Griffiths remembers being on the road with the band in Sweden: "It was clear to me it was Malcolm's band. Bon was just a great guy. But even then, I sensed, off Michael [Browning], that he wasn't sure Bon was the singer to take the band all the way. I didn't get that from the band, I got it from Michael. It sounds terrible to say it, but I think that if Bon hadn't died . . .

"I suppose it was true, he always was sort of separate from the rest. Phil, he was off on his own, he was actually pretty obnoxious. Angus and Malcolm were thick, obviously. And then Mark, you knew Mark wasn't going to last, he was too much of a nice guy. I mean, these were tough guys, they were pretty tough on each other.

"Bon did have an ability to get into trouble. But I've been around some pretty nasty drunks, and I definitely wouldn't put him in that category. I just remember he used to get pretty . . . drunk!"

EVANS: "They would dispute this, but I think they viewed Bon to be ultimately disposable. In hindsight, it seems preposterous, but at the time, he was always in the firing line. And there was a lot of pressure, mainly from George, and record companies. I think within that camp, there's been a certain rewriting of history, about how they felt about the guy—no, that's wrong, how they felt about the guy professionally. Because there was no way you could spend more than 30 seconds in a room with Bon and not be completely and utterly charmed. The guy was captivating; he was gentlemanly, but he had the rough side to him, and he was funny."

MOLLY MELDRUM: "When I was in England, AC/DC were breaking there, and breaking in Europe, and I remember Michael taking me aside, and telling me he had this great dilemma on his hands. The Americans wanted to release this group, but what they said was, You've got to find another lead singer. Because they couldn't understand Bon Scott. So Michael was going . . . But I mean, he was never going to get rid of Bon."

Back in England, the band relocated into new digs, a house opposite the cemetery in West Brompton, which was chosen because it came equipped with a piano. Bon instead moved in with Silver.

With the Marquee residency kicking off on July 26, "Jailbreak" was released as the band's second single. Caroline Coon, wrongly referring to it as "Jail Bait," described it as "a muscle-flexing fine blast of rock'n'roll," but as Charles Shaar Murray observed in the *NME*, "it will not be helped one whit by the fact that "Jailbreak" is also the title of Thin Lizzy's current album and next single."

The Marquee residency was heralded by full-page ads in the music papers, which reprinted Jack Barry's famous Led Zeppelin comparison and pictured Angus holding up a reproduction of a letter Atlantic had received from the City of Glasgow District Council, which read, "We have been advised that the audience in attendance at the recent concert featuring AC/DC which you produced were for the most of the performance entirely out of control and were actually standing up on the seats. This has caused some damage to the upholstery and has also resulted in a back being broken off one of the seats."

It goes to show just how dull most British bands were, unable to generate even this modest amount of excitement. Punk was really still waiting in the wings. The "Lock up your daughters" tour had set the wheels in motion. Playing the Marquee residency, every Monday night through August—and playing other gigs in and around London—AC/DC really caught fire.

Recalls Dave Jarrett, an Atlantic Records promotion man who worked with AC/DC, "Monday night in London is called Swede Night, because they're the only people who go out, Swedes. The first Marquee show, there was about 18 people there. So what we did, the record company just took everybody we could down to the gig, it was an unlimited guest list. I mean, I used to go down to my local pub, say to the guys, Who wants to go out, and they'd say, How much is it going to cost? They had no idea who they were going to see. But it built up very quickly, to the point where you couldn't get in the door."

MICHAEL BROWNING: "There was another group called Eddie and the Hot Rods that were happening in London at the time, both of them had a residency at the Marquee, and it was very much like a competition between the two groups to see who could break each other's record. I think AC/DC to this day still hold the record for the most people in the Marquee. It was quite a small room, and I think we had something like 1,400 people there. I don't think I've ever experienced anything as hot and sweaty as that."

It was a stinking summer in 1976. With the fetid aroma of punk in the air, it was no summer of love; but London when it sizzles is worlds apart from London at any other time of the year—people go out, and get crazy. Hot August nights, indeed.

"You wouldn't believe the weather," Bon wrote to Debbie Sharpe. "It's been a hotter summer than we had in Australia early this year. It's particularly bad 'cause we're 60 miles from the nearest beach and if you happen to fall in the Thames they treat you for a week with tetanus injections."

AC/DC were one of a hot summer's hottest items. Molly Meldrum flew in to shoot a segment at the Marquee for *Countdown*. Phil Sutcliffe reported from deep in the club's mosh pit, "The heat is beyond belief . . . Guys take their shirts off and within half a minute they look as though they've stepped out of the shower. The girls say they wish they could do the same . . . And that's just for the disco!

"AC/DC stroll on unassumingly, Bon grins an evil grin and says, This one's just to warm you up."

Angus was making a ritual of the flashing routine he'd unveiled initially at the Lifesaver back in Sydney in March; and even that spotty visage, in—or rather out of—soiled jocks, didn't turn people off.

"E's the best fing I've seen since Pete Townshend," a punter said to Meldrum, who was down there in the mosh-pit with everyone else.

MOLLY: "It was just this tiny room, and there were all these kids dressed in school uniforms there—which was pretty exciting to me, I can tell you right now! But the thing was, AC/DC weren't doing anything different to what they ever had, and they never have. It was the same as the first time I saw them. They've never had to alter their music."

The Marquee established AC/DC as the only band in London getting anywhere who weren't a punk band. That they were swarmed by female fans backstage was proof of the fact—and welcome relief for the band after a veritable drought of feminine attention.

MOLLY: "By that stage, Bon was certainly drinking a lot. Because it was just part of rock'n'roll, it was part of getting to the next gig, doing the gig . . . Bon would be there, and he would have his bottle of whisky, and so we were soul mates in that respect, I guess, because I was into whisky then too, and so we'd be going arrgghh, you know . . . In those days, quite frankly, you didn't have to worry about it catching up with you. Why would you? You weren't hurting anyone, you were having a lot of fun, and you were doing your job."

SILVER: "He was drinking a bottle of Scotch a day, even back in those early days of success. I mean, what he was getting in wages wouldn't have covered his Scotch bill."

High Voltage may not have cracked the charts—if only because its sales, which totaled 50,000 by year's end, were spread over several months—but with the vibe the Marquee generated, even the mass-circulation tabloid *Sun* (despite being outraged by bare bottoms and bad language) had to admit that "AC/DC are a band we will learn to live with."

RICHARD GRIFFITHS: "What was happening was that AC/DC were playing at the Marquee, and just up the road in Wardour Street at the 100 Club, the Sex Pistols were playing, so they sort of got caught up in the whole thing. But what they were, they were a rock band who were different to what had been going on."

"The Sex Pistols, and bands like the Clash and the Damned, are important because they have brought rock down to earth again," Caroline Coon wrote in *Melody Maker*. "The musicians, unimpressed by the trappings of stardom, are as close to their audience as rock'n'rollers have ever been.

"Their lyrics, eschewing the cultural irrelevancies of American R&B, are committed, searching comments about the new morality and tough environment they grew up in. Their music is fast, intensely emotional, fierce and devoid of presence."

Just like AC/DC. "The trouble with these bloody punk bands," Bon told *Juke*'s Christie Eliezer, "is they try and look tough but musically they've got nothing, not even a hint of originality."

The punks also liked to claim they were working class, but if they were that at all, they were—like Pete Townshend and Keith Richards before them—art school dropouts. The real working-class kids, the punters, didn't know what they were supposed to like, they just knew what they liked. And it became emphatically clear that what they liked was AC/DC. This was especially true outside trendy London, in the industrial wastelands of the North—not just in Scotland but in cities like Manchester, Newcastle and Liverpool, where the London-based music papers held less sway. AC/DC, in turn, didn't condescend to their audience.

GRIFFITHS: When you compare them to what was going on in England at the time . . . They came over, and they were so great, because they'd been playing all these gigs, and English bands hadn't been playing. So you had the raw excitement of the Sex Pistols or the Clash or the Jam or whatever else was going on, but you just had this real rock'n'roll band, with this extraordinary guitarist, showman, and Bon who was just great. Kids just loved Bon."

It probably had a lot to do simply with musicianship. AC/DC, with their greater prowess, got across aggression so much more effectively. With even a measure of flash. AC/DC also attracted older fans—like bikers, who always liked their rock'n'roll loud, hard and fast.

Not only that, they had genuine character and they put on a show. Malcolm, Mark and Phil at the back line—a rhythm section as tight as any—looked like any real, ordinary young blokes. Out front, Angus was pure vaudeville—the errant schoolboy imagery stretching all the way back to comic-book character Billy Bunter—but the thing was, he was a freak, he could really play that guitar. And Bon—Bon was simply larger than life; but at the core he too was all real. If the band mostly copped stick from the press, it didn't matter, because the kids knew what was what.

GRIFFITHS: "It was all word of mouth, the record wasn't doing much;

Sounds was supportive, nobody else, and they were just touring all over. But they were building an incredible live following. Funnily enough, everything was building towards a peak, because by then we were about to come in with the second album, and we thought they were going to explode from the Reading Festival. But in fact, they played Reading and they didn't do very well, and I've never really understood why, because they had a great slot—the Saturday or Sunday afternoon—and they played well, but they really didn't go down very well."

The annual Reading Festival is an institution in British rock, a showcase that can make or break bands. Sharing a bill in 1976 with Brand X, Ted Nugent, the Sutherland Brothers and Quiver, Black Oak Arkansas and Osibisa, AC/DC had the same hopes for Reading that they'd had for Sunbury back home in 1975. But before a crowd of nearly 50,000 they would again be thwarted.

An entourage accompanied the band to Reading, including Michael and Coral Browning, George and Harry, Richard Griffiths, Phil Carson, even Silver. On the way there, they stopped in at Richard Griffiths' parents' place for lunch and a quick game of croquet. Griffiths remembers that Bon, of course, utterly charmed his mother.

But as *Melody Maker*'s "Reading Report" put it: "If you think the Sex Pistols are a gang of untalented jerks, then prepare yourself . . ." John Peel admitted he slept through AC/DC's set—"probably the first person ever to do so"—but somehow still managed to note, "Anticipation was high for AC/DC, and response was agitated—people seemed to think them either absolutely awful or great fun. The loutish element definitely dug them, as did I."

MARK EVANS: "We drove back to London, and George at that stage had come over with Harry, and we had a pretty heavy meeting, because everyone had the shits. George came back, we were going to play cards, and Malcolm and Angus started arguing. I tried to split them up, and it was the first time George ever said anything more to me than, No worries, mate. He'd given Malcolm and Angus a blast, saying, Who the fuck do you think you are? I don't think it was the band's fault, I think it was the crowd, but George blamed us. And he turned to me, and said, And you! He kept calling me Dave, you know, that was the old singer, Dave Evans—and I said, At least you could get my name right. And then they all set on me."

GRIFFITHS: "I didn't like George at all. I felt that George was out to fuck with Michael. In fact, I got the sense that the Alberts people were out to fuck Michael off.

"But then Michael fucked me and took the band away from my agency! But you know, it was probably the right move. Because I was a small little agency, and he needed someone bigger.

"The last tour I booked for them would have been August/September. The first gigs we did with them in London they were getting ten pounds a night; by then we were getting £500 to £750 a night, which was pretty decent money in those days."

Announcing that they'd joined the prestigious Cowbell Agency, which handled such top-line British acts as Jethro Tull, Roxy Music, Rod Stewart and Alex Harvey, AC/DC were "bought on" to a September European tour supporting Ritchie Blackmore's Rainbow. A buy-on is when a band pays for the privilege of playing on the bill with another, bigger band. It cost AC/DC a not inconsiderable sum to open on 19 dates for Ritchie Blackmore. The legendary status of the former Deep Purple axeman guaranteed AC/DC an audience which would be not only large, but also almost certainly the right audience.

Every territory has its distinctive likes and dislikes, and Germany, the third largest market for music in the world, next to producing its own avant-garde strain of rock, has always had a real fondness for the hardest of hard rock. To the Germans, AC/DC must have seemed made in heaven.

AC/DC had excited Germany even before they arrived there. The *High Voltage* album shifted 16,000 copies in its first week of release. Prior to the band's joining the Blackmore tour, they played three gigs of their own, and a fourth—a major show for *Bravo*—in Duisburg. *Bravo* was the top rock magazine in the country, and every year it held its own hit-pick concert. Sharing the bill were Suzi Quatro, Slik and Shaun Cassidy.

The band arrived in Hamburg by ferry at 9:00 on the morning of September 15. They were greeted by George, who had made his own way over, and brother Alex, who was based there at the time. It was a family reunion. Bon checked into his hotel room where a letter was waiting for him from Atlantic's German International Product Manager Killy Kumberger.

"Welcome to good old Germany," it read. "May I tell you that we at WEA are sure you will be one of the major rock'n'roll bands in the future. Your sound seems to be perfect for our market. With your fantastic live appearances, you should soon be able to attract a wide audience. The first reactions to the single and the album have been very positive."

Accompanying the letter was a schedule for the day, which was typical:

On tour in Germany, October 1976. Mark Evans: "Jeez, Bon was on the turps early that day."

9:00 - Arrival harbor Hamburg
12:45 - Pick up at hotel by Hannelore Kring, promotion co-ordinator
1:00 - Interview at Cafe Boheme with Martin Meister, journalist for music magazine *Joker*
2:00 - Interview at Cafe Boheme for magazine *Pop* with Brigitte Weckelmann
3:00 - Interview at Cafe Boheme for daily newspaper *Morgenpost* with Mario Scheuermann
4:00 - Fabrik open for road manager
6:00 - Rehearsal
8:30 - Concert
11:30 - Dinner at Bratwurstglockle with journalists from *Sounds*, *Pop-Foto*, *Musikexpress,* etc and WEA people

In Hamburg, the boys in the band indulged in the not-so illicit pleasures on offer in the world's most notorious red-light district. All except Bon that is, who delighted as he was by window displays of real live naked ladies, had a date lined up with a fräulein he had met when Fraternity visited Germany.

Apart from an uncooperative stage prop—a huge model rainbow which, like Spinal Tap's miniature Stonehenge, kept falling over—the tour was marred only by Blackmore's bad temper.

AC/DC played with Rainbow in Geneva, Marseilles, Paris and Belgium before returning to England by mid-October. If the French have any particular predilections, it's for the wild men of rock, its gutter poets; and so again, AC/DC must have seemed like a dream band.

Back in London, the band had barely a week off before it was due to go out on the road again, headlining, for the first time, their own British tour. The plan was to do that, and then in mid-November go to America en route to Australia.

A return tour of Australia was booked for December. *RAM* suggested that promoters Evans-Gudinksi had considered calling the tour, "The little c**nts have done it." In America, at least two gigs at the Starwood in LA were on offer.

Meantime, *High Voltage* was released in the US, and both the *Dirty Deeds* album and single were released in Australia. Britain would see the release of the "High Voltage" single and the slightly amended *Dirty Deeds* album by the beginning of November.

Reviewing *Dirty Deeds*, *RAM* suggested the band was simply repeating itself, though had to admit "they've shown positive signs of a NEW DIRECTION"—even if it came down only to "Ride On" and "Jailbreak."

America bore both good and bad news. *High Voltage*—surprise—had polarized reaction. With new cover artwork yet again (Angus struck by a bolt of lightning), industry bible *Billboard* listed it in its "Recommended LPs" column: "Australia's newest entry is a cross between Led Zeppelin and the Sensational Alex Harvey Band. Lead singer has a very unique sounding voice and the twin guitars are front and center from the first cut. Expect airplay on progressive stations."

Rolling Stone, on the other hand, was contemptuous. "Those concerned with the future of hard rock may take solace in knowing that with the release of the first US album by these Australian gross-out champions, the genre has unquestionably hit its all-time low," said Billy Altman. "Lead singer Bon Scott spits out his vocals with a truly annoying aggression which, I suppose, is the only way to do it when all you seem to care about is being a star so that you can get laid every night. Stupidity bothers me. Calculated stupidity offends me."

As it transpired, the band wouldn't make it to America in 1976. Michael Browning was unable to arrange visas, since not only Bon but he himself had Australian criminal records for pot convictions. This certainly wouldn't have impressed Atlantic—not so much having been busted in the first place, but not being able to get around it, and not coming to America to make some promotional appearances.

Critical reaction to *Dirty Deeds* in Britain echoed that in Australia. Comparing *Dirty Deeds* and *High Voltage*, Geoff Barton said, "So alike are they that tracks could be interchanged quite easily" (which was of course perfectly true). The single "Jailbreak" was inexplicably omitted, thus undermining the album's killer ending; so too was "Rock in Peace." Replacing them were "Rocker," the *TNT* track dropped from the first English album, and "Love at First Feel," a track the band had up its sleeve which would only see release in Australia as a single the following January. *Dirty Deeds* was more of the same, but in Britain, the groundswell of fans had only one previous album to go on, and so it was quite welcome.

Nevertheless, neither the album nor the "High Voltage" single went anywhere near the charts. AC/DC's rise was a live phenomenon.

DAVE JARRETT: "AC/DC and Van Halen, who I also worked with, did a very similar thing. Van Halen did two tours of England, very, very quickly, one supporting Black Sabbath, and then headlined themselves. When they came over and supported Black Sabbath, we'd never heard of them. So it was the young turks with the old warhorses. And they were so exciting, I mean, Dave Lee Roth was in the band. The audience was very responsive. It was fantastic, and again, a very similar situation to AC/DC.

"What you had to do, you only had to do a good support or two, and you could cover the whole country, and kids would come out and see you the next time, you didn't need hit records."

On October 27, the band played the first gig of its headline tour at Southampton University. Oxford Polytechnic refused to grant them permission to perform because their repertoire contained "blatantly vulgar and cheap references to both sexes."

Heading towards Scotland always brightened the band's spirits.

"Glasgow would be our favorite place in Scotland, in the whole of Britain, because the kids are really mad—like, half of them are Angus and Malcolm's relatives anyway," Bon told *RAM*. "The first time we ever played down there, there were about two rows of seats just demolished. And so this time they had extra men inside and the riot squad outside. But if the cops had stopped the show and arrested Angus the kids would have gone mad. And no one goes mad like Glaswegians, believe me."

Arriving back in London and playing the Hammersmith Odeon, even the *NME* had to admit AC/DC was here to stay: "The emcee only just ducks into the wings and out of the firing range when the Odeon stage explodes deafeningly. Bruised about the head, their breath stolen by the sheer impact of noise, the security men are caught off guard and trampled to the floor as the audience immediately besieges the front.

"And then this schoolboy brat up on the rostrum smirks maliciously as his opening power chord painfully rattles through our bones and makes the unnecessary triumphant gesture of wildly tossing his cap to the floor, as if to say: This is our day.

"The day, Gawd 'elp us all, AC/DC conquered London."

Dave Dee and Phil Carson, and Michael Browning and Coral, and everybody, knew that they'd cracked it. The 4,000 seat theatre was only just over half full, but it wasn't so much the quantity as the quality of the crowd that convinced them. It was clear then, with even a few kids in the audience dressed in school uniforms, that the band's appeal extended beyond the merely musical. Particularly satisfying to the band itself was the fact that this success was achieved without having to alter its act.

Even the *Times* reviewed the show. Said rock critic Clive Bennett,

"My objections are to their music, not their words, which simply express without inhibitions what most of us have discussed innumerable times with equal frankness in private. Music of any sort must surely require more from performers than just the capacity mindlessly to bash their instruments into oblivion. It is in this primal state that AC/DC exist."

Any sort of acknowledgement by the *Times* was signal enough: AC/DC had arrived. It was, indeed, a meteoric rise. Their standing in Britain could certainly still be improved upon, but the new frontier now was America.

MICHAEL BROWNING: "There's an amazing photograph of Bon from that first time they headlined a major venue in London. Bon said he'd make his own way to the gig, which of course, we were all a bit nervous about, but anyway . . . We were all there backstage worrying that Bon wasn't going to turn up. In the meantime, because the band's name was on the marquee out the front, I asked this photographer if he could go around and get a picture of it, you know, "Sold Out—AC/DC." So he did that, and then Bon turned up and everything went fine.

"Anyway, this photographer brought the proofs in to show me the next week, and who should be walking past on his way to the gig in the picture but Bon! He was just casually walking to the gig. And that just really summed up Bon, you know, the first ever big headline gig, no lights or anything like that. He's just casually strolling along. He would have just got off the tube at Hammersmith station.

"And to his credit, he would do things like that."

Welcome home at Melbourne's Tullamarine Airport, November 27, 1976.

12. THE LITTLE C**NTS HAVE DONE IT

The story ran on the wire around Australia on November 26:

> A small crowd of screaming girls today welcomed home the
> controversial rock band AC/DC. The screams, the hugs and
> the odd tears assured the five member group that it had not
> been forgotten during an eight month absence in England and
> Europe. And the members said they ensured that the English
> public and police force would not forget their act too quickly.
> At almost every performance the local police vice squad
> turned up. Guitarist Angus Young provoked the attendance
> of the law by stripping off his clothes on stage. In two cities,
> Glasgow and Liverpool, he was threatened with arrest.

The media was intent on getting something out of AC/DC. Another story
went out that teenage female fans were getting tattoos in emulation of the
band, which led to an uproar (as the papers put it) among health officials,
who feared the risks of backyard tattooing. But if this was a storm in a
teacup, it was only the beginning.

AC/DC themselves were happy to be home, although on a professional level, they weren't so sure. They were in line to cop more shit than
they ever had before. The matter of AC/DC even got so far as parliament,
where one particularly crusty old member expressed fear at the threat
the band posed to the nation's morals.

The controversy only confirmed AC/DC's suspicion that Australia
was a backwater, and even though the band would make a tradition of
coming home every year for Christmas, after this tour they would never

play an Australian show again (at least not an official one) while Bon was alive.

AC/DC would ride out the so-named "Giant Dose of Rock'n'roll" tour—or what was left of it after bannings and protests—and then go back into Alberts to cut a new album in January.

Bon and Silver had not traveled out together. Bon flew in with the band; Silver went overland from London to Adelaide, where she spent Christmas with friends. She then joined Bon in Sydney in January as the band worked on the album.

Michael Browning went via New York, where he was going to have to pull some rabbits out of a hat if Atlantic was to continue its relationship with AC/DC. Support was building for the band in Britain and Europe, but they weren't selling truckloads of records. And in America, they'd sold next to none. Then they'd failed to get into the country to make personal appearances, and the album they'd presented as a follow-up to the first, *Dirty Deeds* stunk—at least as far as Atlantic was concerned.

MICHAEL BROWNING: "The band really didn't want to do that tour [of Australia]. I can remember arguing about it. But we needed money, because that was the time when the Atlantic contract was in question, so it was one of those things we had to do just to keep the machine running. I think the band thought Australia was all just a bit rinky-dink, after doing things on a reasonably professional level in England."

Alberts was determined to distance the band from punk rock. They issued a press release in which the closing question "Were they a punk rock band?" was answered decisively by Bon. "No," he said, "we are a straight ROCK'N'ROLL band." But it was the specter of punk that was constantly evoked as the band was broadly decried as obscene and disgusting.

With all the hype—plus the fact that *Dirty Deeds* was still sitting in the top 10—AC/DC might quite reasonably have expected the tour to sell out. But the other major disappointment of the summer was that attendances were down. This was probably largely due to the fact that at that stage AC/DC were caught between audiences. The teenyboppers had lost much of their interest in the band in its absence. Yet the image of AC/DC as a teen phenomenon still persisted, so the emerging headbangers were still very wary of them. What made all this especially galling for the band was the fact that they were in such fine form, playing like demons.

Some muck-raking wowser had actually bothered to listen to an AC/DC record, and found that the songs' subject matter was quite frequently less than squeaky clean. At the same time, as *Truth* gleefully reported under the banner "POP HIT MAKES WIDOW'S PHONE RUN HOT": "A wealthy widow was shocked and upset when she began to receive obscene telephone calls." Kids had taken to dialing the number 36-24-36, which Bon suggests calling in "Dirty Deeds Done Dirt Cheap." Chris Gilbey issued a profuse public apology.

But it was the sight of Angus's spotty behind at every turn that really upset the media. Bon gasped in mock shock. "You see his backside in the papers more than you see his face—which is preferential as far as I'm concerned," he told *RAM*.

The tour kicked off in grand fashion at the Myer Music Bowl. The full complement of tickets, at $5.50 and $4.50, was sold out. The show was the triumphant return everybody had hoped for. But things only went downhill from there.

Molly Meldrum reported in *TV Week* that AC/DC was the "cause of yet another hysterical riot," bringing "a 5,000 fan crowd to fever pitch" (other reports had a further couple of thousand outside the cyclone-wire fencing).

"With scenes like this," Molly went on, "there is no doubt that AC/DC have become a huge threat to the top positions held by Sherbet and Skyhooks."

The scene in Australia hadn't changed much. The most successful new talent was a cabaret nostalgia act called Ol' '55, whose debut album *Take It Greasy* won out over even Sherbet's *Howzat* as the year's biggest local seller. Split Enz were still too weird for *Countdown*, although sophisticated *Rolling Stone* readers voted them "Best Band." Hush had already faded away. Punk was still just grumblings in the underground, not taken seriously at all.

Debbie Sharpe said of the Bowl show in the *Herald*: "Lead singer Bon Scott played with the audience, singing to them, acting to them . . . and oh, that glint in his eye." Bon was, in fact, doing everything short of what Jim Morrison got arrested for in Florida in 1970 (when he exposed himself) in an attempt to incite the crowd.

Sharpe went on later that night to see the Bay City Rollers, on tour in Australia for the second time in 12 months, and whilst she conceded that the scenes at Festival Hall were not as hysterical, "for both bands Sunday night was successful."

AC/DC and company repaired to the Tiger Lounge, a pub in Richmond, where the band took over the stage. An unsuspecting punter who happened to be there remembers the occasion: "I'd never seen AC/DC, I mean, I wasn't a fan. But they came down to the Tiger Lounge, and they just got up and had a blow. They played some blues songs and some rock'n'roll songs . . . Elvis songs. The room was really small and really packed, and it was great. I realized how good they were, even as pissed as I was. But the amazing thing was Bon. He was just this scrawny, ugly little guy standing up there, but he had every woman in the place eating out of his hand. He had this incredible sexual energy, magnetism, and the whole room was electrified by it. No one, men included, was unaware of it."

AC/DC turned a few heads that night. The Tiger Lounge was a musicians' watering hole, and when the cognoscenti (who had only ever condescended to AC/DC as a teenybopper band) saw them that night—just jamming, away from the usual pressure to put on a show, ripping up old blues tunes—they were impressed. Underneath the set moves, it was clear that they had the chops as well.

Malcolm and Angus didn't care whether they were respected or not. They just wanted to make the money and run. Or at least, that was what they claimed. Certainly though, they knew themselves how good they were. And though Bon too had developed a thick skin—England had inured him to criticism—he was delighted that his peers at last saw the worth of what AC/DC was doing.

The band hit the road on Tuesday, December 7. They had barely made it to the Victoria/New South Wales border town of Albury on Wednesday, for the second gig of the tour, when the shit started rolling in. Sale of their tour program was stopped after the first gig as some other wowser had found a stray four-letter word in it. Bon was quoted explaining the theme of "Ain't No Fun Waiting Around to Be a Millionaire" as follows: "It means it takes a long time to make enough money to be able to fuck Britt Ekland." Albury's town clerk claimed to have subsequently received complaints from parents. "If AC/DC want to come here again, they'll have to change their act," he said. "I'm a professional artist myself, and their act isn't entertainment. I'm broadminded, but when you get children going along . . ."

All over the country, AC/DC would face such self-appointed moral guardians and petty bureaucrats who were determined to place every obstacle in their path. Gigs in Canberra and Wollongong over the next two nights were tempered by warnings from police: they would pull the plug if Angus pulled down his pants. He withheld his brown-eye.

Support acts for most of the tour were Stars and Punkz. Stars were the Adelaide band Michael Gudinski signed to Mushroom instead of Cold Chisel, because they seemed more manageable. They were that, but they were also less enduring, the appeal of their cowboy boogie sound wearing thin after "The Mighty Rock," their biggest hit. Punkz later became known as Cheek, Punkz being something of a misnomer from the first. Managed by Glenn A. Baker and also signed to Mushroom, Punkz were a Sydneyside sixties-style act with which Baker perhaps hoped to repeat the success he'd enjoyed with his other retro proteges, Ol' '55—but he failed to do so.

"As a young player, in my first serious band, the thing that made a real impression on me was AC/DC's utter professionalism," says Mal Eastick, then lead guitarist in Stars. "And I've never seen anything quite like it since. They just knew exactly where they were going."

After playing Newcastle on Saturday December 11, on the Sunday the tour played the rather more urbane Hordern Pavilion, in the center of Sydney. AC/DC put on a full-scale show—and no one was known to have gone off into the night speaking in tongues and raping babies. The 4,500-capacity Hordern was barely half full, however. As *RAM*'s review of the show reported, with the teenyboppers dropping off "AC/DC, like Skyhooks, must start the whole slow progress of winning over and earning the trust of a more musical audience." But their prospects looked good, since "the bulk of the audience resembled the Status Quo crowd who raged and boogied to their heroes just a week before."

The band's appeal was irresistible either way. "Loud seems too tame a description for the volume they inflict on an audience," *RAM* continued, "it's more a 'living sound' that actually penetrates the flesh and bones until movement and rhythm come involuntarily and the audience is swept into the same current . . . behind the insistency lies an excellent rock/blues outfit with an amazing singer out front in Bon Scott . . ."

Heading out of Sydney, the band played Orange and Dubbo before the Mayor of Tamworth, Australia's country music capital, stepped in and refused the band permission to play in his fair burgh. Channel Nine's *A Current Affair* had a crew following the band around like the Keystone Cops, waiting for the something sensational to happen—which it didn't, even then. The gig was blown out, the band just had to hole up in their motel, and then move on, according to schedule, to the next town. No savage retribution, no trail of rape and pillage.

MAL EASTICK: "We actually had to pinch ourselves to believe it, you know, This is really true, they're not going to let us play. And then the next thing, Mike Willesee arrives in a helicopter, and Willesee was a very big deal on television at that time, and so it was, Hey, this is getting serious! Up to that point, I don't think they were at all perturbed by the controversy, I think they were probably quite amused. But when it was actually loudly expressed that AC/DC were not welcome to play in Australia, in certain parts, they just couldn't believe the pettiness, the small-townness of it. I think they were then inclined to adopt the attitude, Well, fuck Australia, we'll go back to Europe, seeya later."

The juggernaut pressed on, from Tamworth to Toowoomba. AC/DC made use of any spare time they had to prepare for recording.

EASTICK: "We traveled together in a small bus. They were always working on songs, all the time. It wasn't like, Hey, I'll wait until I've got some privacy, or until I've had a couple of drinks, gotten loose—none of that. I can remember Angus playing guitar on the bus, and Bon used to stomp up and down the aisle, he would stand behind the driver and he always had a pad and would work on titles first."

After Toowoomba, which a police spokesman said was "quiet and without incident"—if quiet is the right word—the band played Brisbane Festival Hall on Saturday, December 18. Strangely, Joh Bjelke-Petersen's blue-shirted stormtroopers failed to exert their presence.

The papers in Sydney still wouldn't let go of the story. "'Members of Australian punk rock group AC/DC must decide if they are strippers or musicians,' the General Manager of radio station 2SM said today," read one report. "'Until they do, the station will not associate with them in any way,' Mr. Garvis Rutherford said. Mr. Rutherford said 2SM would not advertise the group's concerts or play their recordings." 2SM may have been one of AC/DC's original champions, but the station also happened to be owned by the Catholic Church.

The band headed north out of Brisbane to tropical Bundaberg and Rockhampton, before doing a U-turn and heading back down the coast again. At Surfers Paradise on the Gold Coast, the band checked into the Pink Poodle for a well-earned day off. Bon made a beeline for the surf, where the diversions were many besides just swimming. He watched the guy with a spray gun full of suntan oil anointing barely bikini-clad beach bunnies.

But as occupied as Bon was, he still desperately missed Silver.

SILVER: "Where I was staying at the beach in Adelaide, this girl didn't have a telephone, so I was just bombarded with telegrams. Bon was a prolific letter writer, when he was on the road, he wrote almost every day. All those letters I lost. It was sad, because some of his song lyrics were born in those letters, too."

EASTICK: "Bon was probably one of my strongest early impressions of a rock star living that rock star life, a hard life, you know, where he wasn't really sleeping much, nursing a lot of hangovers—there must have been something inside him that was lonely, or unhappy, for him to have acted the way he did. But at the same time, he was a totally dedicated professional. With that strong obsession, like, We're gonna be better than everybody else."

On Thursday, December 22, the band played in Murwillumbah, just an hour or so's drive south of the Gold Coast, in the lush Northern Rivers of New South Wales, next door to the Aquarian Age commune town of Nimbin. AC/DC made as much sense to the hippies as they did to banana farmers. At least Bon scored a bag of killer home-grown.

The following night, the band played on the Gold Coast itself, at the Miami High School Great Hall, with the Saints. As if from out of nowhere—or at least from the wilds of the western Brisbane suburb of Oxley—the Saints had set faraway England on its ear with "(I'm) Stranded," the blazing, pioneering single they'd recorded and released themselves, which went on to become a punk classic. Chris Gilbey had got wind of this and located the band to offer them a gig. They arrived at the gig in a couple of beaten-up old station wagons, a few of the Oxley boys lugging their gear just so they could hang around.

Even at the height of school holidays, the hall held only a smattering of suntanned teenagers. Michael Browning was manifestly unimpressed by the Saints, although Chris Gilbey would go on to manage the band briefly. AC/DC themselves were equally unimpressed, the Oxley boys narrowly avoiding a confrontation with their crew since all they were doing was getting in the way.

At eight the next morning, the band climbed in the bus to do the thirteen hour drive back to Sydney. "THEN," as the worksheets put it, "EVERYBODY FUCKS OFF! BUT MAKE SURE THAT YOU MAKE ARRANGEMENTS TO BE BACK IN MELBOURNE BY THURSDAY 6TH JANUARY."

It was almost as if Michael Browning had only just sat down to Christmas dinner with his family in Melbourne when the phone rang. Phil Carson was calling from London. A problem. Atlantic in New York had decided not to release *Dirty Deeds,* and were quite possibly not going to pick up their option on AC/DC.

MICHAEL BROWNING: "There's no doubt that Atlantic Records in America were really lukewarm on the group at first, in point of fact, would have preferred to have dropped the group. They had a guy called Jim Delahant, who was head of A&R at the time, who quite clearly wished to have them dropped. Jerry Greenberg, the president of the company, was kind of half into it. It was only because Phil Carson in London talked them into dropping the advance commitment that they held onto the group. Which was the difference between having to pay twenty thousand dollars instead of thirty; nothing by today's standards, but then, it was the only way we could keep the deal."

Carson was confident that AC/DC could do good business in Britain to start with, and then in America. He shared with Browning and the band members the belief that the forthcoming album would take AC/DC up to the next level.

The band, as usual, was unaware of these goings on. Bon checked into the Hyatt Kingsgate in Sydney's seamy Kings Cross, and spent Christmas with the Youngs at Burwood. But with the news coming through that the city fathers of the Victorian coal-mining town of Warrnambool had barred the band from appearing there on January 12, something was going to have to give.

"ROCK BAND THREATENS TO LEAVE COUNTRY" read the head-line on New Year's Eve. "AC/DC—Australia's raunchiest rock group—have threatened to quit the country and settle in England because of alleged 'hounding' from local authorities," the story opened.

"It's no good if we drive half way across the country to stage a concert to find that someone has cancelled it because they consider us obscene," Angus was quoted as saying. "It will only take a couple more hassles from the authorities and we will leave Australia."

The point was academic. Leaving Australia, so to speak, was what the band was doing anyway; they were never in one place long enough to call anywhere home. But from this point on, AC/DC almost disowned Australia, even if they all continued to return there every year for Christmas. They would go so far as to play down being an Australian band, proclaiming instead their Scottish roots.

On New Year's Eve, Bon went out to see the debut performance by Rose Tattoo. They were guys he knew: singer Angry Anderson had fronted

Buster Brown, Phil Rudd's old band; slide guitarist Peter Wells was previously in Buffalo, and bassist Ian Rilen in Band Of Light; the line-up was completed by rhythm guitarist Mick Cocks and drummer "Digger" Royal. Overnight, the Tatts became notorious, a self-styled gang of rock'n'roll outlaws intent on mayhem and destruction. Bon loved them; it was his tip, in fact, that led to their signing with Alberts.

MICK COCKS: "In the early days, when we first started, we could only work two places, the Lifesaver and Chequers, everybody hated us. But Bon was a big fan. And that's basically how we met. If Bon was in town, he'd pop up somewhere, and we'd go and have a drink.

"In those days, Angus and Bon used to get up for a blow. 'Cos Bon would be out drinking with his girlfriend, just having a good time, and we got on really well. I suppose we were one of the few bands he could get up and have a sing with and feel comfortable. We'd just do standards—Little Richard, "Johnny B Goode," "Goin' Down," old blues songs. We were a rock'n'roll band, in a period when everything was a bit glam, or whatever."

AC/DC got out on the road again on January 5. They played out the rest of their tour, six gigs, without undue incident. Bonds were paid in Portland and Bendigo, $500 and $2,000 respectively, and they were not forfeited. After the last gig on January 14 in Ballarat, the band was simply relieved it was all over. Now they could get in the studio. They hightailed it immediately to Sydney, where they all checked into the Hyatt Kingsgate. Silver joined Bon there.

The band was back in the familiar—indeed, familial—confines of Alberts' Studio One. Bon added Silver's name, in silver spray-paint, to the graffiti wall at one end of the studio, such was his devotion to her. Such was everyone else's suspicion of her, it was promptly erased.

MARK EVANS: "The band sounded different in the studio. We were all playing well, we were all happy to be back in Sydney, we were enjoying that, and so recording that album the confidence was right up. We were recharged because we knew we had to go back over to England again and really do it. And I think that album was one of the better ones of the whole lot, it was a real turning point for the band."

RAM asked Bon whether there would be any change in AC/DC after three straight rock'n'roll albums. "But that's all there is," he replied, "there's no more than that. You play what you were brought up on, what you believe in. I can listen to other bands that play really intricate stuff and I can appreciate it, and I even like some of it, but I'd never attempt to play it. Like Alex Harvey took the rock'n'roll thing and told stories but that's going too far for me. I wouldn't try to tell anything more intricate than "Jailbreak" 'cos that's still basically rock'n'roll."

George and Harry were just as fired up as the band. If George accepted that *Dirty Deeds* had been rejected by Atlantic in America because his production of it was poor (rather than blaming Michael Browning), then he was going to make amends with *Let There Be Rock*, as the next album would be called.

Alberts had continued on its winning streak in Australia during 1976. The Ted Mulry Gang trailed only Sherbet and Skyhooks as the biggest band in the land. John Paul Young was the leading male solo artist. George and Harry themselves won a *TV Week* King of Pop Special Award for Best Australian Songwriters. Late in the year, when they released their own first single under the Flash and the Pan aegis, "Hey, St Peter!" it went to number three.

By now ensconced at Kangaroo House, George and Harry were raring to go with AC/DC. Sessions progressed smoothly, in typical AC/DC fashion—George, Malcolm and Angus honing riffs and ideas, with the addition of Bon's lyrics, into structured songs, and then putting it all down in rapid-fire sequence. One of the most repeated stories concerning AC/DC's studio method emanates from these sessions. At one time, as Angus was overdubbing a guitar solo (and guitars and vocals were about all that was overdubbed), his amplifier started smoking, fusing out. George gestured wildly from behind the desk, Keep going! Keep going! "There was no way," he later explained, "we were going to stop a shit-hot performance for a technical reason like amps blowing up!"

Let There Be Rock was the first fully rounded AC/DC album. The band had finally found itself. George and Harry gave the band plenty of room, and the band rose to the occasion and brought it all home. George and Harry got AC/DC sounding better than they ever had on vinyl before, capturing with clearer definition and crisper dynamics all the savage attack of the band's live sound. Bon's writing too was more assured, more coherent. The band stretched themselves to wring the most out of every bar of every song—and still they never overdid it.

Let There Be Rock saw AC/DC abandon the last vestiges of the pop band they had once been. "That album sort of put us on the road," Angus agreed, "and I think it also set the style of the band."

Its feature track, "Whole Lotta Rosie," was, of course, a play by Bon on Led Zeppelin, and his tribute to the self-same Rosie, an ode to making fat ladies sing as fine as Jimmy Castor's like-minded funk classic "Trog-lodyte." If Bon had returned to Melbourne in 1975 for that song's inspi-ration, others betrayed the same source: "Go Down" was inspired by supergroupie Ruby Lips, and "Overdose," which appropriately borders on the turgid, harks back to Judy King.

On previous albums, simple stomps like "Dog Eat Dog," "Bad Boy Boogie" and "Hell Ain't a Bad Place To Be" might have been filler tracks, but on *Let There Be Rock*, they more than justify their presence. Only the requisite slow blues, "Crabsody in Blue" (a creaky play on the title of George Gershwin's "Rhapsody in Blue"), falls short lyrically, like "The Jack." The title track, however, is a masterpiece; its extended instrumental passage enters a realm of pure white noise equaled at the time (ironically enough) only by the Saints's anarchic opus "Nights in Venice," from their first album.

AC/DC had almost finished the album—and a new, previously recorded single, "Love at First Feel" had been released—when they went out to play a special show for the Festival of Sydney on January 30. Five thousand people turned up at the old Haymarket warehouse to see them headline over Taste and Chariot, and blow away any echoes of the "rock" stars of the festival—the Little River Band—who had earlier played the same venue.

MARK EVANS: "When we finished the album, we had to go back to England. We did a couple of gigs in Sydney, then we went back to Mel-bourne to do some gigs; we did a gig in Melbourne on Thursday night, then we did Friday and Saturday in Adelaide, then we did Sunday night in Perth, then we did the following Wednesday night in Edinburgh."

"Can't wait to get back [overseas]," Mark said at the time in *RAM*. "They treat you properly, food and booze provided, none of this hassling with hall managers shit."

The band had had enough of Australia. Australia had failed to show the required amount of respect, so Australia could go fuck itself. AC/DC just wanted to be where the action was—in America. "Love at First Feel" performed even less well than "Dirty Deeds"; it would be the last AC/DC single to chart in Australia until "Highway to Hell" over two years later.

After playing to a mixed reception in Melbourne and Adelaide, AC/DC played its last Australian date in Perth, which at least enabled Bon to see his folks. His mother didn't quite know what to make of this mysterious, dark lady by the strange name of Silver. But Bon seemed to cherish her—that was the right word—so like always, she just had to go along with him. Silver was extended every hospitality, and she could see just how devoted to Bon his parents were.

Like the other four members of AC/DC, Bon had received a missive from Ted Albert just prior to leaving Sydney which he was still clutching proudly. It contained a royalty check for the second half of 1976, and a letter, which read:

> As you will see from the enclosed statement, the total record earnings for the whole group for the period total $24,733.06. After deducting the manager's one-fifth, the total of $19,786.45 remains and your one-fifth of this is $3,957.29. A check for this amount is enclosed.
>
> My personal thanks to you for all the many hours of hard work that you have spent in the studio during the last few weeks. Also on behalf of the whole company our thanks for your efforts overseas and our best wishes for the coming year.

Four thousand dollars in six months was a paltry sum when expressed as barely three cents for every $7 album sold—but to Bon, it was a fine old going-away present.

Isa saw Bon and Silver off at the airport. Chick couldn't be there as he had to work. The band was glad just to get on the plane, putting Australia and all its petty aggravations behind them. They would not return to play again until after Bon was dead.

Now, not only Britain and Europe but also America beckoned. And they had a new album in their pocket that was so hot it was burning a hole.

Bon's feet had barely touched the ground in London before he was back in the bus on the way to Edinburgh, where the band commenced a 26-date British tour on February 18. "Dirty Deeds" had been released as a single in January.

AC/DC was playing like a band possessed. The evident quality of *Let There Be Rock* had given them another injection of confidence, although none of its material had yet been introduced to the set. The ecstatic response back in Britain was encouraged by kids who had bought the *Dirty Deeds* album over Christmas and were now getting a chance to catch up with the band.

The majority of critics still failed to appreciate AC/DC, but Bon hit the nail on the head when he told the *NME*, "The music press is totally out of touch with what the kids actually want to listen to.

"These kids might be working in a shitty factory all week, or they might be on the dole—come the weekend, they just want to go out and have a good time, get drunk and go wild. We give them the opportunity to do that."

Critic Lester Bangs once celebrated a "no-jive, take-care-of-business band . . . churning out rock'n'roll that thundered right back to the very first grungy chords and straight ahead to the fuzztone subways of the future." Because their music was "so true to its evolutionary antecedents," he went on to say, "it was usually about sex, and not just Sally-go-to-movieshow-and-hold-my-hand stuff . . ., but the most challengingly blatant flat-out proposition and prurient fantasy." Bangs also praised the band's "consistent sense of structure and economy," noting: "I don't think any of their songs ran over four minutes, the solos were short but always slashingly pertinent, and the vocals were . . . raspy and cocky and loose and lewd."[1]

Bangs was extolling the drooling, banal raw glory of sixties punk prototypes the Troggs (creators of "Wild Thing" and "I Can't Control Myself")—but he could just as well have been describing AC/DC. Devoid of artifice and stripped down to the essentials, the rhythm and the blues, AC/DC got to the point with an elemental force, allowing Bon, with a glint in his eye and tongue in his cheek, to tell his tall tales.

"You get on that stage," said Bon, "and the more crass, gross and rowdy you sound, the more they love it. So I just go up there and scream away, sometimes to a point where I can't talk the next day.

"We're on the crowd's side," he said, "because we give 'em what they want, and everybody gets into our show—because it's a band/audience show. We're not like performing seals, we're all in it together."

Back in London by the end of March, the band had a moment's peace prior to taking off for Europe to tour with Black Sabbath at the end of April. Malcolm and Angus moved into a flat together in Ladbroke Grove; Mark and Phil moved into one just around the corner. Bon was snugly shacked up with Silver, who was still living by somewhat dubious means and dabbling with increasing enthusiasm in heroin.

Heroin was in plentiful supply in London in the late seventies, and

---

[1] Lester Bangs, "James Taylor Marked for Death," in *Psychotic Reactions and Carburetor Dung* (Alfred A. Knopf, 1987), pp. 55-56.

of a consistently high quality and low price. It was enough to tempt anyone. Bon resisted it, maybe because he knew how dangerous it was, maybe because it just wasn't his style of drug—he preferred anything more social—or maybe because he knew that as far as the Youngs were concerned, it was just not on. Silver, however, had no such reservations. And Bon was happy if she was happy.

SILVER: "As far as my life goes, I don't think anyone has loved me as unconditionally as Bon. He had no complaints—they were all on my side. It gave me the guilts for quite a long time. Because Bon was really good to me. He accepted me exactly as I was. He was really attentive too, you know, two or three letters a day bombarding you when he was on the road, and he was always bringing flowers and little presents. I mean, it was full on, right up until we split up.

"No one gave Bon drugs. He could have used any time he wanted, but the thing was, we just wouldn't let him. Partly because he wouldn't metabolize them well, and also, if he was in that devil may care frame of mind, he wouldn't stop to think that the person he was using with may have had a tolerance, and he had none at all, and so he would have ended up blue on the floor.

"Bon wanted to get married and have kids and all that sort of stuff. At the time, I just couldn't get my head around that, it seemed like the world we were living in was so mad, it didn't make any sense.

"Bon was very pipe and slippers. He liked peace and quiet. He had this public image, but he was probably the most domesticated male I've ever known. He liked everything to be clean and tidy. When he was home he liked to just see people, you know, sit around, entertain—at home, not going out. He liked having roast dinners on Sunday and all that. But he could go very quiet and somber if he was hurt. He was a typical Cancer."

Silver's recollection of the kind of records they used to listen to together throws a different light on Bon as well. He had a special fondness for female soul singers—Millie Jackson, Gladys Knight, Lorraine Ellison, even Joan Armatrading—and he also liked Roxy Music and Bryan Ferry, Steely Dan, the J Geils Band.

SILVER: "He knew the lyrics to an enormous number of songs. Everything from *Oklahoma* through to . . . all that Broadway musical sort of stuff. He had a great memory for lyrics . . . well, his short-term memory was stuffed, he couldn't remember which plane he was supposed to catch! But yeah, his taste in music was very different."

He still felt an obligation to live up to his image though, as a profile he filled out at the time suggests:

Favorite Drink: Whisky
Favorite Bike (Don't Like Cars): Harley Sportster
Favorite Color: Silver (Preferably Metal), Black
Guitarist: Don't mind the Young brothers
Singer: Don't mind Jess Roden
Record: Don't mind *Tres Hombres*
AC/DC Record: "Carry Me Home" (as yet unreleased)

Before the band left London for Europe, they shot a video for their new Australian single "Dog Eat Dog," the first to come off *Let There Be Rock*, for the special fifth anniversary episode of *Countdown*. With "Carry Me Home" on the B-side, it went nowhere. When *Let There Be Rock* itself was released in May, it went in and out of the charts without getting higher than number 20. Ironically though, as Mark Evans put it, "That was the point at which things started to look really strong, that was when America started."

With the British release of *Let There Be Rock* in the offing, Atlantic in New York was finally starting to come around. New A&R manager John Kalodner was much more sympathetic to AC/DC than his predecessor; plus there were two other new executives, Michael Klenfner and Perry Cooper, who were prepared to pin their own careers to the band's. At the same time, AC/DC signed up with a new booking agent, Doug Thaler of American Talent International.

MARK EVANS: "The reason the band always had a level head was because there was always something to do, a new objective. We always seemed to be starting at the bottom and working our way up."

The tour with Black Sabbath would prove ill-fated, and precipitated Mark Evans' sacking. Sabbath, by 1976, were well past their prime, and AC/DC were all but blowing them off stage. Only the showmanship of Ozzy Osborne kept Sabbath alive. Substance abuse within the band was rampant. It was in this atmosphere, then, that relations between the two bands came to an ugly head, when Sabbath bassist "Geezer" Butler apparently pulled a flick knife on Malcolm. Fistic retaliation was swift, with the end result that AC/DC were simply shown the door.

EVANS: "I don't think the band took too kindly to being on the road in Europe for some reason. Every time we went to Europe, things seemed to get strained. When we were in England, Scotland, no problems. And yeah, things did get very tense between Angus and me, basically, I suppose, because we just didn't get on. And so what happens, if you've got your brother in the band, and somebody doesn't like your brother . . .

"Europe could be a lonely time for Bon too. He never socialized with the band. It would not be unusual for us to be out, and not return with Bon. He would just wander off in some other direction. Do whatever it was he did.

"The last six months I was in the band, his drinking did escalate pretty quickly, to the point where he started showing up at gigs with a bottle of Johnnie Walker.

"In hindsight, after we had a problem with the Americans, going, What the fuck is this? knocking back *Dirty Deeds,* I think with the negativity of that, and then getting thrown off the Black Sabbath tour, I think I was made a bit of a scapegoat. It was, What's going wrong, we'd better make a change. And it was gonna be both me and Bon!

"I didn't know, and I'm sure Phil didn't know either, that *Dirty Deeds* was knocked back in the States. We just weren't told. We were in Helsinki after the Black Sabbath tour, ready to fly to America, right, we're going, but then it was like, Guys, sorry, we're not going, you're going back to England. Things aren't ready yet."

Next thing, as *RAM* reported on June 3, "Mark Evans, the quiet, well-behaved member of AC/DC has left the group."

All Mark said at the time was, "Both me and the band are better for it." He was sent packing, given a $2,000 golden handshake in lieu of all future royalties. He returned to Melbourne, where he continued a career in music, initially as bassist with a band called Finch. And though it would take him ten years, he eventually won a settlement over the subsequent royalties which had been denied him.

MICHAEL BROWNING: "I got a phone call from Malcolm and Angus, and they said, Could you come over, we've got something important we want to talk about. At that stage I had a sense the Americans were a little bit negative towards Bon, I had a sense it might have been something to do with that. So I got there and I was actually surprised they wanted to get rid of Mark."

MARK EVANS: "When I got the bullet, Michael Browning rang me and said, Listen, the guys are going to call a meeting, what do you know about it? I said, Michael, you've called the wrong guy, I don't know anything about a meeting. He said, Well, it's at Malcolm and Angus's place tonight, I think they're finally going to give Bon the arse. I said, I don't know about any meeting, so I said to Phil, Do you know about a meeting, and he said, Yeah, I do. And I said, Michael, it's me. And Michael's words on the phone were, Oh fuck. He said, I thought it was going to be Bon."

On the road in America. Left to right: Phil Rudd, unidentified ligger, Bon (with perm, and bottle), new bassist Cliff Williams, Angus, unidentified liggers, Malcolm, Michael Klenfer and Perry Cooper of Atlantic Records, and AC/DC manager Michael Browning.

13. AMERICA

The replacement of bassist Mark Evans by Cliff Williams indicated that AC/DC was shifting its operation up a gear, clearing the decks in readiness for its first assault on America, the biggest and most competitive music market in the world. With the stakes now so much higher, nothing could be left to chance, no excess baggage would be trucked. Cliff Williams would be expected to hold his end up, no more, no less. You had to know your place, or else forfeit it. Nobody was indispensable.

There's no reason to believe Bon was beyond this law either, even if the Youngs reserved an inordinate amount of loyalty for him. But Bon knew himself that he'd come too far to throw it all away now. An atmosphere of increasing venality was something he would just have to learn to live with. When he joined AC/DC in 1974, it was a new lease on life for him; but in the end, for the last couple of years of his life, the band became a business, and it was more like a job, a daily grind that Bon endured as the price of finally "making it."

As everything other than the music itself congealed around him, Bon drank more and more just to get through the day. Cliff Williams, it turned out, was a saving grace, a new friend for Bon who relieved some of the day-to-day tedium. Bon told Molly Meldrum in an interview for *Countdown:* "He's a guy who's been playing for a lot longer than Mark, so his technique is far advanced. Cliff's just given us more scope."

It was Michael Browning, again, who found Williams and engineered his joining the band. Malcolm and Angus were keen on a bassist called Colin Pattendon, who had previously been with Manfred Mann's Earth Band. But as Browning said, "He just didn't fit the image. At that juncture, I felt that whoever came in had to look the part as well." Browning was alerted to Williams by a friend. When Williams passed the audition, Browning gave his friend a tenner by way of a spotter's fee.

Williams was born in the Essex town of Romford, just outside London, on December 14, 1949. His musical background was not unlike Bon's; he had spent the early seventies in an obscure English country-rock band called Home. He was playing with an outfit called Bandit when AC/DC's better prospects presented themselves.

SILVER: "It was a bit of a relief when Cliff came in, because Cliff was more our age, our interests. The boys—they were kids. I mean, they were kids from the western suburbs, and they were really aware of it, they had a lot of fronts up, and they weren't going to change. Whereas Cliff, you know, he was 28, he'd been around, and he read books, went to the movies, had a girlfriend. Because none of the boys had girlfriends at that stage."

The band returned to Australia at the start of June to work Williams in, in preparation for touring throughout the rest of the year. America had finally fallen into place. The band would have to be in top form.

Michael Browning had gone over to New York to meet with Perry Cooper and Michael Klenfner. As the new kids on the block at Atlantic, Cooper and Klenfner needed to earn some kudos. When President Jerry Greenberg came to them one day early on with that same old film of "High Voltage" they saw their opportunity.

PERRY COOPER: "He said, Look, we've got this band, we've signed them for the rest of their life, and we put out an album, but we can't get fuckin' arrested with it. He said, Why don't you have a look at it. Klenfner says, I haven't got time, so I go into my office—and I really liked the whole thing.

"So I went back to Klenfner, and I said, You gotta look at these guys, and so we started talking. We thought, What's going to break this band? Obviously, radio isn't. The only thing I could think, If they get over here and tour, if they're as great live as they look, they've got something different. We had to find out, Are they willing to work their asses off, for the next—you know, nonstop, like the Stones. The Stones, in the very beginning, used to just go around in a station wagon. AC/DC ended up doing exactly the same thing.

"We met with Michael Browning, and it was agreed that they would just come over and work their asses off, touring. Michael said, That's what these guys do, don't worry about that."

Browning signed AC/DC on with a booking agency called American

Talent International, and gigs were lined up.

The band arrived in the US at the end of June 1977. Club dates had been booked along a route from Texas to Florida. The South had produced redneck boogie bands such as ZZ Top and Black Oak Arkansas, and if an opening existed in America for AC/DC, it was here. In 1977 punk rock meant about as much to middle America as it did to middle Australia.

MICHAEL BROWNING: "One of the important factors in the group's American campaign was a promoter called Sidney Drashin in Jacksonville, Florida. A radio station down there must have got hold of an AC/DC record and actually listened to it, and just fell in love with it. Programmed about four or five tracks. And so the guy from the radio station was calling up Atlantic, and so was Sidney, saying, you know, What are you doing with this group? So that one town formed the basis, it gave the record company living proof that it could work. And so when we went there to tour, we picked up a couple of dates here and a couple of dates there, we'd play for $500 and travel 500 miles, playing dates with a variety of acts, but we did Jacksonville and played the Coliseum to a packed house."

AC/DC supported REO Speedwagon at the Jacksonville Coliseum in front of as big a crowd as they'd ever faced, nearly 8,000 strong.

BROWNING: "There was Jacksonville and there was Columbus, Ohio, which is a college town, and that was a similar situation there, the radio station people were fanatical for the group. So you just had to go there and build it from the ground level up. It was all done on a shoestring, in hire cars, staying at Red Roof Inns, Holiday Inns."

The band headed north from Florida, through Columbus and Chicago on its way to New York. Bon wrote to Mary:

> I'm enjoying our tour of America. The band is playing good and going over great . . . The money's good . . . The chicks are outta sight (right now they are outta sight) and everything is better than I ever thought it could be. We're touring here till Sept 7 and then it's Europe for eighteen dates, England for twenty, America for another month or so and then Australia for a tour. So I should be able to break your door down early next year. Bon's love life ain't goin' too well at the mo. I haven't seen my lady for four months and it's kinda painful . . . Love will prevail. My hair's getting long and the perm is almost out. I'm a regular shaggy dog . . . But I like it.

In New York on August 24, AC/DC played on the bottom of the bill at Palladium, under old-wave punk band the Dictators. They then raced downtown to the Bowery, to put in an appearance at CBGB's, the decrepit, hallowed home of New York new wave, where they were met with stony silence opening for a nowhere power-pop outfit called Marbles.

Variety at least gave them the thumbs up over the Dictators. Angus's asshole had been deemed unfit for puritanical American consumption, but the band's new set-piece—the walking-the-floor routine, Angus astride Bon's shoulders—had been further improved when Angus acquired a new toy, a cordless guitar pick-up.

When New York fanzine *Punk* interviewed Bon and Angus, Bon succeeded in his attempt to outgross the grossout standards of punkdom. The only telling thing he said was in answer to the question, What's the meaning of life? "As good a time and as short as possible."

In some ways, AC/DC were a little confused by America. Britain, Europe, even punk rock, they could understand, but America is so big and so diverse that contradiction is inherent.

"I hadn't even heard a lot of the music here at the time—I thought there would be more rock," Angus told *Guitar World*. "But when we got here it was a disco type thing. What was real strange was that although the media was pushing this really soft music, you'd get amazing numbers of people turning out to hear the harder stuff. We were playing big stadiums and getting a great reaction."

The band was unimpressed when they met the Atlantic staff, finding the stereotypical image of the gold-sporting, cigar-chomping, cocaine-sniffing record company executive not too far from the truth.

From New York, AC/DC jetted to the West Coast. After gigs in the Northwest with Ted Nugent, they played four well-attended shows at the Old Waldorf club in San Francisco. Then it was on to Los Angeles.

Bon fully intended to make the most of his first ever visit to southern California. He wasn't seen without a blonde on one arm and a bottle in his free hand. He and Phil went to Disneyland on a day off. They rustled up a couple of extra special joints for the occasion. They didn't know what they were in for. The joints were laced with angel dust, a powerful psychedelic, which sent them off on a trip more unnerving than any Disneyland big dipper. It was just a question of who was more put off, Bon and Phil or the regular Disneyland patrons, who couldn't tell if these two tattooed men walking around wide-eyed and legless, holding hands, were one of the attractions or just some sort of terrible mistake.

In their shows at the Whisky A-Go-Go, LA's legendary Sunset Strip equivalent of London's Marquee, AC/DC pulled in a crowd of fewer than 100; but, as *Variety* again enthused, they made an indelible impression. The band boarded the plane back to Britain feeling quite pleased with themselves. The prospects ahead were looking good.

AC/DC had 18 gigs in Europe (France, Holland, Belgium, Germany) still to play before a 14-date British tour commenced on October 12 (though their two London shows at the Hammersmith Odeon were already sold out). Bon was only in London long enough to unpack his bags, do his laundry, then pack and leave again.

The new album had just been released. It could hardly have got off to a better start, gaining good reviews and—for the first time—actually entering the charts.

Sympathetic critics were in agreement that *Let There Be Rock* was a more complete AC/DC offering. It would reach number 75 in the British charts, a quite respectable first entry. George and Harry were celebrating back home, because at the same time, Flash & the Pan's "Hey, St Peter!" was hitting in Europe, going to number six in Belgium, number seven in Holland and also selling well in France.

The tour confirmed AC/DC's stature beyond any doubt. Stalwart supporter Phil Sutcliffe of *Sounds* commented: "Live [they] are the most insanely compulsive heavy rock band I've ever experienced . . . who offer the rare combination of wild excitement and consistency. The schoolkid image will have to go one day but at the moment it's still dead right . . .

"Bon is vital. He's the spice and flavor with the heavy hardtack. An appealing rogue and buccaneer, give him a wooden leg and a parrot on his shoulder and he'd be the image of Long John Silver."

It was the sheer, irrefutable power and appeal of AC/DC's live gigs that accounted for their growing following and its diversity. AC/DC traversed Britain's tribal barriers, pulling punks, bikers, hippies, headbangers, 9-to-5ers, old rockers and young boppers all along.

The band got back to London on the first day of November. Silver was worried about Bon's drinking. This was ironic, as he might well have worried about her increasing drug dependency, which he did not presume to do. But even as Silver let her own habit run away with her, she couldn't bear to watch Bon boozing it up.

SILVER: "When Bon was drinking and I was drugging, I didn't know what I was running from, and yet I could see what Bon was running from.

It's always easier to be in denial about yourself. I see it a lot differently now. We both really had the same disease, it was just a matter of a different drug of choice. But I was judging him. It was also just really painful; I couldn't bear to be around him when he was drinking. He didn't ever nag me, he didn't have a problem with what I did—but then I was a lot more manageable than what he was. Basically, it was just a lot of people in a lot of pain, trying to rage on regardless."

Bon and Silver's relationship was starting to show some cracks, but the couple enjoyed a reprieve on a weekend away in Paris. The Stones were in the studio there recording the *Some Girls* album, and Silver's friend, Stones guitarist Ron Wood, invited them to drop in.

SILVER: "Ron had been in town, and he said, Come over. The strange thing was, a French punk band [Trust] was recording in another part of the same studio, and they were more impressed by the fact that Bon was there than Bon was by the Stones. Though he liked the Stones. It was good actually, because they took us around everywhere—we didn't know a word of French. That was a buzz for Bon."

Let There Be Rock was out in America by now, confounding the critics. Even *Creem* magazine, with its metalesque predilections, was succinct in its dismissal of AC/DC: "These guys suck." Maybe America was just going to be like Britain all over again. The band was succeeding there despite the critics' best efforts to quell them. *Let There Be Rock* cracked the *Billboard* chart at number 187. It's difficult to enter much lower than that, but it was a start.

AC/DC returned to America in November, and spent the next six weeks crisscrossing the country. They would be back in Australia by Christmas, like the year before, to record a new album. Their American home base was New York, where Atlantic had its headquarters, and where Michael Browning had by now also set up an office on Broadway. The band themselves stayed at the Americana Hotel near seedy Times Square. They played a few headline club gigs of their own in the South, with support acts like British bands UFO and the Motors, and then they opened big stadium gigs for Kiss and for pomp-rockers Rush.

"We toured around in a station wagon," Angus told *Guitar World*. "We got put on with Kiss. This was when they had all the make-up and everything—the whole hype. They had everything behind them, the media, a huge show and stuff. And here we were—five migrants, little micro people.

"It was tough to even get into the show with that station wagon. Many a time they wouldn't let us into the venue 'cause they didn't see a limo!"

On the road, Bon drank even more than he did at home.

MICK COCKS: "What happens, you're playing to 5 to 10,000 people a night, an hour and a half on stage, it's fantastic, it's real high; and when you come off, you travel in the bus back to the hotel room, you've got to come down, it can be really difficult to find something to do that makes sense. And if you're doing a long tour, it builds up, you know, and you drink, there's not a real lot of alternatives. I once did a tour without drinking, and phew, you can keep reality."

Silver joined Bon as the band played through a blizzard in Chicago with Kiss. Stoned though she may have been herself, she hated to see Bon drinking himself into oblivion.

SILVER: "I couldn't deal with seeing this incredible, together, really wonderful person that half the world was in love with, and then seeing this dribbling mess that you could have no respect for. I found it just too hard in the end. He wasn't like that all the time either, but when he went, he went. He was one of those drunks, he wasn't aggressive, he was just unmanageable. He wouldn't know what city he was in, he'd just lose it."

Silver was starting to think that maybe she'd had enough.

The band swung back through New York in the first week of December, before returning to Australia, Bon and Silver travelling together. They played a radio broadcast from Atlantic's studios on December 7 (the source of a very collectable promo-only recording, released officially only much later as part of the *Bonfire* box set), then opened for Kiss at Madison Square Garden, and then flew out of JFK to Sydney.

The band hoped and planned to tour Australia again.

Bon and Silver checked into a serviced apartment at Coogee. They needed some space of their own. At Coogee, they were right on the beach—and it was going to be a sweltering summer.

SILVER: "A lot of the hoohah had died down by then, that teenybopper thing was over, so it was much more laid-back. Bon hired a motorcycle to get around. You know what it's like on the road, you get sick of eating out all the time and that, so at least at this place you could have some stuff in the fridge, and a frypan and that, some of your own stuff. Because we were there for three months."

No tour materialized. With an English bass player now as well as a British road crew, the absurdly protectionist Australian immigration authorities refused to issue AC/DC the appropriate visas.

"We used to think of ourselves as an Australian band," Angus told *RAM*, "but we're beginning to doubt that now. The fuckers won't even let us play here." The band found itself with time on its hands, since they were not due to return to Britain until April, after the album was cut at Alberts in January.

With their local profile slipping, AC/DC could have used the exposure afforded by a tour. The 11 months the band had been away from Australia this time had seen many changes on the scene, changes which would have been greatly to AC/DC's advantage—changes which they in fact had played a considerable part in bringing about. Sherbet and Skyhooks had both dropped right off. *Countdown* still held sway, but its reign was no longer dictatorial. Pub rock was taking root, and this was music which by definition sold itself through live performance.

Pub rock left no room for punk. Any Australian new wave was consigned very much to the fringes. The old hippies who had only just got their act together and assumed seats of power in the music industry were hardly about to hand the reins over to a bunch of young punks. First generation Australian "new wave" bands like the Saints, Radio Birdman, Nick Cave's Birthday Party and the Go-Betweens were forced to go overseas to find a significant audience.

"We don't have the kind of culture punk needed," Ross Wilson once explained. "We're quite comfortable. Groups like the Angels and Rose Tattoo transferred that aggression into a macho rock, using better musicianship than the punks."

It was in Sydney that pub rock really came to the fore. Rose Tattoo actually formed in Melbourne but moved to Sydney because their work prospects were better there. Adelaide bands Cold Chisel and the Angels also gravitated to Sydney. Dragon had arrived from New Zealand. And Sydney itself produced Midnight Oil, Mental As Anything and Icehouse. Melbourne bands like the Sports and Jo Jo Zep and the Falcons trailed the leaders.

On almost any given night in the late seventies, Sydney venues like the Bondi Lifesaver, Chequers, the Stagedoor Tavern, the Civic Hotel and the Grand Hotel would be pumping. Suburban beer barns like the Manly Vale Hotel, the Comb & Cutter and Selinas were taking off, too.

But even as Sydney was buzzing with new energies, the most pervasive influence on the scene was still Alberts. The Alberts label put out Rose Tattoo and the Angels, but Alberts' mere presence, its independent heritage and its innovative drive, perhaps did even more to reinforce its patriarchal hold.

CHRIS GILBEY: "I don't think Alberts set out to become a rock'n'roll label, but it became a rock'n'roll label due to the momentum set in motion by rock'n'roll bands like AC/DC."

Everybody, but everybody recorded at Kangaroo House, where the vibe George and Harry generated was palpable—and something they all hoped would rub off on them. With the Angels and Rose Tattoo specifically, George and Harry took the work they had started with AC/DC to its logical conclusion, orchestrating and stylizing a unique—and uniquely Australian—brand of rock'n'roll.

Cold Chisel set the standard for pub bands. But for all their maverick spirit, Cold Chisel owed AC/DC—and Bon especially—an enormous debt. Cold Chisel had come out of Fraternity's alma mater, the Largs Pier, and their singer and fellow Scot Jimmy Barnes (who had briefly replaced Bon in Fraternity) saw himself as Bon's heir apparent. AC/DC had become a given in Australian rock'n'roll.

The Angels and Rose Tattoo institutionalized pub rock. The ferocity which was their trademark became one of the distinguishing fundamentals of the genre. "[People] come to our gigs, or to gigs generally I guess, to let something go, as a sort of catharsis," Angels frontman Doc Neeson once told *Rolling Stone*. "We always feel that there's this implied confrontation between band and audience. They're saying, "Lay it on! Do it to us!" and it's like a veiled threat that if you don't, you'll get canned."

Rose Tattoo's debut single "Bad Boy for Love" was released in October 1977. By December, when Bon arrived back in town, it was near the top of the national charts.

MICK COCKS: "It was the first record I'd ever made. It went top five. I thought, This is easy!"

Cocks was among a number of reprobates, including Joe Furey, living at the time in a big old hotel in Kings Cross called the Eaglefield. "We just took this place over. Downstairs we had a music studio and an art studio—the girls painted, the boys played music."

The scene was riddled with drugs. Killer weed was equaled in abundance by speed, mandies and heroin. In the late seventies, top-grade smack was plentiful and cheap in Sydney, as it was in London.

MICK COCKS: "Bon came back to town, and he would stay at this hotel he liked in Coogee with his girlfriend, and I got into him one night and said, Oh, come and stay with us if you like, because things weren't going so well with his girlfriend, and so he'd come and crash at our place."

Powerage, as AC/DC's new album would be called, was cut like every other AC/DC album—quickly.

JOE FUREY: "Of course, with the album being recorded, and guitar parts going on later, Bon had done most of his stuff; he was sort of hanging loose around town, so he used to drop over. The Tatts were playing around, the Lifesaver was happening, it was pretty rockin'."

Powerage followed closely in the footsteps of *Let There Be Rock*—so much so, in fact, that there was something almost rote about it. It contained some great individual tracks—"Rock'n'roll Damnation," "Riff Raff" (which would become a highlight of the band's live set), "Sin City" and "Gimme a Bullet." "Gimme a Bullet" was perhaps Bon's most accomplished piece of writing to date, in which his penchant for hardcase metaphors finds more genuine pathos and humor than it had before. Even the album's second-string tracks sustain a more consistently high standard than earlier albums' fillers. Yet taken as a whole *Powerage* seemed to lack the uncompromising coherence, the relentless body and soul that made its predecessor so great.

Bon was happy just to finish his work in the studio. He didn't necessarily enjoy recording, with its alternating intensity and tedium. "Recording can be a bit of a pain," he once said. "You have to think. The rest of the time you are just cruising." You might wait around all day till a track was set up, and then have to get your part down within a couple of takes. It was fortunate Bon was so capable. No other singer filled Alberts' Studio One with sheer vocal presence the way Bon did.

His obligations in the studio fulfilled, Bon spent long hot days on the beach, sunning himself, swimming and thinking. He was worried. Silver was acting strangely. He knew she was losing patience with him because of his drinking, and at the same time, she'd struck up a friendship with Joe Furey. Bon liked Joe himself, but even if, as Silver always maintained, she and Joe were never actually lovers—their relationship more akin to that of soul brother and sister—and whether there were drugs involved or not, Bon still felt threatened. Knowing the independent Silver as he did, though, he just had to grin and bear it. He decided to try to get off the grog, which he thought might win him back some favor.

He was delighted when Graeme showed up to see him. "He knew that drink was getting to him. He was going to a hypnotist, to stop from drinking. But a hypnotist, you've got to do it all the time, not just once or twice. And so of course, touring all the time, I think the loneliness got to him. You drink."

Sitting on the beach all day at Coogee, the only thing Bon wanted to do once the sun went down was go out raging. He fell off the wagon. It was too much to ask, he had too little to do otherwise.

GRAEME: "He'd go down to the Bondi Lifesaver, and he'd be drunk most nights, and he'd still go home on his bike."

MICK COCKS: "Bon was one of the last true rock'n'rollers, a real person. It wasn't a business to him, it was an addiction, something he had a gut feeling for. He lived it. You know, he had that dream—because you're talking about a period of time when it was a dream, a romantic dream. You were outlaws, that was the only way to look at it. You only sort of paid lip service to the social side of things—like paying tax, or registering to vote—when you had to. You didn't have any sense of community, you weren't really interested in what was going on, you didn't have the same problems the average person had. It was like you were in a different world.

"And when you did achieve it, it's still a dream, you know, it's not like it ever becomes a job, going up on stage."

Perhaps it's just everything else—the soul-destroying rootlessness of life on the road, the phoniness endemic in show business, the purely exhausting demands of celebrity—that becomes hard work. Bon wasn't tired of it all yet, and he still had a fair way to go to get to the top, but maybe the only way to do it was in a numb, alcoholic haze.

With Bon going on tour in Britain and Europe, Silver had arranged with Joe to go away together, off on the hippie trail through southeast Asia. They had arranged to meet Bon's brother Graeme in Bangkok.

SILVER: "I made the decision to break up when we left Australia. Bon couldn't accept it, he was still very emotionally dependent on me, so we said, Okay, 12 months, have a 12 month break."

Before Bon and Silver went their separate ways, AC/DC played a couple of shows at the Lifesaver under wraps. Billed as "the Seedies," as the band was affectionately known, word got out, as it was doubtless meant to, and more than 4,000 people tried to get into the Lifesaver over the two nights.

Let There Be Rock might have only sold a miserable 25,000 copies in Australia, but as Bon pointed out in RAM, it had sold nearly ten times that internationally, and "word builds up when people hear you've been going well overseas. People want to see you. A lot of people just haven't seen the band." AC/DC had by now completely shed the stigma of being a teenybopper band. They were acknowledged as a force to be reckoned with—and as godfathers of Australian rock. And when they played those two nights at the Lifesaver, they proved the point.

JOE FUREY: "It was probably one of the best shows I've ever seen. I mean, you had a band that had moved into virtual stadium mode, a big rock band, playing in the Lifesaver, to a capacity crowd, and the band was on a real high then, playing really well . . ."

In Australia, like Britain and America, AC/DC had to take the step that only a hit record makes possible. A lot hinged on *Powerage*.

Bon left for London with the rest of the band, clinging to Silver's promise that he would see her there in a couple of months' time, after he'd been to Europe and before he went to America again.

Critical reaction to *Powerage* was generally positive. Any suggestion that the band was merely repeating itself was offset by the fact that this would only make the album an easier sell. And indeed, it got a strong start out of the blocks.

Bon defended the album. "Look what happened to the Rolling Stones," he said. "They started looking for a new direction, going off on tangents, and they produced shit. And then the punk bands came along and scared 'em, and now you will notice, they are going back to producing what they've always done best—rock'n'roll. You progress, sure you do, but you move forward in the same direction. You do not shoot off on some tangent."

On April 28, the band embarked on its most comprehensively mounted British tour to date. A full range of merchandise—T-shirts, patches, posters—was available—a first for AC/DC and an early example of what is today standard practice, and extremely lucrative, for rock bands.

DAVE JARRETT: "They were right in that era when patches on denim jackets started happening, all that, and so the AC/DC logo was just everywhere. It was really easy for kids to identify with."

AC/DC were making the transition every band has to make in pursuit of American superstardom, and at which many falter—the transition from a club band to a stadium band; that is, a band able to project to the farthest reaches of a venue so big and cold that rock'n'roll should never have been put into it. The trap is that as every gesture is amplified, the act becomes bloated, bombastic, impersonal. AC/DC somehow managed to avoid that. They scaled up but not out, retaining their trademark leanness and vitality even as they drew so much broader strokes.

Bon wrote to Irene:

Hi sugar . . . I'm writing from Birmingham. We're about half way through the Brit tour and most of us are suffering from the flu or bubonic plague or something. It's been great so far gig wise as most have been sell outs and we've been getting good reviews for the concerts and the album. Stand to make a bit of money at long last . . .

Our album went into the British charts first week at 26 so it looks like being a Top 5 at least. We only have about ten gigs to go on this tour and then it's off to Germany for two TV shows and then we have three weeks off before America. Cliff and I are going to Paris for a root around. I have some friends in a band there who'll put us up for a few days. They're a punk band called Trust. They recorded a couple of our songs in French and just last week got banned from French TV for singing suggestive lyrics. The song they did was "Love at First Feel." So I've struck again!

"Rock'n'roll Damnation" was released as a single in Britain at the end of May as the band left for Europe. It went to number 24, the best performance yet by an AC/DC single.

Bon and Cliff returned to London from Paris in mid-June. Bon was anxious because Silver was finally on her way there too. She and Joe hadn't got far down the hippie trail. They waited around in Malaysia for an old girlfriend of Silver's who never showed, and then went on to Bangkok, where they met up with Graeme and got "bogged down," as Silver put it. People go to Bangkok for two reasons—sex and drugs. And these weren't people who had any kind of interest in either little boys or girls. The best and cheapest smack in the world was available in Thailand.

SILVER: "Bon was in London when I arrived there, he was staying at a friend of mine's place, and I was a bit pissed off actually, because I'd planned on staying there myself. I felt intruded upon by that, because we had this agreement, and he was just there all the time. He couldn't kind of let go."

Angus was dispatched to Australia to promote the release of *Powerage*. "We drew straws to see who'd come, and I lost," he grumbled. Neither the album nor "Rock'n'roll Damnation" made any real impact on the charts there, but at least the album sold steadily enough to go gold by the end of the year.

By the start of July, the band was back on the road in America, where the album was now out, playing support spots anywhere and everywhere with the likes of Rainbow, Alice Cooper, Journey and Aerosmith. They were starting to get a reputation as a bad support act, because they were so good, often upstaging the headliner.

In Chicago, playing in front of 40,000 Summer Jam revelers, they pulled the rug out from under bands higher on the bill, like Foreigner, Aerosmith and Van Halen. Working their way to the West Coast, they did the same thing in Oakland, as Pasadena's *Star-News* reported: "While the big name on the bill was Foreigner . . . it was little known Australian group AC/DC that brought 70,000 fans to their feet . . . The quintet's 10:30 a.m. show aroused the crowd with a moving set of power rock'n'roll."

AC/DC were connecting because they were rock'n'roll and they were real, and American audiences, at least in part, were starting to tire of bland FM radio fodder. It was another sign of the emergence of the new wave.

Back in New York by the start of August, the band repeated a familiar routine, blowing Ritchie Blackmore's Rainbow off stage at the Palladium, before pulling out again for the South. *Powerage* was selling respectably, especially considering it wasn't getting any airplay to speak of.

The road was simply a way of life for AC/DC. On August 12, they headlined over Cheap Trick and Molly Hatchet in Florida stronghold Jacksonville, and sold out 14,000 seats.

"I enjoy touring; I've had some great times," Angus told *Sounds*. "I think touring is what you make of it. I do get fidgety if we have a day off, because touring is geared around twiddling your thumbs and getting ready for the show. If the show's missing, the day just doesn't feel right."

MICHAEL BROWNING: "There were grumblings sometimes, because it's hard for these young guys to appreciate that you can play to 14,000 people in Jacksonville, Florida, and earn whatever it was, 20 or 30 grand, and then you could drive 100 miles up the road and play to 20 people! There were a lot of gigs, I guess, that they questioned. But it was all part of the building process."

"It's sometimes a drag being in a different hotel every night," Bon allowed, "but it's not as bad as being stuck in front of a lathe every day of your life for 50 years. I am here and I am free and I'm seeing new faces every night and touching new bodies or whatever. It's great, there's nothing like it."

"Bon is fine," said Angus. "We call him the old man, but he's always there. And he will be in the future." It was almost as if Angus was trying to convince himself of the fact. He admitted, after all, in a contemporaneous interview, "You can have so many women and so many drunken nights, but it's going to take its toll some day."

Rock'n'roll bands on the road in America don't have to pursue sex and drugs—sex and drugs pursue them. Cocaine is chopped out under your nose. Bon found it difficult to just say no.

Vince Lovegrove and Bon hadn't seen each other in a dog's age when Vince met up with the band in Atlanta, Georgia. After wearing out Adelaide, Vince had moved to Sydney, and then Melbourne, where in 1978, after a stint producing Channel Nine's *Don Lane Show,* he worked up a proposal to make a documentary for Channel Seven on the international emergence of Australian rock'n'roll. AC/DC naturally occupied a prominent place in his script (along with the Little River Band and Air Supply), and so he sought them out. They were playing a show that night at the Atlanta Symphony Hall, with Cheap Trick supporting.

Vince found a lump coming to his throat as he watched from the side of the stage, his old mate "struttin' across the boards like the eternal Peter fuckin' Pan he was . . ." After the show, when Bon had changed out of his ragged denim stage threads into a very flash plaid drape coat he'd just bought, and grabbed the bottle of Scotch that was always included in the band's rider for him, he and Vince repaired to his hotel, the very plush Peach Tree Inn, to catch up.

Vince wrote in *RAM*:

Very impressed, I was. Personal driver, ritzy hotel, the best lookin' groupies I'd ever set eyes on. I mean, it was the real thing. I thought, if anyone deserves it, Bon does. He's been at it for long enough, and at last, he was showing 'em. He said he'd make it and he was making it . . . in style.

Out of the car, and up into Bon's room. Not yer average hotel room, but one that reeked of a very determined effort to emulate all the comforts of a luxurious home away from home.

So there we were. Bon and me, an Australian photographer, a few groupies, and the odd Seedie wandering in and out in an attempt to find the action. Not that there would be too much action in Bon's room that night. The groupies would eventually be bored, the photographer would almost nod off to sleep, room service would be cut off at 2 a.m., and Bon and I became self-indulgent about the good old days . . . and to top it off, there was nothing to smoke. We used the completely legal drug of Scotch to ignite the memory cells.

"I'm getting tired of it all," he finally confessed. We were both wasted. Totally. There were no inhibitions. His burbled confession came as a total, almost sobering shock. I mean, his scenario appeared complete. Success was almost there, and so were its trimmings. And Bon tells me he was getting tired of it; he must be joking.

"No way, Vinnie. I really am getting tired. I love it, you know that. It's only rock'n'roll and I like it. But I want to have a base. It's just the constant pressures of touring that's fucking it. I've been on the road for thirteen years. Planes, hotels, groupies, booze, people, towns. They all scrape something from you. We're doin' it and we'll get there, but I wish we didn't have these crushing day after day grinds to keep up with."

I'd never seen Bon like it. He managed to laugh it off and have another swig. He set a fast pace, the old Bon, but if you dug deep enough, you found an accumulative exhaustion that threatened to sap his upfront energy.

"Rock'n'roll, you know that's all there is," he said. "But I can't hack the rest of the shit that goes with it."

From the South, the band dashed across the continent to the Northwest, where they played shows with Aerosmith, before dropping in on LA for a headline show of their own at the Starwood. In September, they played a few more dates with Aerosmith through the Midwest before heading back to Britain.

Aerosmith, then hitting their drug-addled midcareer crisis, suffered in the face of AC/DC's hunger and were regularly blown off stage. In LA, AC/DC managed to drive a typically jaded LA audience "wild and calling for encore after encore."

The band wasn't exempt from crises of its own though. If Bon was beginning to feel, if not show, the strain, it also was around this time that Phil Rudd buckled under it. Phil had always been highly strung, and in the bleak American Midwest heartland, he was suffering what might only be described as an acute case of white-line fever.

SILVER: "When Phil cracked up, Bon was pretty upset about it. I mean, Bon wasn't one to rock the boat, but he was pretty freaked out by the way they just propped Phil up and made him perform.

"I think it was a bit of a strain for Bon too, because he did all the PR. Like, if there was a radio station, Bon had to do all that, pretty much.

"And I mean, that's what happened to Phil, because he was doing a lot of the driving as well. And because he was the quiet type. I mean, I'm getting this second hand, I'm getting this from Bon, what happened to Phil."

Like Bon, Phil was a dedicated pot-smoker. He was also always partial to a toot. Put that together with life on the road itself, and the result can be pure paranoid dementia. Phil was a mess. On a couple of occasions, he had to be hauled off to hospital for sedation.

SILVER: "Instead of, like, giving him some time out . . . there was no actual concern for Phil's long-term well-being. And basically, that was pretty much their attitude to Bon too, with his drinking. Nobody really seemed to give a shit that he was killing himself, as long as he got out there and did it. If I wasn't there to make sure he caught the right plane, then someone else would be, and that was it. As long as they could do the job on the night."

Bon wrote to Irene:

Hi there. Tis about four in the morn (Mon) . . . the bar's closed . . . the bottle of Black Jack [Daniels] is empty . . . we're outta dope . . . the TV's finished . . . I don't have anybody to fuck . . . I've dropped a quaalude [downer] . . . I could go on all night but I won't . . . We're two days from the finish of our US summer tour . . . It's been fourteen weeks and of course we did a month in England before that. We have six days off before touring Europe and England again for a month . . . Boring innit. I should be back in Sydney around Nov 16th. We're recording for maybe a month and hopefully January will be off . . . Now I've had days off since I joined this band . . . But not one whole thirty-one day month.

The band landed back in Britain in October, just as the live album *If You Want Blood, You've Got It* was released, a mere six months after *Powerage*. Alberts had been planning a greatest hits album called *Twelve of the Best*, but at the last minute changed its mind. The greatest hits in live form would obviously extend the album's appeal and indeed, while *If You Want Blood* wasn't exactly planned, it turned out to be the record that paved the way for AC/DC's breakthrough. Live albums, which tended to be double or triple sets in which songs short in their studio versions were stretched out into extended tedium, were for some reason popular in the seventies. *If You Want Blood* reversed that trend. Culled by George and Harry from tapes "recorded live" (as the sleeve notes asserted) "during Australian, UK and American tours," the album was indeed just like an AC/DC gig. Packaged simply, bearing the indelible image of Angus impaled by his own axe, with Bon glancing over his shoulder, it boasted a blunt ten tracks and, allowing for nothing extraneous, got straight to the point, that being raging AC/DC rock'n'roll. For a band whose forte was live performance, it was the perfect souvenir, and the punters responded accordingly. In Britain, they pushed it to number 13, a new high for the band.

In America, it propelled AC/DC into the top 50 for the first time. In Australia, the album went unreleased until Christmas, by which time it was quite apparent the authorities were still not going to relent and allow the band to tour the country, which would ideally have promoted the release of *If You Want Blood*. The band was suffering for this stupid stalemate. The album sold slowly.

At the end of October, the band embarked on yet another British tour, playing 16 dates in 18 days. They would return to Australia after that—as had become their tradition—to spend Christmas at home, and cut a new album at Alberts.

The British tour was an unqualified success.

At the Glasgow Apollo, legend has it, Bon got lost backstage after walking the floor with Angus, and then managed to lock himself out of the theatre. The only way he could convince the stagedoor bouncers that he was, in fact, the evening's attraction, was to ask them, Why else would I be running around in the freezing cold without a shirt on? Asked about the incident a couple of days later, Bon said, "I can't remember that—it was two days ago."

DAVE JARRETT: "They had this incredible work ethic, and the fact was that each time they made a record, it seemed to be so much better. So it became a matter of how many Hammersmith Odeons you were going to do."

In America too, they were finally taking off. The success of *If You Want Blood* reflected on *Powerage*, and by year's end, its sales, at over 150,000 units, outstripped those of the previous two albums combined. Even *Rolling Stone,* which had studiously ignored the band since mercilessly panning *High Voltage* in 1976, was starting to take notice. A news story ran in its November 16 issue. It read in part, "Bon Scott mentions some influences that are difficult to glean from listening to his music. He is particularly impressed by the way Frank Zappa has been able to manipulate his image over the years. Fondly remembering the old PHI ZAPPA KRAPPA poster of Frank sitting on the toilet, Bon suggests a successor: 'Bon Scott pulling himself.'"

In London to play two concluding shows at the Hammersmith Odeon, Bon was shunted into Atlantic's offices to drink the liquor cabinet dry whilst doing phone interviews with the press in other parts of the world. He spoke to the *Herald* in Melbourne, claiming success hadn't spoiled him. "All that has changed is my intake of alcohol. I can now afford to drink twice as much."

Talking to David Fricke in New York for a feature on the band which would be published in *Circus Weekly* in January, he bemoaned the lack of critical acuity applied to AC/DC in Britain even as the band scaled the heights. "This guy came to see us at Leeds University. We did two encores that night and the crowd went wild. Then I read the review next week and he puts shit on the crowd—"How could 2,000 mindless people like this bunch of idiots". He didn't see what we were doing for the crowd and what they were doing for us."

Bon went on, "There's been an audience waiting for an honest rock'n'roll band to come along and lay it on 'em. There's a lot of people coming out of the woodwork to see our kind of rock. And they're not the same people who would go to see James Taylor or a punk band."

Asked about the band's unrelenting touring, Bon kept up a brave face. "It keeps you fit—the alcohol, nasty women, sweat on stage, bad food—it's all very good for you!"

But Fricke asked, what if his voice ever gave out?

"Then I'd become a roadie," Bon replied matter-of-factly.

The two sold-out Odeon shows the band played on November 15 and 16 merely confirmed their status. Atlantic threw a party backstage after the first night's show. Bon proceeded to get so drunk that in the wee hours, according to *Melody Maker*'s Steve Gett, he "needed the stomach pump before getting to his feet again."

Success, for Bon, was bittersweet. He had no one to share it with and no home to go to.

Angus and Bon: definitely not the Glimmer Twins.

14. HIGHWAY TO HELL

"If Bon Scott is lucky," Pat Bowring reported in the Melbourne *Sun* on December 9, 1978, "he'll see his parents in Perth at Christmas."

"I haven't seen them for three years," Bon, back in Sydney, told Bowring. "I hope they recognize me."

"Some of the guys in the band are buying places here this time," he continued. "I'm not. I've bought a bike. That's all I want. I'll sleep on that. Besides, I'm too young to settle down!"

With his Kawasaki 900 throbbing between his legs, Bon found a flat in O'Brien Street in Bondi. Moving in, he said to Pat Pickett, "You know, Pat, this is the first time I've ever had a flat of my own." Bon was still aching for Silver, but this new, forward-looking experience was some compensation.

The band was waiting for the nod to go into Alberts to start work on a new album. Bon threw himself into a strict regimen, getting up at 8:30 every morning to go for a swim, eating well, and drinking only sake—in moderation—in anticipation of a likely tour of Japan in February. He was working up ideas for the new album.

All the band's plans, however, were about to come undone. Bon wasn't lucky enough to make it to Perth for Christmas or anything else. In fact, the developments of the next month or so would be the most traumatic AC/DC had ever endured.

The story broke late in January when Pat Bowring reported, "The Vanda-Young songwriting and production team may not be working on the next AC/DC record." The storm had been brewing for some time, right back, perhaps, to the very beginning of AC/DC's relationship with Atlantic in America. The records AC/DC were selling in America were due to the band's live profile, not because they were getting any airplay.

MICHAEL BROWNING: "Atlantic, at that time, quite clearly felt that they weren't getting records delivered that were radio-friendly, soundwise, for the American market. And it was true."

First thing in the new year, Atlantic's Michael Klenfner flew in to Sydney from New York. His mind was already made up. AC/DC needed a hit single. George and Harry were off the case. Within a week, a new producer had arrived in Sydney and started working with the band.

BROWNING: "Klenfner's idea was to get a guy called Eddie Kramer involved. And so Eddie Kramer was flown out to Australia and met the band, and then the band flew over to Florida and did some pre-production with him—they were virtually forced into using this guy."

Never one to give anything away, especially to the press, George seemed to take it all in stride. Privately, though, he was fuming. He had made all this possible only now to be unceremoniously dumped. Malcolm and Angus were equally taken aback.

BROWNING: "Outwardly, there were no signs, but I think Malcolm and Angus felt very strange. I think they felt like their brother had been shafted, and that I was part of that process, or that I'd allowed the record company to get away with it."

Bon too was perturbed, but he also knew that his was not to reason why. He'd seen the axe come down before, and though blood might be thicker than water, Malcolm and Angus were also extremely ambitious. Maybe the Yanks were right, anyway. Besides, if the band didn't go along with the idea, they could expect few favors, if any, from Atlantic in the future. They agreed to work with Kramer. Kramer's claim to fame was that he had engineered Jimi Hendrix, and more recently he'd produced Kiss. He came on more like a cigar-chewing hustler than a music man.

Malcolm and Angus assuaged their guilt at George's sacking by blaming Michael Browning. From this point on, things would never be the same again. What had been defensive insularity now escalated into full-blown paranoia. It was an atmosphere of fear and loathing that would increase for years to come, and it only exacerbated Bon's growing sense of dislocation.

BROWNING: "I think it was really a question of, all bets are off."

Bon was running late, as usual, when he was due one night at the Darling-hurst studios of alternative radio station 2JJ for an interview. Presenter Pam Swain was becoming anxious. She'd been warned about Bon; she'd been told, among other things, that she should have a bottle of something waiting for him. All she could afford was a can of beer. It sat on the desk getting warm.

When he did finally show up, he didn't touch the beer. He and Pam became so absorbed in the interview that they continued talking together in the studio even after the show was over. Pam liked the guy, found him funny, warm, and sincere, for all his ladykiller charm. When Bon finally climbed on his bike to leave, he promised to give her a call, maybe they'd go out together sometime.

The band was rehearsing at Alberts, putting material together. Kramer was sitting in. Bon took Pam to the speedway out at Parramatta. It was a lovely night, Pam remembers, marred only by the speeding ticket they got on the ride home.

Pam invited Bon over to a lunch she was having the next day, not expecting him to come. But come he did. The scene was quite outside Bon's experience—polite society almost, the intellectual types that tend to work at the Australian Broadcasting Corporation (2JJ's parent company)—but Bon was the life of the party. Pam was smitten.

All this was enough to keep Bon's mind off his deeper woes. The theft of his bike a couple of days later, however, threw him back into a spin. At least it wouldn't be long before the band left for Japan. A farewell party was held at the Strata Inn, a pub in Cremorne. Bon, Malcolm and Angus got up with George on bass and Ray Arnott on drums and played a few numbers. It would be Bon's last ever performance on Australian soil.

On his last night in town, Pam arranged to meet Bon at the Lifesaver after she'd finished work. When she got there, he was nowhere to be seen. She raced back to the radio station, thinking he might have got the arrangements mixed up. He wasn't there either. She went back to the Life-saver, but still he hadn't shown up. She was dismayed more than anything else. Bon was about to go away indefinitely, and they weren't going to see each other again. She drove home across the bridge cursing him. Bon, meantime, had managed to climb through a window into her bedroom, and was in repose when she got there. All that was missing was a rose between his teeth.

Needless to say, Pam's flatmate was horrified when this ravaged, tattooed figure emerged the next morning and went straight to the fridge for a beer for breakfast.

But the band wouldn't be going to Japan, after all. At the last minute, visas were denied. Bon killed a couple more days at Pam's place while new flights were booked—the band would now be going straight to Miami.

RAM's Stuart Coupe met up with the band in the departure lounge. Bon, he said, who had Pam on his arm, was "batfaced." "True to form and reputation he informs my female companion she 'should look after that great body.' He looks me up and down and continues, 'and if he doesn't, let me know and you can have my phone number.'"

AC/DC were not enamoured of either Eddie Kramer or Miami. "This time of year, it's an Elephant's Graveyard for geriatric Jews and totally boring," Bon wrote to Maria. Maria and her husband Jim had just had their first child, and Bon extended his hearty congratulations on the "wean."

Bon wrote further to Uncle:

> Atlantic reckoned we should use a top Yank producer and appointed one Eddie Kramer to the post. It turns out the guy was full of bullshit and couldn't produce a healthy fart. He was a good engineer with a big mouth ("I can hear this note . . .") and a lot of front. We gave him the arse and got hold of one John Lange who we start work with on Wednesday in London.

MICHAEL BROWNING: "I got a phone call from Malcolm in Florida, to say, This guy's hopeless, do something, he's trying to talk us into recording that Spencer Davis song, "Gimme Some Loving", "I'm a Man", whatever it was . . .

"Three weeks in Miami and we hadn't written a thing with Kramer," Bon told *RAM*. "So one day we told him we were going to have the day off and not to bother coming in. This was Saturday, and we snuck into the studio and on that one day we put down six songs, sent the tape to Lange and said, Will you work with us?"

These demos were cut by Malcolm, Angus and Bon, with Bon playing drums, as had become their practice.

BROWNING: "I was at that stage based temporarily in New York, I'd met some people who'd invited me to stay with them, one of whom was Mutt Lange's manager, Clive Calder. I got the phone call from Malcolm, and I got off the phone, and Mutt was there, in the apartment, and I said, You've got to do this record. At the time, Mutt had really only done City Boy, the Boomtown Rats, but I happened to think he was incredibly talented. So within a couple of days they agreed to do the record."

But not before Michael Klenfner lost his job over the matter. It was Klenfner who had foisted Eddie Kramer on the band, and he disagreed violently with the idea of now getting in Lange. But if Michael Browning ever had a reputation for being soft, he stood firm this time. Klenfner was left out in the cold. The band flew to London to start work with Lange.

Bon's letter to Uncle continued:

A couple of days later: Landed in London yesterday on one of those beautiful rain-drenched two-degree mornings. Today's not much better. Gee, it's great to be back . . . We meet our new producer tonight and hit him with fifteen songs that need shaping. My fingers are crossed.

Robert John "Mutt" Lange was a South African who, after getting his start in music as a singer and songwriter, crossed to the other side of the mixing desk. He was reported to have felt on trial with AC/DC initially. But the band—unused to outsiders in the studio—felt vulnerable, too. Over time, they developed a guarded respect for one another.

BROWNING: "It turned out, he was the best person on earth to do it."

The band virtually moved into the Roadhouse Studios in Chalk Farm, spending the best part of three months there. That, to start with, was a shock to AC/DC, who had never previously spent more than three weeks on any one album.

Highway to Hell—as the completed album was called, after the name Angus had given the band's last American tour—was as much of a progression upon *Powerage* as *Let There Be Rock* was on *Dirty Deeds*. But more than that, it was ground-breaking in any terms.

"Mutt was brought up on the rough side of town, which helped him in the studio," Malcolm told *RAM*. "He's like Harry, a bit more commercial. We learnt a lot. You really need an outsider because we can all go too far and disappear up our own anuses."

Sessions for the album—15 hours a day, day-in day-out, for over two months—were grueling. Songs were worked and reworked. Staying at the Swiss Cottage Inn, Bon bore up under the prolonged pressure, maintaining a brave face, but none felt it more deeply than he did.

SILVER: "He was a bit lost. I mean, I still ran his bank account for him. He was never in one place long enough to keep it together. He got used to me organizing everything, keeping the bills paid, all that sort of stuff. Plus the emotional stuff—like, he was no longer in a relationship that he was dependent on—stuff like that."

Silver was herself by then a fully-fledged junkie.

The album was finished at the end of June, having been mixed relatively quickly at Basing Street Studios, near Ladbroke Grove, in eight days. Lange managed to inject a greater sweep into the band's sound on *Highway to Hell*, and it was this, plus the smoother touch of melodic backing vocals, but without losing any of the band's characteristic dynamic crunch, that gave the album its poise and potency.

The title track, which opens the album, assumes anthemic proportions even before Bon's vocal comes in. Few albums in rock open quite so ominously, and few, as this one proceeds, are ultimately quite as monolithic. Bon's lyrics were more universal—few characters appeared in the songs and the narratives were more compact—but they were no less evocative. His turn of phrase, and better-balanced vocalizing, counterpointed perfectly the band's controlled explosive grind. Every track except "Love Hungry Man," which the band quickly disowned, became an AC/DC staple. Mutt Lange had achieved precisely what George and Harry couldn't—a blend of accessible polish and raw power which satisfied both the band and Atlantic.

MICHAEL BROWNING: "When they were in England recording, I spent a fair bit of time in Australia, so I wasn't really part of that process. I was also having a few immigration problems with America, so I was waiting for that to be resolved too. I next saw the group in New York, after they finished making the record. By that time, I think a few American management companies had started to sniff around.

"At that point we were strapped financially, the whole thing had put such a strain on the whole financial system, and so this guy Peter Mensch, from Leber & Krebs [one of the most powerful US artist management companies at the time], had damaged my position, and so I think they were quite impressed by the prospects in that."

Alberts was already deep in the hole (touring America as a support band is a money-losing proposition), and simply couldn't afford to increase the amount they were putting into AC/DC. Michael Browning had been talking to an upstate New York promoter by the name of Cedric Kushner with regards to him buying in on the operation. Malcolm and Angus were understandably reluctant to see another outsider staking a claim on them. It didn't help, either, that Kushner was questioning the band's deal with Alberts, among other things. It was clear that it was now time to give Browning the chop, too.

PERRY COOPER: "He [Browning] was getting pressured by a lot of people; people were going over his head at times. The band had its own mind—and when they make up their mind, they don't talk to anybody about it. So whatever happened—Michael gave his all for that band. But they're as tough as nails, these guys. There's an old saying, Off the charts, outta your hearts, and when you're off their charts, forget it. But the guys, I've gotta say, they always were very cooperative with us."

Leber & Krebs co-founder David Krebs first encountered AC/DC in England in 1977. After the band's American agent Doug Thaler took him to see them, Krebs proposed a co-management deal to Michael Browning. Browning rejected the idea, but nevertheless Thaler worked with Krebs to get AC/DC some choice support slots with top acts Leber & Krebs represented, such as Aerosmith and Ted Nugent.

Leber & Krebs had been formed in 1972, when Krebs and Steve Leber left the William Morris Agency to set up their own operation. They made a mint out of musicals like *Jesus Christ Superstar* and *Beatlemania;* then, in 1974, whilst also acting as US agents for Focus, Argent and Hawkwind, they took on management of Aerosmith and Nugent. In 1977, those two clients alone grossed them nearly ten million dollars.

Leber & Krebs capitalized on the fact that, as Steve Leber once explained to financial magazine *Forbes,* "an unknown group couldn't walk into Citibank and get a loan if they tried to use their talent as collateral. But we're willing to be the banker for the artist."

The marriage of Leber & Krebs and AC/DC was made in heaven. Not only could Leber & Krebs inject cash into AC/DC, but the band was impressed by their aggressive, evasive style. In return, AC/DC was just the hot prospect that might give Leber & Krebs a further boost. Malcolm himself wanted Peter Mensch to handle the band personally. Though Mensch was a relatively lowly Leber & Krebs accountant, he'd befriended AC/DC when they were on the road supporting Aerosmith.

Michael Browning still had a year to serve on his contract, but he accepted a payoff. His removal provided some comfort, at least, to the smarting George back in Sydney, though he thought the settlement was too generous. Browning, of course, thought it was too little.

Bon had no strong feelings either way about Browning, but he was saddened to see the end of Coral, whom he'd always liked. He stayed in contact with her when she moved to LA, calling her regularly.

Browning himself returned to Australia and continues to this day to work at a high level in the music business. On the immediate rebound from AC/DC in 1980, he formed Deluxe Records, the label that first signed, among several other fledgling pub bands, INXS.

MICHAEL BROWNING: "It was hurtful, no doubt about it. I personally think I did a pretty amazing job. Sure, we made a couple of mistakes here and there, but it was a pioneering situation. And what made it more hurtful was that over the years, everyone, me included, with the Youngs and AC/DC, tends to get written out of history. It's like you never existed. Even Mutt Lange, who did an amazing job of delivering to Atlantic Records exactly what they wanted, it's like, Mutt Who?'

AC/DC hit the road again in America in 1979 at the end of June, with *Highway to Hell* due out in a matter of weeks. *If You Want Blood* was still selling, had by then, in fact, surpassed the quarter-million mark, neatly maintaining the rising curve of the band's sales. The band would play its own first stadium headline tour, through partisan territory like Texas and the South.

Atlantic had high hopes for *Highway to Hell*. Perry Cooper said at the time: "I don't believe you can break an act in the United States 100 per cent by touring. It takes you to a certain level and then drops dead. The only thing I can equate AC/DC with over here are Cheap Trick and Van Halen. They've both toured extensively over the years and neither one of them has broken from touring. They've created albums that are a little bit more acceptable and bang! they've become platinum artists. AC/DC can do that too."

Bon called Pam Swain to invite her to join him on the road. He also asked her a favor—could she get him some money from Alberts? A thousand dollars would do. The request struck Pam as strange, but she told Bon she'd do what she could.

Highway to Hell was released simultaneously in Britain and America on July 27. It immediately registered the desired response—good reviews in Britain, and airplay in America.

Even the arch *NME* now had to come to the party, though it wasn't without snide qualification. "THE GREATEST ALBUM EVER MADE (IN AUSTRALIA)," read the headline, the review going on to describe AC/DC as "a band who practice the science of overstatement to a ludicrous degree and succeed."

Highway to Hell quickly became AC/DC's first British top-ten album, going to number eight, and their first to crack the American top 20, peaking there at number 17. European returns were also very encouraging. Stalwart support continued in Germany and Scandinavia, while the single went to number 15 in Holland in its first week of release, and France too

AC/DC promo shot from 1979 featuring bassist Cliff Williams (second from left), who joined after Mark Evans was fired.

looked better than ever.

This was the big time. Strangely, Bon was still harping on to Pam about the money. Maybe it was because the band was caught in the transition between Browning and Leber & Krebs that there was no cash around; whatever, Bon seemed desperate.

In Australia, the single was released first, in August, and it climbed to number 24, marking the return of AC/DC to the charts after an absence of nearly three years. When the album followed in October, it completed the strategy of reestablishing the band in Australia. After the last two albums had failed to chart altogether, *Highway to Hell* went up to number 13.

The road snaked its way to the Midwest. Billed as an "Australian-Scottish new wave punk band," AC/DC were special guests on good friends Cheap Trick's gala fourth of July show in their hometown of Rockford, Illinois.

Pam Swain joined the band in Chicago, and traveled with them to Omaha, Nebraska. She felt like she really shouldn't have been there. Bon seemed distracted, a different person altogether to the one he had been in Sydney. It wouldn't have helped his mood that Pam couldn't bring any money either. Alberts had refused to write a check. But Bon still tried to accommodate Pam.

With a full entourage numbering 25, the band was by now travelling in greater style, which meant a fitted-out bus. It was a home away from home that could never be. But Bon didn't have a home to go to anyway. He was just another weary traveler on that lost highway.

"Some days you wake up and you never want to see the blokes again," tour manager Ian Jeffery told Pam. "But those days never come near the others when you can see what you're working for—five, ten, 15 thousand people shouting their heads off for the group."

That was what kept Bon going too. "I'm in love with rock'n'roll, that grows, you know," he told KSJO San Jose radio show *Livewire*. "I'm more in love with a couple of things, but . . . I was in love with one, but, ahh, she left me . . . I just hope rock'n'roll never leaves me."

Bon fed off the crowd, finding fresh inspiration for songs he'd sung literally hundreds of times. Fifteen thousand faceless heads, all bobbing in unison, hair swinging, arms outstretched, fists punching the air, just a-spittin' at the moon.

The band was still playing a lot of the same songs they were when they first arrived in Britain over three years ago, still opening the set with "Live Wire," and running through "Problem Child," "The Jack," "High Voltage" and "Rocker." "Riff Raff" and "Sin City" were more recent, off *Powerage*, but even "Let There Be Rock," "Bad Boy Boogie," "Hell Ain't a Bad Place To Be" and "Whole Lotta Rosie"—the band's standard encore—were over two years old. But as a support act, you can't afford to muck around.

They say that performing is like making love to an audience, and yet then at the end of the night you find yourself alone in a hotel room. But if the experience is less like making love than having sex, Bon was always prepared to personalize his audience. A lot of artists won't do that, preferring to remain inside their cocoon. But Bon was too much a true man of the people. He happily spent time with fans—and not just groupies—having a drink and a smoke, entertaining them; perhaps it allayed his loneliness.

"Often he would trail off with fans who came back after a show," Angus later told *Sounds*. "He took people as they were and if they invited him somewhere and he was in the mood to go, he went."

For a story she wrote for *RAM*, Pam asked Bon on the record whether life on the road was glamorous.

"Bloody oath," he replied almost indignantly. "What do you think I do it for? The money, or the music? I do it for the glamour. The women and the whisky . . . What else is there in life? Let me think . . ."

"You get used to being on the road," Malcolm said. "You can get boozed up like Bon. He can get right out of it. Then you get sick and have to stop drinking. Now I've learnt to pace myself it works better, because you've got so many hassles all the time."

Privately, Bon was talking a lot about settling down. He was telling Pam he wanted to buy a house somewhere.

On July 30, 1979 a headline ran in the Melbourne *Herald*: "TWO SHOT AS FANS RIOT AT AC/DC SHOW." Sharing a bill with Ted Nugent, Aerosmith, Journey and Thin Lizzy, the band had appeared at a huge open-air gig in Cleveland, Ohio, which turned very ugly. One youth was killed and another seriously wounded when a gunman let loose among the crowd of over 60,000. Three hundred police were called in. Over the course of the day, nine people were treated for stab wounds and 75 were arrested, mainly on drug charges.

Bon later claimed that AC/DC knew nothing, at the time, of this unrest, but it can't not have touched the band. At least, that's what Pam Swain thinks. She had got off the bus in Omaha to go to New York for a stay, and when the band got there, a few weeks later on August 11—to open for Ted Nugent at Madison Square Garden—she found Bon to be more remote, dark even. Maybe it was just her, she thought, but maybe it was other things too. Maybe it was the kid shot dead in Cleveland. Maybe it was just all the pressure. Maybe it was the booze and drugs—Bon was gobbling down pills by the handful. Maybe he was just having a bad few days. Pam would never see Bon again after that.

Molly Meldrum was in New York for the Madison Square Garden show. He saw a different Bon. "He was as fine as ever. He was being warned by the doctors, Stop drinking, and I said to him, Are you going to stop drinking? He said, Of course not. I've never been sick for a day in my life, and I think that's one of the reasons why! Any germs that get into my body, Johnnie Walker goes, Pow!"

PERRY COOPER: "As far as the drugs and stuff? I mean, he did a little blow—and everybody was doing it—and he had his marijuana, but he never got to the point where he had to have it, or he was paranoid."

The band had been invited by the Who to appear with them on a one-off London show at Wembley Stadium on August 18. It was an offer even AC/DC couldn't refuse. The Who were one of the few bands Malcolm and Angus had any time for, and so it was an honor to be asked to share the stage as they made their return to live performance after a three-year hiatus, and debuted new drummer, former Small Face Kenny Jones, who had filled the chair left vacant by the death of wild man Keith Moon. As such, the Who wanted to make a grand entrance, and so a bill was assembled that was meant to stand as a sort of state-of-the-rock roll call. It featured the latest American guitar-slinger Nils Lofgren, and new wave old farts, the Stranglers, as well as AC/DC. The gig stamped AC/DC with a seal of approval and broadened their scope further.

Checking into the Swiss Cottage Holiday Inn, Bon was pleased just to get back to London, where at least he had a few friends. And old friends were becoming dearer to him as it became increasingly difficult to tell who your real friends were.

JOE FUREY: "Touring all the time, you can become cut off from people, you're unable to sustain friendships. You just end up living the whole rock'n'roll stereotype on the road. Bon knew how important it was, keeping that family of friends he had together. People like percys, they keep that side of an artist's life intact. You've got to have that infrastructure, and I think when Coral Browning went, you lose that, when you suddenly go with another management company that doesn't know."

SILVER: "Once they signed with Leber & Krebs, it was getting to be big business by then, the personal touch was gone. That social thing, where you saw everybody around, was over. The band had their respective lives they were leading. Angus was close to getting married. Malcolm was with Linda. Cliff had a girlfriend, and an ex-wife he saw as well. So it was fragmented socially."

JOE: "A lot of the time, when Bon lobbed into London, he was just completely hanging loose. So in a lot of ways, that was the relationship Bon and I had, because he could always get in contact with me when he got to town, and I'd know where so-and-so was, you know."

Joe was then working as a Percy for UFO guitarist Paul Chapman.

JOE: "The feeling in London when Peter Mensch came in and started trying to run AC/DC was that he was just like somebody's nephew or something, you know, an accountant who was related to the boss at Leber & Krebs in New York, where it was like, let's give Peter a job, you know—and he came in, like, This is the way it should be done. He was treating it like you would have run a factory, you know, and it doesn't work like that. Bon would only get a phone call from them when they had something for him to do.

"But he worked within it. Those last couple of months, there was defi-nitely the feeling, I mean, they were the hottest band in the world. They knew they could blow anybody off the stage. And Bon was aware of that too. But he was never one to bitch about things, and that comes back to his professionalism. He was smart enough not to do that. He was going to reap the bounty of what he'd just spent 20 years pushing to do."

The Who's Wembley show was indeed a "gathering of the tribes," as hippies, punks, old and revival mods, and headbangers alike all made their way in the summer sun down to the famous Twin Towers. But between the tepid Nils Lofgren and the turgid Stranglers, it was only AC/DC who aroused the crowd's unanimous enthusiasm. Read *Juke*'s review of the show: "AC/DC are not "good" or "bad". They are perfect AC/DC, a heavy metal archetype overblown to the point where stereotype meets parody. Is Bon Scott serious or what? Is he just playing out a real-life comic strip of an HM lead singer? Do they smirk when they write those giant three-chord riffs? Or do they just know that the world will love something this crass?"

After repeating the performance supporting the Who again at a couple of similar European summer festivals, the band flew back to America more confident than ever. The rest of the year was mapped out for them: after doing another lap of America, they would return to Britain in late October to tour, then tour Europe, and then they'd be free to head downunder, as usual, for Christmas.

Bon wrote to Irene late in August:

Hi kid, how's tricks. At the moment I'm in California to start our Fall tour. We've been running round like blue-arsed flies this past couple of months between America, Europe and the UK doing all kinds of concerts, TV shows and promotion shit for the new album. Have you heard it yet? I don't even know if it's been released in Australia yet. It's on the charts all over the world and selling like hot crumpet. I think we've done it with this one. Should be able to pay the rent for a couple of years. I wanna buy a house in California, a place like Fraternity had. I have some friends here who are in the real estate business and I've had some good offers but it'll take another year and I'm in no hurry. It's just a nice feeling to know you can do it at last . . .

I might get a chance to see you round Christmas-New Year. I plan to get to Sydney round the 23rd of Dec, buy a bike and ride to Perth. I've got a couple of weeks off and I just want to take it easy and unwind (this touring takes it out of you) . . . I'm still a very single man and having a ball right now. America's certainly the place for a good time. I've become a bit of an alco (what's new) but I'll cut down when I go on holiday and leave off for a couple of hours . . . I'm not doing a lot of letter writing at the moment you might have noticed but I'm always thinking of you. Say hi to Graeme if he's still alive.

The band toured America through September, into October, headlining exclusively in big venues over bands like Molly Hatchett, Sammy Hagar and Pat Travers. Bon somehow still managed to find enough energy to get into trouble.

A famous incident was recalled by Angus: "We were going from California to Austin, Texas, and we stopped off at Phoenix for fuel. We were just taking off again when someone says, Where's Bon? He'd followed this bird off the plane and we reckoned he'd drunk so much he wouldn't even know which country he was headed for . . ."

"We'd been drinking in the airport bar for about ten minutes," Bon picked up the story, "when I says, Don't you think it's time we caught our plane? She says, What do you mean our plane? I'm staying here. I run back and the fuckin' flight's gone." Bon went on to describe, true or otherwise, the night he spent in a Mexican bar whipping all the regulars on the pool table, before he was chased off by a fierce-looking black lady of Rosie-esque proportions. He managed to get on another flight to Austin just in time to make the gig.

With "Girl's Got Rhythm" out as a single in Britain, the tour the band was due to start there on October 26 was practically sold out before they left America. They didn't even stop over in London on their way to Newcastle, where the first gig was at the Mayfair.

DAVE JARRETT: "I flew up to Newcastle, and when we got there, there'd been a small fire in the hall, so they had to cancel that night's show. So I thought, Alright! Back to the hotel, party time! The band all went to bed. It was just me and the road crew. I think they were all just so tired."

Prior to concluding in Leicester on November 9, the tour played an unprecedented four-night stand at the Hammersmith Odeon, which unequivocally confirmed AC/DC's status in Britain as, simply, one of the biggest bands on the circuit.

The band then headed to Europe. They were accompanied by freelance photographer Robert Ellis, who had somehow convinced a "loud American" (Peter Mensch) that he could serve the band well. He wrote later of

Bon: "Like Keith Moon, he was a real danger to himself and needed constant minding . . . but he was nearly always the first down in the lobby of a morning, spruced up and ready to go. I warned him and anyone within earshot of the impending danger, but no one took much notice, least of all him."

Due to public demand, another, albeit shorter, tour of Britain had been hastily arranged for the first week of December. Two more shows at the Hammersmith Odeon were locked in. The tour's first gig, at Southampton, had to be cancelled when a leg muscle Bon had pulled in Europe became inflamed.

JOE FUREY: "That was the sort of period when Bon . . . well, when he'd come to town before, he was very much the rock'n'roller on the make. But at that point when he came back to London, he almost had a statesman's air about him, a sort of serenity. I said, So you reckon you've made it? and he said, Yeah; not boasting, but satisfied. He knew that he was financially set for the rest of his life regardless."

Getting back on his feet, Bon climbed aboard a bus bound for the Midlands. He had an unexpected passenger in tow, Mick Cocks of Rose Tattoo, or rather, formerly of Rose Tattoo. Mick had arrived in London in November, after leaving the Tatts under something of a cloud.

MICK COCKS: "Bon said, Look, I'm going on tour with the band, why don't you come? I said, yeah, alright. He wanted some company, he was pretty lonely. I figured, he was playing in a band, but that doesn't mean he's got friends, right?

"What Bon would do, was go and have a drink with people he didn't really know, and because he was sort of famous, you'd get a lot of hangers-on. He knew who was leeching off him and who wasn't, but he'd reached the stage where he didn't really care. He just wanted the company.

"The first four days on the bus, I just sat there before anyone actually spoke to me from the rest of the band. It was a coach, a 40-seater coach, and so Malcolm would sit up the front with his entourage, and Angus had his posse, the rhythm section theirs, and so I just sat up the back there with Bon. The band gave me the impression they were very set in their ways. Every band has its own way of doing things, but it was like, This is what we have to do. If I had any respect for them it was for that. Then I remember one day, one of the roadies came down and said, Malcolm wants to have a word with you. Just this message. So I went down to Malcolm and said, Yeah, g'day. And he said, Well, what are your intentions? I said, What do you mean? He said, What's the story? I said, Well, Bon asked me to come along with him for the ride. Malcolm knew me well enough, but he was playing the grandfather. So I said, Look, mate, if you think I'm taking advantage of him you've got it all wrong. I was sharing a room with Bon; it wasn't as if they had to spend money on me or anything. And he was just very lonely at the time.

"It gets like that. I'm not putting anybody down, but if you've been in a band for a number of years, it's a bit like having five wives. So what you try and do is, if you can, set up your own little situation that doesn't create friction, then you go with it. It's not unfriendly, it's just the way it is.

"Bon was drinking a bit at the time. But he'd give it a nudge for a while, and then he'd go off it. I think he was looking for some sort of romantic love he knew didn't exist. You know, because he'd stopped chasing girls. He was thinking about other things. In those days he was talking a lot about his ex-wife, saying he had some things there he wanted to sort out. He was doing a lot of thinking, in terms of how he saw things working out."

The two additional Odeon shows were merely a postscript to AC/DC's ascent.

MICK COCKS: "You got the sense, Shit, they're going to go up another level again. That they were really comfortable with what they were doing, and they just needed a bit of luck to kick on even further."

JOE: "I think it was at that point in time that everyone knew it was going to happen. I remember we went to Tramps one night, and we were joking about the bill, which Bon picked up, so things were obviously going well."

MICK COCKS: "He said, Look, I'm going to take you to this restaurant tonight, and he was all giggly. I said, What's the matter? He said, We're going to have steak tartare. I said, I love steak. And so these two piles of pink, raw mince [ground beef] show up, and I say, I'm not eating that! And Bon's sitting there, he says, Okay. He says, Taste it. I say, No. Of course, I'm getting hungrier and hungrier, and so in the end I ate it. It was good.

"The food he'd eat, he was quite fussy about it. After a gig, he'd say, Let's find a restaurant that's open; and we'd go and eat. I was shocked. I mean, I used to tell people, I'd say, Oh, I ate this last night, and they'd say, Ah, get away. They'd say, Who took you? I'd say, Bon. They'd say, Piss off. And liqueurs. He had a cultured side that he liked to . . . I used to call him a toff. He used to laugh at that.

"He never gave me the impression money meant anything to him. The guys in the band, Phil, he'd go out and buy a couple of Ferraris; the bass-player, he was just happy with the security; Malcolm and Angus, I'm not sure, but they always gave me the impression they were pretty level-

headed about it. But Bon was like, well, Fuck the money.

"He was very aware of not owing anyone anything. I remember actually giving him some money one night, not because he didn't have any but because he didn't have any cash, and I remember at the time thinking, well, you know, he'd spent hundreds of pounds on me, wining and dining, and he was like, You've done me a big favor. I thought, it just didn't match the ten quid I'd given him. It was a bit silly, really."

Mick lost sight of Bon then, because Bon went to Australia. AC/DC dropped in on Paris to play a single show with Judas Priest—which was filmed and subsequently released on video as *Let There Be Rock*—and then Bon flew on to Melbourne. He went straight to Mary Walton's place in Prahran, where he was always welcome. Mary's future second husband Peter Renshaw provided him with a serious drinking partner.

Since *Highway to Hell* had put them back on the charts, the band was all the more determined to get an Australian tour together; but now it depended more on Japan falling into place, which would justify the expense of hauling the huge AC/DC roadshow to the eastern hemisphere.

Bon was doing the rounds of all his old haunts, looking up all his old mates. Irene and her boyfriend Nick arrived home one day to find a bottle of Scotch and a few bottles of beer awaiting them on the doorstep. "That'll be Bon," said Irene, who was six months pregnant. "He'll be back."

He did come back, and he got stuck into the grog as Nick fired up a barbie. He talked to Nick about music—Nick was an aspiring musician himself, a blues buff. Bon told him about the solo album he wanted to make (Silver also confirms he wanted to make a solo album).

MARY WALTON: Bon was just fine. He was Bon, as he always was. He was drinking a real lot. Too much probably. And really wasn't eating that well. But that was just because he was partying. He was, by that stage . . . you know, I can imagine Bon getting lonely, getting bored with it all, and really just wanting to settle down, because that was the sort of guy that he was too."

Bon picked up after Christmas and headed west; first stop, Adelaide, where he stayed with Bruce Howe. Band commitments required him to be back in Britain by the middle of January. They were set to record a new album, and Bon was already toying with a few ideas.

BRUCE HOWE: "Bon wasn't particularly happy when I last saw him. He was talking about permanent relationships, having children, stuff like that. He looked dreadful. He seemed to sense, the closer you get to the top, you've still got the same personal life, and that's when he started, for the first time, to have this philosophical conversation with me. You could see, he'd been overseas, it was all starting to get really big, and he was still . . . where do you go? You either have a family, or you chase endless relationships with women that make you feel good, but don't really make you feel good, and the more popular you get, the more money you make, the more you question if it's you people really love or whatever. It was almost like he was admiring the fact that I'd stayed behind. I said, Well, I think I'm as happy as you are, I'd love to be doing what you're doing, but I can't trade off what I've got here.

"We were talking about love. Bon always had this trouble with the word love. That day he drank a full 40-ounce bottle of Johnnie Walker. He got really out of it. He was talking about how I'd stayed in Adelaide, and had a wife and son, and he was saying how he could never do that, and then we started talking about love, and I said, It's only a word, and he said he felt like he could never commit himself totally to one person. He wanted to know why?"

From Adelaide, Bon went to Perth, to see his folks.

ISA: "That time he was home, that's when he told me, This one I'm working on now is going to be it. They were going to hit the top this time. So that must have been that music that was written; they called it *Back in Black*. They had to give it a name, you see, but Ron, I think, did all the words.

"Oh, he used to open the fridge in the morning, and I had to bite my tongue, because I don't like drink. But it was his way of living, I couldnae . . ."

CHICK: "You'd go into any of the rooms in the house and you'd find an empty bottle."

ISA: "He wanted to buy us a house. But we already had the duplex we were in. I said, Ron, we don't need it. He did take us out one day and we went around looking at a bit of ground, to build a house. But it fell through or something.

"And then he went away again. I said, Ron, you ought to make a will. He said, I'm not going to die.

"He said, I don't need to make a will, I'm not going to die."

Although Bon returned to Australia from late 1979 to early 1980, he did not make any public appearances. This photograph shows his last performance on Australian soil, an impromptu one at a party for AC/DC at the Cremorne Strata Inn in Sydney, February 5, 1979. Left to right: drummer Ray Arnott, Angus, Malcolm, Bon, and George Young on bass.

15. FEBRUARY 1980

Bon arrived back in London at the start of a new year and a new decade. He had just over a month to live.

Before anything else, he found a flat in Victoria, not far from Buckingham Palace. Located in a block called Ashley Court, it was small but nice. Silver lent him a few things to help set up house. He liked things neat and tidy.

Bon then went off to France, to play seven gigs in seven days (January 16–23) and still manage to drop in on the annual MIDEM music industry convention in Cannes, where AC/DC collected a pile of precious metal records. France awarded them two golds—one each for *If You Want Blood* and *Highway to Hell*—Canada gave them a gold, and Britain, a gold and silver for *Highway to Hell.*

Returning to London, there was little on the calendar to interrupt time designated for writing songs for the new album. Bon was very excited about that, constantly scribbling on scraps of paper and in little blue exercise books that he carried around, in and out of the studio where he was working with Malcolm and Angus, manning the drums. The band still had to honor ticket holders to the two gigs that were cancelled on the last tour, the Newcastle Mayfair and the Southampton Gaumont, which were rescheduled for January 25 and 27 respectively. A *Top of the Pops* appearance was also being organized, to promote the current single "Touch Too Much." And Angus's wedding to his Dutch girlfriend Ellen was on. But that was all.

A great deal of this time Bon spent with a Japanese girl he met known as Anna "Baba," who moved in with him. Anna was a friend of Ian Jeffery's Japanese wife Suzie. They had been at boarding school together in London in 1976. Anna went back to Japan to complete her education and as soon as she was able she returned to London, which she loved so much. "The best time in my life it could be. Indeed it was. The best thing and the worst thing happened to me there then."

Anna got in contact with her friend Suzie as soon as she arrived back in London. On January 27, she was invited over to the Jefferys' for Sunday dinner, and afterwards, maybe they'd go to Southampton to see AC/DC.

ANNA: "Had a Sunday dinner with Bon and Jefferys and ridden in the bus to Southampton with them. When their show starts, I mean, when the singer turn up the stage with shiny smile and rhythm, I knew I was naturally in it. After the music over, all the audience gone and the roadies fixing all the instruments on the stage. Busy. Bon stands there with contented smile. How did you like the show? It was beautiful.

"Back to London, highway to the town. By the time bus stopped around his flat, I've seen him being quite high with a bottle of booze in his hand. Being drunk but not so quietly and gentle. And his back going home alone, unsteady on his feet."

The next morning, Bon phoned Suzie to ask her to ask Anna if she'd like to come over to his flat and cook him a Japanese meal. Anna obliged. Bon wooed her "like the sweetest gentleman."

After going with him to the BBC on February 7 to tape the band's *Top of the Pops* appearance (they performed "Touch Too Much," which would prove to be so prophetic), Anna spent her first night with Bon: "Waking up in the morning with him playing Billy Preston. 'Get dressed,' he says, 'We go to your place and get a couple of things.' We got a cab to Finsbury where I was staying then, but on the way back not a couple of things but all my belongings were with us."

Mick Cocks had by then moved into a flat in Kensington with Joe Furey. "I ran into Bon in Victoria; I went to a gig there one night, and after the gig I just bumped into him. He said, Come back for a drink, so I said, Okay. He was into sake because his girl was Japanese. We'd just be sitting on the couch, and she'd come out with this warm sake in a pot, and we'd get rat-arsed. And then she'd cook. It'd just arrive, so we'd eat.

"She couldn't speak English. Bon was teaching her a bit, and he was learning a bit of Japanese. She was more like the mothering type. She was a sweet girl. Bon liked her. I think he was experimenting. But it was fairly obvious she wasn't going to satisfy any of his deeper needs.

"Drugs were rampant at the time, but I know drugs were not a problem for Bon. It was alcohol, it was a social thing. I'm not saying Bon didn't have the odd toot . . . everyone did, but he was busy writing the new album. He was really positive. He wanted to experiment with his lyrics. He was always

Bon's last appearance with AC/DC, performing "Touch Too Much" on *Top of the Pops*, February 7, 1980.

reading them to me over the phone, and I was encouraging him."

JOE FUREY: "He was constantly having to simplify stuff to fit in with the Youngs' format of the band. Lots of stuff he just didn't even bother showing to them. Like, that line, 'She had the body of Venus with arms'—that would have gone straight over their heads. Like, Who's this Venus, some chick without arms?"

SILVER: "For quite a while after we broke up, I still cashed his checks for him. It was probably only a matter of a couple of months he'd been doing that sort of stuff for himself.

"Getting that flat was a big thing for him. He was kind of really proud of that. I lent him a lot of stuff, because he didn't have anything, you know. But he was quite pleased with himself.

"He was probably a bit more tired in that last while. I think his health just started deteriorating very early in his life."

Bon was in fact seeing a doctor for problems with his liver.

ANNA: "Just the way things seemed to rush us. Going to Albert Hall, London Zoo, horse riding he'd teach me how, and to Hyde Park to listen to the Sunday speeches there, and this summer, just drive through Europe by bike without a map. How wonderful! And more and more Bon suggest: We go there too. Never made it.

"I realized, in those days, that when we were holding hands, he often take fast hold of my hand like he's saying something doing that. Something not for our bright future but something so hopeless. Maybe in a tormented hell."

Bon was drinking heavily, as Anna testifies: "Waking late in the morning, start with a glass of Scotch and music." He was listening to Eric Clapton's *Slowhand*, John Lennon's *Imagine*, the Pretenders' first album, which had just come out, and Tchaikovsky.

Suddenly though, something snapped inside Bon. He told Anna she would have to leave. He said he had to start working. Anna was devastated. Bon had told Ian Jeffery that Anna was distracting him. Suzie explained to Anna that she was smothering Bon.

ANNA: "So next morning, before he wakes up, very quietly I packed my suitcase and left. I went to the shop on the street to get some fresh milk, as it was running out and he always liked it in the morning."

Anna rang Suzie from the public phone in the shop to ask if she could stay with her that night.

ANNA: "She says, Okay, but Bon just phoned and said you're gone. Going back to the flat, and just taking time opening the door as it's heavy, hard to unlock always. And there was Bon's back at the record player, playing "Wonderful Tonight", my favorite song on *Slowhand*.

"Where are you going? Bon seeing my suitcase packed. Just trying to get close to the moon, I answered. Who's gonna cook for me if you go? Bon said. And the plans for coming days. This Sunday, he wants to invite his friends from Paris, Trust, for Japanese food party."

Bon had dropped in on his French friends while they were doing a session in London on February 13. It was then that he made his last recording, a version of "Ride On" that would eventually be released in 1998. "That's why I'm lonely," he bawled. "So lonely . . ."

ANNA: "Till then, I said to myself, I'd be with him here just till then. And another day busy being happy . . . He said, It's been the best for a while, like he's angry with it."

Trust came to dinner on Sunday. Mick Cocks was there too.

ANNA: "It was like the Last Supper. Had lots of fun. Bon seemed that he didn't want me to smoke though. Why?"

The next day was Monday, the 18th, Bon's last. He left the flat in the early afternoon. Anna got dressed after about an hour, and left too. She bumped into Bon on the way out. "My bank is closed," he said. "I'm hungry."

"Do you want me to cook something?" she asked.

ANNA: "Quick cooking of Japanese soup and fish cake. Doing dishes, I turn back and saw him giving me such a sad look as if he's the one who's hurt separating tonight. Dishes done, he calls my name, says, Thank You. Too formal, we've never been like this. And, See you, he said firmly."

Anna went over to the Jefferys' in Maida Vale.

ANNA: "Ian came back, said nothing. Plug, the roadie who's staying there, came back later, said that Bon didn't come to the studio. About 11 o'clock at night, he phoned and says: How are you doing?

'Fine.'

'Just checking if you are okay.'

'Fine, I'm fine. How are you?'

'Just sitting on my own. Drinking and writing lyrics. I didn't go to the studio today, maybe tomorrow. (That means I can't see you tomorrow either?) Do you have a blanket?'

'No, I'm sleeping in the sink. No, I have a blanket. And you? Do you have a blanket?'

'I have too many for one.'

'I don't think so.'

'Well, I just wanted to check if you were okay. Is Ian there?'

"And he spoke to Ian and the night fell. I was wrapped up in a blanket that Plug left on the couch. In the middle of the night or before dawn, I woke up and saw this white light coming through the door. Pain in the abdomen but it went through to the window next second and back to sleep unaware. Maybe I was dreaming."

Next day, in the afternoon, Anna went shopping with Suzie. But all her strength had left her. The city seemed dusty and unreal. Back at Maida Vale, when Ian came home, he said Bon hadn't shown up at the studio again. When Plug came back later, he was irritated. "Where the fuck's Bon?" he demanded.

ANNA: "Suzie suggest I phone him at the flat. I was afraid. Say no. But can't face this. Decided to ring him up at 12:00 a.m. Up to 12:00, I'll wait for him. No phone rings. Time goes slowly. And finally at 12:00, when I put my hand to the phone, I jumped back for fear. The phone started to ring. Suzie nod. So I pick it up. Is Ian there? Not that dear voice, husky, but the biting businesslike manner. I handed the phone to Suzie and left the room.

"After a while, I heard some sort of screaming. I walked into the room. And there Suzie is sitting with Ian having his arm around her and crying.

"For some tragedy she was crying. I fell down on my knees, asked, Is it Bon? She took my hand and nod. Her face furrowed by tears. Has Bon died? I asked again.

"Soon, many people walked in the sitting room. They all look tamely. But no one aware that a petal of the cyclamen Ian gave to Suzie on Valentine's Day fell down without a sound."

CERTIFIED COPY   OF AN ENTRY

Pursuant to the Births and   Deaths Registration Act 1953

DEATH	Entry No. 74

Registration district   **Lambeth**

Sub-district   **Lambeth**

Administrative area

London Borough of Lambeth

1. Date and place of death

**Dead on arrival on Nineteenth February 1980
Kings College Hospital, Denmark Hill**

2. Name and surname

Ronald Belford SCOTT

3. Sex   **Male**

4. Maiden surname of woman who has married   ——

5. Date and place of birth **9th July 1946
Forfar, Scotland**

6. Occupation and usual address

**Musician
15 Ashley Court, Morford Crescent, Westminster**

7. (a) Name and surname of informant   (b) Qualification

**Certificate received from M B Levine, Assistant Deputy Coroner for
Inner South London. Inquest held on 22.2.80**

(c) Usual address   ——

8. Cause of death

Acute alcoholic poisoning

Death by Misadventure

9. I certify that the particulars given by me above are true to the best of my knowledge and belief.

——   Signature of informant

10. Date of registration

Twenty-second February 1980

11. Signature of registrar

C R Harris   Registrar

Certified to be a true copy of an entry in a register in my custody.

268 A Thorpe Deputy Registrar 22nd February 1980   **IR   681321**

16. TOUCH TOO MUCH

The news first appeared in London's *Evening Standard* on the afternoon of Wednesday, January 20th. By Thursday morning it was in all the dailies, under such predictable headlines as "ROCK STAR DRINKS HIMSELF TO DEATH." The same story was repeated in all the articles: Bon had died in a car parked outside a friend's flat in South London, having been left to sleep off a drunk on Monday night, or more accurately in the early hours of Tuesday morning. Bon's friend, identified as Alistair Kinnear, a "bass guitarist," had found him unconscious on Tuesday evening. Bon was subsequently pronounced dead on arrival at nearby Kings College Hospital. Police said there were no suspicious circumstances.

The *Evening Standard*'s John Stevens located Kinnear, and reported:

> Speaking from his third floor flat in Overhill Road, East Dulwich, a distraught Mr. Kinnear described the drinking bout which led to the Australian star's death.
>
> "I met up with Bon to go to the Music Machine, but he was pretty drunk when I picked him up.
>
> "When we got there, he was drinking four whiskies straight in a glass at a time . . .
>
> "I just could not move him so I covered him with a blanket and left him a note to tell him how to get up to my flat in case he woke up.
>
> "I went to sleep then and it was later in the evening when I went out to the car and I knew something was wrong immediately."

These comments were the first and last that Alistair Kinnear offered publicly. After that, he seemed to vanish from the face of the earth.

As a result of Kinnear's apparent disappearance, combined with the twin rumors—both well founded—that some people had wanted Bon out of AC/DC, and that Bon moved in heavy drug circles, conspiracy theories began to spring up almost immediately.

These conspiracy theories grew more and more elaborate over the years—right up to the moment when Alistair Kinnear was effectively flushed out by an article in London's *Guardian* newspaper on the 25th anniversary of Bon's death in February, 2005, written by Richard Jinman. In it, this author was quoted exasperatedly asking the one final question neither he nor anyone else had ever been able to answer: What happened to Alistair Kinnear? His disappearance was so complete, his identity so nebulous, it was as if he had never even existed.

Indeed, it was this idea—that Kinnear never existed—that formed the basis of the principal conspiracy theory: that "Alistair Kinnear" was merely another alias among many used by Joe Furey, and, relatedly, that drugs were involved in Bon's death. Just weeks before Jinman's *Guardian* piece, veteran metal journalist Geoff Barton had written a cover story for *Total Rock* magazine based on the shifting memories of various former members of UFO, which placed Bon with them on that fateful Monday night, and going off to see "Alistair Kinnear" (whoever he might have been) to score smack.

It's true that Bon was friendly with UFO (two weeks before he died, he was photographed backstage at a gig of theirs at the Hammersmith Odeon); it's also the case that Joe Furey was one of their dealers; but the garbled and conflicting accounts of these recovering addicts never added up, any more than any of the other conspiracy theories did. Joe Furey may have been able to pass himself off as someone else to his junkie clients, but to the police? The press? The coroner? If Alistair Kinnear didn't exist, how come Bon had an entry under his name in his phone book? If drugs were involved, how could an autopsy fail to find them in Bon's system?

No, the way Bon died was pretty much the way the "official" version always had it, as this book concluded from its very first edition in 1994 onward. And when the real Alistair Kinnear, who had been living in Spain since the early 1980s (he still works as a musician there, in the bars of the Costa del Sol), released a statement later in 2005 to *Metal Hammer* magazine,[1] the final piece of the jigsaw fell perfectly into place.

---

[1] Printed in "Metal Hammer & Classic Rock Present AC/DC," *Metal Hammer* magazine special issue, 2005.

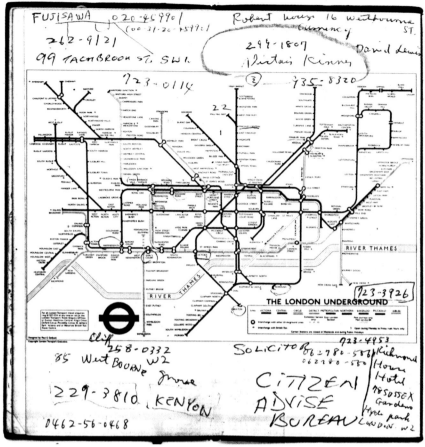

The inside back cover of Bon's pocket diary, showing Alistair Kinnear's phone number.

Bon was at home in the early evening on February 18, 1980, trying to write. He was drinking, of course. Trust's Bernie Bonvoisin would later sing in "Your Final Gig": "Everything had gone great, we'd laughed the night before"—but Bon's mind was wandering. Mid-evening he called Silver (he also called Coral Browning in Los Angeles, as well as Ian Jeffrey and Anna). He had never gotten over Silver, who by then was a fully-fledged heroin dealer. Joe Furey was still heavily involved with her, as he was with UFO.

SILVER: "Bon phoned up, he wanted to go and see someone, I think at Dingwalls, just check 'em out, and he didn't want to go by himself. So Alistair and Bon went. I didn't hear from Bon again. I got two more calls from Alistair."

Kinnear was a fringe figure on the London rock scene. He'd first met Bon as a result of sharing a flat in Kensington with Silver in 1978. He told

Metal Hammer: "On the night of 18 February 1980, Zena Kakoulli, manager of the Only Ones and wife of bandleader Peter Perrett, invited me to the inaugural gig of her sister's band at the Music Machine in Camden Town. I phoned Silver to see if she wanted to come along, but she'd made other arrangements for the evening. However, she suggested that Bon might be interested, as he had phoned her earlier looking for something to do. I gave him a call, and he was agreeable, and I picked him up at his flat on Ashley Court in Westminster."

Bon was at home when Kinnear got there around midnight, and then the pair drove across town to the Music Machine (the venue was renamed the Camden Palace a couple of years later).

KINNEAR: "It was a great party, and Bon and I both drank far too much . . . however, I did not see him take any drugs that evening. At the end of the party I offered to drive him home. As we approached his flat, I realized that Bon had drifted into unconsciousness. I left him in my car and rang his doorbell, but his current live-in girlfriend didn't answer. I took Bon's keys and let myself into the flat, but no-one was at home."

Even if Kinnear had entertained the idea of carrying Bon inside, somehow in the process—he was drunk, after all—he managed to lock himself out of the building. As Anna Baba has already said, the front door was "heavy, hard to unlock always"; this is corroborated by a note the caretaker at Ashley Court left for Bon and Anna the following day, which Anna picked up later. It read: "On morning duties on arrival on 4th floor found door of Flat 15 open, all lights and radios on. Also found one set of keys to flat, on mat inside of front door. Awaited someone to come, and having heard nothing, reported matter to managing agents. [Signed] Mr. Burke."

So Kinnear found himself stranded on the street, with Bon out cold in the car: "I rang Silver for advice. She said that he passed out quite frequently, and that it was best just to leave him to sleep it off."

SILVER: "I said, Well, why don't you take him back to your place? He got him back to his place, and by then, Bon had completely blacked out. By then it was probably three in the morning."

KINNEAR: "I drove to my flat . . . and tried to lift him out of the car, but he was too heavy for me to carry in my intoxicated state."

Kinnear rang Silver's place again.

JOE FUREY: "Alistair rang again, about three in the morning, saying Bon was passed out in the car, what could he do about it? It was three flights up or something to his flat. Alistair wasn't the sort of guy who was built to throw someone over his shoulder."

SILVER: "He said, What'll I do? And this had happened many, many, many times, so I just said, Just take some blankets down to him. Bon had never been to this place—it was in South London—so I said, Leave a note for him, saying which flat's yours, so when he comes to, he can come up."

KINNEAR: "I put the front passenger seat back so that he could lie flat, covered him with a blanket, left a note with my address and phone number on it, and staggered upstairs to bed. It must have been four or five a.m. by that time, and I slept until about eleven, when I was awakened by a friend, Leslie Loads. I was so hung over that I asked Leslie to do me a favor of checking on Bon. He did so, and returned to tell me my car was empty, so I went back to sleep, assuming that Bon had awoken and taken a taxi home. At about 7:30 that evening I went down to my car, intending to pay a visit to my girlfriend, and was shocked to find Bon still lying flat in the front seat, obviously in a very bad way, and not breathing."

Kinnear immediately drove Bon to Kings College Hospital, but it was too late: as the death certificate states, Bon was pronounced dead on arrival. "Hindsight being 20/20," Kinnear explained to *Metal Hammer*, "I would've driven him to the hospital when he first passed out, but in those days of excess, unconsciousness was commonplace and seemed no cause for real alarm."

He gave the hospital Silver's name and number, as the nearest person he could think of to Bon's next of kin. The hospital called Silver.

SILVER: "I went down there with Joe. Joe had worked in hospitals. They didn't tell me he was dead. They told me he was there, and it was serious, would I come down. When we got there, we got shown into a little room, I mean, English hospitals are pretty bloody basic. So it was a bit of a surprise being put in this little room. And then they brought us a cup of tea, and Joe said, Look, this isn't right. They don't do this, he must be dead, they're going to send a doctor in to tell us."

JOE: "The body was already identified, he had ID on him."

SILVER: "I just freaked right out. I mean, I didn't get hysterical or anything. I just shut down. I gave them Mensch's number."

JOE: "After that point, the machine took over, all of a sudden they were interested. It was inexperience; they were like, We've got to control the media, otherwise it might affect our career, we're on the verge of . . . It wasn't like, Hang on, Bon's just died, we'll worry about anything else later. I'm not saying any of that came from Malcolm or Angus. But this was the way the new management was handling it.

"I mean, it was devastating, at the time, but the real hurt came in the way it was all handled by the management."

Although she can't actually remember doing so, it had to be Silver, in shock, who phoned Angus. Angus later told *Sounds*, "Peter, our manager, got to the hospital as soon as he could to find out exactly what had happened and identify him, because everyone was in doubt at the time. I immediately phoned Malcolm 'cos at the time I thought maybe she had got the wrong idea, you know, only *thought* it was Bon. And Ian, our tour manager, said it couldn't be Bon 'cos he'd gone to bed early that night. Anyway, the girl gave me the hospital number, but they wouldn't give me any information until the family had been contacted. Anyhow, Malcolm rang Bon's parents 'cos we didn't want them to be just sitting there and suddenly it comes on the TV news, you know."

Ian Jeffery, who went with Peter Mensch to the hospital, identified the body. He was struck by the fact that Bon's neck was twisted, and showed bruising. However, it was accepted then—with an autopsy yet to be performed—that like Jimi Hendrix, Bon had choked on his own vomit.

ISA: "It was the day after my birthday, on the 18th, we got the phone call on the Wednesday. I nearly tore my hair out."

CHICK: "We'd been over to the club for senior citizens ..."

ISA: "...and the phone was ringing when we came in the door, couldnae get in quick enough, and I heard the voice, and I said, Oh, Ron, and it wasnae Ron, it was either Angus or Malcolm. it wasnae Ron at all, he used to phone me ..."

CHICK: "He always used to phone home."

ISA: "He used to give us a ring wherever he was. We got a shock."

Isa rang Irene, in Melbourne. Irene had spoken to Bon only a few days earlier, when he rang her and told her he wanted to set something up for her; and she had just been talking about him then, on the phone to Mary, about how he had a Japanese girlfriend, and they were laughing together, Well, he's had every other nationality ...

Irene rang Vince in Sydney. The papers were soon ringing Vince.

The news then hit Australia. Even the cynical tabloids, beneath their sensational headlines, seemed genuinely shocked and saddened. "When Bon Scott died in London yesterday," the Sydney *Telegraph*'s Roger Crosthwaite wrote, "a little piece of Australian rock history ended."

There was, indeed, almost a sense of national mourning.

PETER HEAD: "I was playing in a piano bar in Alice Springs. My wife rang and told me, I was half way through a show, playing to about 20 people I guess, quite a few Aboriginals. So I just went out and said, I'm sorry, I can't go on. The audience was shocked too, they just got up and left."

Pat Bowring reported in the Melbourne *Sun:* "No funeral arrangements have been made [yet] and the offices of EMI Records in Perth, where his parents live, are handling the flood of flowers and other tributes pouring in from Bon's friends and fans."

Ted Albert wrote to Chick and Isa:

We have just heard the tragic news and are completely stunned. I would like to try and express to you both, and to Derek and Graeme, our feelings for you at this time, and to send you the deepest sympathy from all of us.

We have lost a really good friend. There are not many people in the entertainment world, unfortunately, who you could call a friend, though the public often are made to think differently, but Bon was one of the real exceptions—a genuine person with a generous nature and a real wish to make others happy—a gentleman in the truest sense.

His only interests were his family, his music and living. He was not one, as so many of us are, to always be dreaming of better days and hoping for better things. He was a realist who lived for the present and was quite happy to live each day for itself and to be content with his lot. He gave absolutely everything he had to his music and the living of life—and you cannot ask for more than that.

Unlike many who pass through life without leaving any trace, Bon has left behind a heritage through his music, records and films, that will be for the benefit of others for many years to come. Only today we learned that the boys' latest album had sold one million copies in the USA alone, which to me represents a million people whose lives have been enriched by Bon's work.

I can't tell you how saddened we are by our loss, but we know that this can in no way compare with your own loss, and we want you to know that our thoughts are with you at this time.

GRAEME SCOTT: "I was in Bali. There was a telegram for me. Funny thing was, I was on the ship in Hong Kong, at Christmas, and when you go there, there's these guys, they set up shop, in the alleyways, and I bought a cassette of *Highway to Hell*, and there was no picture of Ron on the cover. And then a couple of months later, he died. It was strange."

The autopsy was held on Friday, February 22. The verdict was "Death By Misadventure—Acute Alcoholic Poisoning."

The Coroner, Sir Montague Levine, said Bon was "the captain of his own destiny," and concluded that "this young man of great talent was a consistent and heavy drinker who died from acute alcoholic poisoning after consuming a very large quantity of alcohol."

PERRY COOPER: "You know what I think it was? I think it was just a bad night. Like John Belushi. We had John Belushi on the label too, and he used to come in, and he'd have his bag of cocaine, but I never knew John to inject himself, and so when I heard how he died, I've gotta tell you, it just had to be one of those unforeseen things that happen, maybe he was depressed or something ... The same thing happened with Bon. It was just a bad night."

Bon was alone when he died. Under the accumulated strain of more than 15 years on the road, and in a conspiracy of circumstances, his ailing system finally gave way. He was already receiving treatment for liver damage, it was later revealed. He hadn't eaten, and he was extremely drunk. His heart was heavy, his head spinning. The temperature outside was around freezing point. Unable to find a comfortable position, curled around the gearstick, his neck cricked. His dental plate dislodged. The bile rose up in his stomach and his asthmatic windpipe constricted. Whether it was hypothermia, asphyxiation, liver failure, or even cardiac arrest, a combination of those things or none of them, he would be a free man in the morning.

ISA: "When they did the autopsy, I thought, Oh God, don't tell me there's going to be something else."

JOE: "That's what they were supposed to find. It would have been directed at finding that. That huge Fleet Street system would have been paying people to find something."

But not even Fleet Street could find a scandal, even though, as Australian *Rolling Stone*'s London correspondent Bruce Elder reported, "AC/DC's manager Peter Mensch did his best to play the whole story down," which only further fuelled the conspiracy theories.

But one rumor that swirled around at the time did prove to be essentially true: Bon's flat was mysteriously broken into and rifled through, although not on the night of his death, as was first suggested, but rather a few days later.

SILVER: "There was a lot of weird shit *after* he died. The flat was closed off, and that's probably the sort of thing that would send people off on conspiracy theories, because it suggests there's something to hide, and there's nothing to hide.

"I rang up and said, Look, can I go around to the flat and get my stuff, because I'd lent Bon a lot of stuff. Forget it. Mensch was friendly, polite and pseudo-helpful right up until the time Bon died, and after that, I was no longer relevant. The other thing was, Bon wanted to be buried in Kirriemuir . . ."

Anna was shut out, too, even though she was still staying at the Jefferys' place, the virtual center of the storm.

JOE: "She was ringing us—and her English wasn't that good—saying, Do you know what they're doing? She was in a totally foreign environment, her key in the whole situation was Bon, so imagine how she would have felt. She was really distraught. Also, you know that if Bon was there and that was going on, he would have got fairly pissed off! That generated a lot of hate towards Mensch."

Anna was desperate to know what happened that night, what might have been going through Bon's head. It was more likely Bon was thinking about Silver, or even Irene—certainly, he called Coral Browning in LA, but all he got was her answering machine—but Anna didn't know that. She phoned Alistair Kinnear. "When I saw him at the flat, he was already so drunk," he told her. After they'd been to the Music Machine, he said, "I took him to the flat but you weren't there."

ANNA: "I couldn't have kept Alistair on the phone so long, as he sounded depressed, shocked and so weak."

Anna thought Bon's feelings may have been reflected in something he wrote that night. All she had to go on otherwise were some lines he had written earlier and shown her, which she learnt off by heart:

I'm enjoying myself while
I could be writing a song
that's the end
They're bye bye
Everybody knows
Everybody accepts
Everybody knows

Let them talk about you
As they think about me

The only other documentary evidence of Bon's frame of mind around
that time to surface is a scrap of paper on which he'd written a few lines.
It wouldn't do to read too much into a verse titled "Hairy Kerry," but given
Bon's predilection both for things Japanese, and for word plays, it is tempt-
ing. "Hairy Kerry" read:

Who's gonna clean it up
Someone's gotta clean it up
Is nothing sacred?

Anna went around to Ashley Court on the weekend hoping she might find
Bon's notebooks. But the flat was closed. She did bump into Mr. Burke, the
caretaker. It was then that he gave her the note he'd written on the Tuesday morning, which had gone uncollected. He also told Anna that on the
Wednesday "two big men" came by and got into the flat. He protested, he
said, but they went on about their business, picking through things.

Even Graeme Scott can confirm this, seemingly—and strangely—
unconcerned. "When he died, some people went around and took a few
things. Someone had not broken in, but just gone there, and took what
they wanted."

Anna could only presume that the "two big men" were Ian Jeffery
and Jake Berry, another AC/DC roadie, because they were the ones who
brought her suitcase and other belongings from the flat to her. When she
asked after some other things that were in the flat, sentimental items, Ian
told her, "Everything is packed and taken to the office to send to Perth to
his parents."

JOE: "All of a sudden, they're telling us we have no right to get into
his flat. It was like, Whaddya mean, you didn't drop by a week ago to see
if he had anything in the fridge. It comes back to management, and they
are playing it far too hardball.

"At the level AC/DC were operating, with the financial infrastructure
Leber & Krebs put around them when they came in, there was always the
feeling . . . you see, most people working at that level have a percy, who
would just take care of his house, that sort of thing, and make sure he
didn't end up somewhere where he forgot to go home. It's pretty standard
for management, record companies, to put those people on. So you'd have

Note left by the caretaker of Ashley Court, where Bon lived.

the situation covered.

"Bon wasn't that chronic. He had that sense of satisfaction about him, as I said, but physically, he wasn't that well. So from a rock'n'roll perspective, it was negligence. You take care of people better than that. Because that's the way the system works. It was a conspiracy of neglect more than anything else."

After the autopsy, Bon's body, accompanied by Malcolm and Angus, was flown to Australia to be cremated. Anna eventually went back to Japan, but she was haunted by Bon, by the questions she never found answers to. On the first anniversary of Bon's death, in 1981, she went to Perth, to visit his grave, pay her respects to his parents, and hopefully to see his notebooks, which his parents should have had, since Ian Jeffery told her everything was to be sent to them.

But all Chick and Isa got was a suitcase containing a few items of clothing and a couple of personal effects. No papers, no musical instruments, no records, let alone Bon's treasured photo albums—nothing else.

Bon was cremated in Fremantle, on Friday, February 29; his ashes were buried the following day. He lies in the Fremantle Cemetery's Memorial Garden, shaded from the restless dusty sun by tall gum trees.

Memorial notices had run in papers all around Australia in the preceding days, placed by friends, family and fans. The funeral notice itself appeared in the *West Australian* on the Thursday:

> Scott: The [public] funeral of the late Mr. Ronald Belford (Bon) Scott is appointed to arrive at the Crematorium Chapel NEXT SATURDAY MORNING for a Uniting Church Service at 11:00 o'clock.

"Bon's parents were obviously in a bit of shock about it," Angus told *Sounds*, "and they had people from our record company in Australia there with them to look after all the details, but they never got the word about what really happened until we flew out there.

"The funeral itself was more or less quiet, though there were a lot of kids outside, you know. It was better being quiet, because it could have been very bad if a lot of people had just converged there."

Bon's friends felt left out. Alberts' Fifa Riccobono went to Perth to organize everything, and the result, in typical style, was overprotective. Not that the funeral wasn't open, just that arms weren't. Mary Walton only learned about it because Isa kept Irene informed, who in turn kept Mary informed. Irene couldn't make it because she was just about to go into labor. Vince, too, was tied up in Sydney, now managing the Divinyls. Mary tried to ring Isa to say she was coming, but Fifa wouldn't let her talk to her. Even Isa admonished Fifa, "But she's an old friend."

The funeral went unreported even by the local media. A handful of fans congregated harmlessly outside the church. There were no television cameras, newspaper reporters, not even rock journalists.

MARY WALTON: "I was surprised by that. And that there was no one there from the music business. Maybe that was because it seemed like it was a private affair, maybe because it was Perth, I don't know."

The band arrived in limousines. Unschooled in the social graces, Malcolm and Angus didn't know how they were supposed to behave. They were pleased to see a familiar face in Mary.

Maria was there with her family. So were all the Hendersons. Vince's parents. Brian Gannon, Bruce Abbott, the Valentines who'd stayed behind. Ted Ward.

MARY: "Everyone was just in shock more than anything else—I know

I was; no one really showed much emotion. So everyone just sort of stuck together."

Still nervous, Malcolm had to ask Fifa if it was alright for Mary to ride in the limo with them after the service.

MARY: "We went to the parents' place afterwards, and then I went with the boys back to their hotel. I went out sailing with Phil in the afternoon, then had dinner at the hotel, then caught the last flight back to Melbourne. That was it."

Phil and Cliff went on to Melbourne too, while Malcolm and Angus flew straight back to London. Pressure was already mounting to get back on track. After the breakthrough made by *Highway to Hell* a huge amount of expectation now surrounded AC/DC, and with or without Bon Scott the machine couldn't just stop.

Then a few days later, a strange, eerie thing happened: everyone got cards from Bon. Christmas cards. He hadn't put enough postage on them, so they arrived late. For the recipients all around the world, it was a touching postscript to his final sendoff, a reminder of one reason why they held him so dear in the first place—Bon always made an effort.

The obituaries, testimonials and tributes hit the music press, all echoing the same sentiments—that Bon was a great bloke, a great talent, but tragically, yet "another victim of rock's deadly grind." In *RAM*, alongside its four-page cover story obituary by Vince, the names "Harry & George" appeared undersigned to a full-page testament which read simply, "A great singer, a great lyricist, a great friend, one of a kind. We'll miss you."

Vince wrote: "How or why you died, Bon, I don't give a damn. I only know and care that it was too soon."

MOLLY MELDRUM: "Bon dying hit me like John Lennon dying [which happened only nine months later]. People say to me today, How can you still have the enthusiasm? Well, it's been our lives. If Bon was alive today, he'd have the same enthusiasm he always had. If you have to react to it like, Oh, I've got to get up and do this, go to the recording studio—that's when it's time to pack it in. It's got nothing to do with age—you just love it."

Fittingly, the man who replaced Bon in AC/DC, Brian Johnson, would pay him a tribute which was not only full of humility, but also cut through the bullshit. "That poor boy was loved by thousands of people worldwide," he said. "When we did a warm-up gig in Holland, this kid came up to me with a tattoo of Bon on his arm and said, This bloke was my hero, but now he's gone, I wish you all the luck in the world. I just stood there shaking.

I mean, what can you say when people are prepared to put their faith in you like that? Since then, I feel like I've been singing for that kid and so many others like him.

"I think Bon Scott had a bit of genius. It annoys me that nobody recognized that before. He used to sing great words, write great words. He had a little twist in everything he said. He had such a distinctive voice as well. Oh great, when the man died they were starting to say, Yeah, the man was a genius. That was too late, too late."

ISA: "Angus always used to say, It should never have happened. We used to say too, If only he'd done this, if only he'd done that. But you only said that long after he'd gone. Why didn't somebody watch him? But you couldn't watch him. He went his own way, and nobody could stop him.

"If only someone got onto him and made him dry out somewhere, that's all I say."

GRAEME SCOTT: "I always thought he was meant to die when he did. A lot of times earlier, he could have died."

Unable to articulate his grief more appropriately, Malcolm took a swing at Mick Cocks one night when he bumped into him.

MICK COCKS: "That was when they were looking for scapegoats. He put everybody off side—Angry [Anderson], everybody. It was a moment of sadness for everybody, so it was just stupid. Normally, I would fight back, but under those circumstances, I didn't. I thought, This is not right. A lack of respect. I don't mind celebrating somebody's death; I don't have negative thoughts about Bon in terms of, Oh, he was hard done by, or that he missed out on this or that, or that he was emotionally not together, or that he was drunk. To me, that means nothing. To me, he lived and died the way he wanted to. We were friends.

"I just took it as everybody not being sure how to react, I mean, sometimes it's nice to be able to blame somebody. And maybe they felt a little guilty, maybe they felt they should have been paying a bit more attention to what he was doing. But I don't think that's true either, I think it was just one of those things that can't be helped. Bon was his own man, and one thing you couldn't do was tell him what to do."

JOE FUREY: "I thought it was nice that he got right to the top. Chronologically, it might look like the top came with *Back in Black,* but he was aware that was happening. It's like letting go, you maybe feel the sense that the angels are calling and you look back and think, I've done it, I don't need to keep fighting. The body's not enjoying this anymore. That's the way I like to see it. He'd done it and he was called."

274

Of course, the question always remains, What if? There's no doubt that Bon was really only just hitting his stride as a writer. He was capable of so much more, and indeed, he was talking about a solo album; he may even have contemplated leaving the band sooner or later. But such musings are hypothetical and pointless, if not presumptuous. The legacy Bon left is rich enough as it is.

AC/DC, it's true, went on to much greater success. But Bon never defined success in terms of numbers. He wasn't so naive as to deny it—because it put money, however filtered down, into his pocket—but what was just as important to Bon as people buying his records was that they were listening to them, "getting off on it," as he would have put it.

Bon's life and work were inevitably intertwined, but it wasn't as if he had trouble distinguishing between art and reality. It was more a matter of whether or not, besieged by the pervasive loneliness of life on the road, he chose to know. Because in the end, he was painfully aware of what was important and what wasn't. In that, Bon was like most of us, a spiritual battler who grappled with the bigger questions and was probably just befuddled by them. He just wanted to do the right thing.

Larger than life in his own time, in death Bon became an icon. That's how most of us remember him—the public figure. His friends remember him according to their individual catalogues of memories. Bon chose his own way of life and he lived it to the full, realizing most of his dreams. That was one of his successes.

That he is remembered so fondly by all who knew him, almost without exception, as a person of sincerity, humor and great generosity of spirit, is another success.

But if the commercial success AC/DC found even in Bon's lifetime seemed in itself empty to him, if he found he still had the same personal problems, it was not a failure that he was unable to resolve them—because that's the nature of life: it doesn't necessarily provide a novelist's neatly resolved ending.

Transcending a life's fleeting fame, Bon's soul became public property as he assumed immortality.

It is cold comfort for the loved ones left behind.

EPILOGUE: BACK IN BLACK

On *Countdown* Molly Meldrum was spouting that Stevie Wright would replace Bon in AC/DC. It seemed an obvious conclusion to jump to, but Alberts quickly stood on it. "We don't know where he got that from," a spokesperson said, "but there's absolutely no truth in the rumor. Stevie's got his own thing to do, and AC/DC have theirs." Stevie's "thing" was his heroin addiction, which had effectively seen him frozen out of Alberts altogether.

Molly himself was attacked for tastelessness in even raising the issue of a replacement. "That's just absurd," he snapped back. "I've known Bon for 12 years, longer than most of these other people who found it tasteless, and I know he wouldn't have minded. Life goes on; if I dropped dead, I'd expect *Countdown* to announce a replacement immediately and keep going."

And indeed, as soon as Malcolm and Angus returned to London from the funeral, they "got straight back to work on the songs [they] were writing at the time it happened."

Given the band's deep suspicion of the press it was amazing, as Dave Lewis wrote in the *Sounds* feature "The Show Must Go On" of March 29, that "the ever articulate Angus allowed himself to become the band's spokesman at a time when many others would sulkily shun the glare of publicity." But Peter Mensch wanted it to be known that AC/DC would not fold—were in fact auditioning new singers even then.

Bon meant little to Mensch personally; his primary concern was simply that the band's momentum was not lost. And everybody, Bon included, had believed this next album was going to be the one. For Malcolm and Angus, their supreme ambition was a bulwark against grief.

Besides, they had been granted the highest approval. When they were leaving the funeral, Malcolm has recalled, "Bon's dad said, 'You've go to find someone else, you know that.' He said, 'Whatever you do, don't stop.'" Quitting the band would have been the travesty, not continuing it, and Bon himself would have expected no less.

"We got a little rehearsal studio and songwriting became our therapy," Angus said. "Then our manager kept pestering us about what we all dreaded: don't you guys want a new singer? We kept putting it off . . ."

They can't have resisted too strongly: after getting back to work two days after their return to London from Bon's funeral, they were auditioning singers within a couple of weeks; within a month, they'd settled on Brian Johnson, and within six weeks, they were in the Bahamas recording *Back in Black*. If leaping back into the fray with their blood brother still warm in the ground seems in any way graceless, well, no-one ever called the Youngs great sentimentalists.

What was perhaps even more extraordinary, though, was that they made it work. Where bands like the Doors—and later Nirvana and INXS—failed, AC/DC succeeded, and then some. Not only is *Back in Black* the greatest resurrection act in rock history, it is one of its biggest selling albums.

The gift in all this was Bon's anointing. Bon's generosity of spirit, even in death, outdid anything most people could muster in life.

In their Pimlico rehearsal room, Malcolm and Angus worked over song ideas. It was a bit weird without Bon, but they could still hear him, ghost-like, when they got really pumping on a riff. Even in absentia, he was still, as he himself had said, "the lightning bolt in the middle" that charged the two poles on either side.

Alberts' Fifa Riccobono announced, "Nine names have already approached them for the job, although of course I can't say who they are. It will be quite a gap to fill, but the band will be auditioning lead singers almost immediately."

Speculation was rife. *Melody Maker* ran with the Stevie Wright rumor; *NME* and *Juke* suggested it would be one Allen Fryer. Fryer, erstwhile front man with a small-time Adelaide band called Fat Lip, was George's choice. Hailing from Elizabeth, near Adelaide, he was another Gorbals boy, a mate of Jimmy Barnes. But George's opinion was carrying less and less weight, given the way everything was going. (Ironically, Fryer would go on to sing alongside Mark Evans in Heaven, an '80s heavy metal band managed by Michael Browning.)

Other names bandied about included Steve Marriott, the former Small Faces/Humble Pie frontman, who was even older than Bon (and a singer Bon had covered and greatly admired); former Heavy Metal Kid Gary Holton; ex-Back Street Crawler Terry Slesser; and another couple of Australians: Adrian Campbell, who'd previously sung for a band called Raw Glory, and Scottish-born John Swan, who—along with his half-brother, singer Jimmy Barnes—had joined Fraternity (on drums) after Bon left in 1974.

Holed up in the rehearsal studio, Malcolm and Angus conducted the cattle call under the scrutiny of Peter Mensch and Mutt Lange. Gary Holton might have seemed like a good fit but the team was wise to decide against him, since he too would die young, in 1985. They were wiser still to pick Brian Johnson. Johnson at the time was working in a garage back in his hometown of Newcastle upon Tyne, after abandoning the musical career he had dreamed of since the first time he saw local hero Eric Burdon in the early sixties. His band Geordie had enjoyed a couple of minor hits in the early '70s, but by the latter half of the decade their run was over.

The story goes that an AC/DC fan in Chicago sent Peter Mensch a tape of a Geordie album, and Mensch was immediately interested. Geordie was an undistinguished sort of hard rock outfit, but Johnson possessed a pair of lungs of the capacity required by AC/DC. Malcolm and Angus knew who he was—Bon had told stories of seeing this guy sing one time when Fraternity supported Geordie in the UK. Johnson was located, he squeezed an audition into his "busy" schedule, he impressed with versions of "Whole Lotta Rosie" and "Nutbush City Limits," and he got the gig. "He's got the range," declared Mutt Lange. Bon wasn't five weeks in the ground and Johnson was already the new singer in AC/DC.

Meanwhile in Newcastle, New South Wales, just north of Sydney, AC/DC's original singer Dave Evans sat by the phone, dressed head-to-toe in leather and studs, waiting for a call which would never come.

Bon was one of a kind and the band knew he could never truly be replaced. Angus would now be the sole front man, the star attraction. Any singer would have to fall in behind him and just bellow. Which is what Brian Johnson did, and still does.

The next best thing to a Scot is most likely a Geordie, and in terms of temperament Johnson was just the sort of character AC/DC were looking for—down to earth, self-deprecating, and with a salty sense of humor. And Johnson—like Bon—was older, and wise enough to know not to overstep the mark.

The announcement was made on April 8. The band claimed Bon would have wanted it that way, and they were right. To have come this far and not gone on would have been a betrayal of all Bon's efforts. Bon wouldn't have sat around feeling sorry for himself. The ultimate irony, of course, given the American label's complaints about Bon, is that Johnson's shrieking style is essentially as unintelligible as Bon's! He may never have rivaled Bon's songwriting ability, but—helped by superior technology—Brian Johnson has served AC/DC, and Bon's memory, well.

The band spent the first two weeks of April rehearsing with Johnson and Lange in London, and then set sail for the Bahamas, where they were booked into Compass Point Studios in Nassau.

In the same way they'd claimed they didn't want a Bon clone—and in Brian Johnson, didn't get one—the band also claimed they weren't interested in "grave-robbing" any of Bon's last song ideas.

But given the way the famous Young/Scott/Young writing team worked, it's hard to imagine that, at the very least, some of Bon's ideas didn't seep into *Back in Black*, if only indirectly. And if some of these ideas were used—which would not have been unreasonable, since Malcolm, especially, had provided Bon with more than a few lyric lines and themes over the years—at least Bon might have been awarded a credit—but he wasn't.

Highway to Hell had succeeded because Mutt Lange made the band sound bigger and smoothed out some of its rough edges. *Back in Black* succeeded because it sounded even bigger still, and because within that huge, enveloping ambience, it could afford to restore some of the sharper edges (culling a lot of the backing vocals). *Highway to Hell* is a warmer-sounding, more well-rounded album than *Back in Black*, but the overarching sonic vista of *Back in Black*, the vastness of its dynamic crunch, makes it irresistible, and although the later album is uneven (several of its songs are relatively weak), the superior half of it is so overwhelming, it sweeps everything before it. It is no surprise that by 2006 it had sold over forty million copies world-wide.

But *Back in Black* is more than just dedicated to Bon's memory, more than a fully fitting tribute to him; it's like a haunted house, a voice from the grave: Bon not going gently into that good night. It is significant that the graph of AC/DC record sales traces a steady ascent up to *Back in Black*, and after hitting that peak, begins to decline. It's hard not to ascribe that to Bon's fading presence.

Bon's death was "the defining moment for AC/DC," David Christensen wrote in the online journal *fakejazz* in 2001. "It solidifies the band as the hard living thugs they'd always played themselves to be, but is the inevitable end of the lifestyle they led and championed in their music. It gives everything they had previously released a dark pall and a bitter edge. And it was the event from which they could never recover. Though they released another strong record—*Back in Black*—the AC/DC of 1974-79 was gone and in their place was something else entirely, as evidenced by the tonal shift of *Back in Black*."

Back in Black's opening track, "Hell's Bells," is one of the slowest dirges AC/DC have ever recorded. Slowing the tempo a bit generally was one of the keys to opening up the band's sound, but this track, obviously enough, was a funeral march . . .

AC/DC had a tradition of making ten-track albums, five songs per side. Of the remaining four songs on Side One, only "Shoot to Thrill" and "Giving the Dog a Bone" barely measure up; "What Do You Do For Money Honey?" and "Let Me Put My Love Into You" are both pretty ordinary.

The real riches lie on Side Two. The double punch of its opening, first the title track (the Greatest Riff of All Time), followed by "You Shook Me All Night Long" (the ultimate frat-house party-starter and pole dancer favorite, the only pop record AC/DC have ever made), cements the album's impact. The side continues strongly too, with "Have a Drink On Me," "Shake a Leg" and "Rock'n'Roll Ain't Noise Pollution."

"*Back in Black* is a Bon Scott album," concludes David Christensen. "Though he does not appear on it, his presence, or lack thereof, defines every aspect of it. Though some songs were as menacing (the astounding epic opener "Hell's Bells") or as furious ("Shake a Leg") or as nasty ("You Shook Me All Night Long") as earlier AC/DC songs, the album feels emotionally heavy and dark. The fun is gone. The jokes fall flat. It's obviously intended as a tribute to Scott, and it is effective enough in that sense. But the wild abandon is now tempered by an ever present sense of doom."

But it's one thing to say that *Back in Black* is driven by Bon's spirit, that he was its "ghostwriter"; it's something else again to find concrete evidence of his input. Listening closely to it, it is possible to hear things that sound like they could be Bon's work—but also other things that quite clearly aren't.

"Some songs on *Back in Black*," says Anna Baba, "I could have explained too well, with much confusion and tears. They who call themselves mates and declare they don't do it, but have done it, with cool cheek—sneaky! 'Shake a Leg,' 'Rock'n'Roll Ain't Noise Pollution,' 'Have a Drink on Me' and others, obviously his, no-one else's."

Bon's mother Isa has also said that Bon had already written a lot of lyrics for the next album when she saw him over Christmas in 1979. The band was always working on new material in the tour bus, Malcolm and Angus constantly trading licks, Bon and the Youngs trading tags and hooklines. This is classic organic rock songwriting, and if *Back in Black* was born anywhere, it was born there. But more specifically, Bon was in and out of the rehearsal room in London in late January/early February, playing drums behind Malcolm and Angus, trying out vocal lines and honing lyric ideas.

Angus actually told Australian *Rolling Stone* in 1997, "We were in doubt about what to do [after Bon died] but we had songs that he had written and we wanted to finish them."

Bon had already sat in on sessions for "Have a Drink On Me" (which had its final title even then) and "Back in Black" (which didn't). It seems unlikely that he wrote his own epitaph (despite the online myth of a boot-leg demo of the song on which Bon sings!), but certainly Angus as well as Anna Baba dates the very Stonesy "Have a Drink On Me" to the period prior to Bon's death.

"Rock'n'Roll Ain't Noise Pollution" is another song whose provenance is confused. The party line goes that it was built from the ground up in the Bahamas—the only track to have been created this way. But while this confirms the fact that the other nine were all developed in London, Anna Baba says that this song, too, had its origins in London. Bon was inspired to write the lyric, she says, after the caretaker at Ashley Court, Mr. Burke, asked Bon to turn down the loud music late at night. And it certainly sounds very Bon . . .

Anna Baba isn't the only one who believes that an examination of Bon's notebooks would end all this speculation. But although Ian Jeffery, one of the "two big men" who turned over Bon's flat after he died, has admitted that he has a "folder of lyrics of 15 songs" written by Bon, these lost scrolls remain hidden from view. And the credit for every track on *Back in Black* reads uniformly "Young/Young/Johnson."

As if to reconfirm the truism that death is a great career move, interest in AC/DC ran at an all-time high in anticipation of the release of *Back in Black*. The UK's *Music Week* top 75 singles chart for July 9 contained no less than four AC/DC "oldies"—"Whole Lotta Rosie" (at 38), "High Voltage" (48), "Dirty Deeds" (54) and "Long Way to the Top" (55). When the album was released at the end of July, less than six months after Bon's death, it became an instant world-wide smash.

In Britain, it went straight to number one. In the United States, although it only reached number four, it stayed in the *Billboard* top ten for over five months. In Australia, it went to number two, held out of the top spot only by the Police's *Zenyatta Mondatta*. By the end of the year, it had already sold three million units internationally, earning the band 27 platinum and gold awards in 8 countries.

It was AC/DC's crowning achievement, and irrevocably established the band as one of the biggest in the world. As a result, the back catalogue—the six albums Bon made with the AC/DC—has never been out of print, and continues to sell strongly to this day.

JOE FUREY: "Again, a lot of the animosity at the time of his death, people just wanted to convey to his parents just how successful he was. Wanting to say, Do you realize now, you are going to become rich. There were people that wanted to make sure that was passed on, didn't get lost in the vaults."

Alberts sent Chick and Isa to Singapore for a holiday after all the fuss had died down. They were delighted with that.

GRAEME SCOTT: "Our accountant told us it would probably last two years, but it's still going. We can't really say anything, because it's between the Youngs and the Scotts, AC/DC and us."

It's unfortunate Bon didn't get around to providing anything for Irene, as he so clearly wanted to do, when his estate by now must have accrued millions. Irene stood by Bon through his worst period, and as much as she sometimes must have thought, If only I hadn't pushed that divorce through, it's testimony to her strength of character that she hasn't become embittered.

Irene was pregnant when Bon died, and she went on to have a second son. She lives happily to this day—or like anybody, as happy as you can be with all the troubles you can have. But happy at best. In 2005, she put her collection of Bon memorabilia up for auction at Leonard Joel's in Melbourne, including the letters published in this book; one item, a leather shaving kit his mother had given him, attracted a bid of $12,540 from an Australian collector. The letters are on now display at a bar called the Cherry, in Melbourne.

Bon may even have legitimate heirs who've missed the boat too. Over the years there's always been talk of children he may have sired. No paternity claims have been made, however, even though a thirty-something Melbourne man was revealed in 2005 to have a very convincing case, and face. This man, a sometime musician, has neither played on his father's name nor preyed on the estate, opting to protect his privacy and make his own way in the world.

Silver Smith got busted in London not long after Bon died. It was a bad bust: she lost her passport, and had virtually nothing to fall back on, so she went down hard. Bon invested a lot emotionally in Silver, and though she eventually made good—got clean, had a child, and is now a contributing member of the community back in Adelaide—she was probably the wrong woman for him at the wrong time. The sort of domestic dream Bon harbored for them both could never have come true.

Mary and Vince would both have kids, too, but Vince would lose his wife Suzy and son Troy to AIDS. Graeme Scott went to Thailand to live, where he ran a bar.

AC/DC hit the road for the first time without Bon, with Brian Johnson in his stead, in August 1980, after testing the water with shows in Holland and Belgium. They toured America for two months, playing 64 dates into September. It was business as usual. The album was approaching platinum status in the US. In November, the band toured the UK, then went on to Europe.

On the first anniversary of Bon's death in February 1981, just after they had toured Japan for the first time, AC/DC finally returned to tour Australia for the first time since *Dirty Deeds Done Dirt Cheap*. It was only four years, but it seemed like a lifetime. It *was* a lifetime.

Bon's death was deeply felt in Australia. BON LIVES! graffiti spread fast. Yet Brian Johnson already had a hundred AC/DC gigs under his belt.

With shows in the five major capitals, Jake Berry came out to do a recce on the venues. Now armed with the props (the Hell's Bell) and pyrotechnics they'd once disdained (their lighting rig was bigger than Kiss's, the advance publicity claimed), at the dawn of the decade AC/DC led the charge into '80s arena rock.

Despite the high ticket price, an extra show had to be added in Brisbane and also at Melbourne's Myer Music Bowl. AC/DC was already one of the slickest big touring operations on the international circuit (certainly one of the loudest!), and this visit to Australia was a triumphant homecoming of sorts—but again, this success was tainted somehow.

The Melbourne shows were the last of what ended up as a 119-date world tour. The gig in Sydney, the Young family's adopted home town, was the wrap party. After opening the Australian tour in Perth at the Entertainment Centre on February 13, at which gig Bon's family were guests of honor, the band moved on to Adelaide to play Memorial Drive on February 17. On Thursday the 19th, a year to the day after Bon's death, a typical late summer storm rolled in over Sydney. It probably wouldn't do to read too much into all the thunder and lightning, but the next day, when the gig was scheduled to take place at the Showgrounds, the wet weather turned bitter, and the show had to be postponed.

The show was postponed again on the Saturday night, but when it finally happened on the Sunday night, it was hailed as "a triumphant return." Angus gets itchy fingers if his routine is interrupted, and he doesn't know how to give less than 130%. With the Angels and John Swan's band, Swanee, supporting, a 30,000-strong crowd as generous of spirit as Bon himself took his replacement to their hearts.

But as warmly as Brian was received, as celebratory as the crowd and the band's experience was, there was still something incomplete: the absence of the prodigal son was conspicuous. The echo of Bon Scott reverberated in every song, every note and beat the band played.

After the performance came another trophy night. Everybody was there: George and Harry, the entire Young clan, Ted Mulry, Ted Albert and all the Alberts people, Mark Evans, Peter Mensch, Ian Jeffrey, Sherbet, Angry Anderson, Pat Pickett, Lobby Loyde, support bands the Angels, Swanee, Rose Tattoo—everybody except Angus, who slipped away. AC/DC's backstage set-up now included a hospitality area in the form of a complete mock-English pub. Brian liked an ale or ten, and so did Malcolm. The band was presented with 40 gold and platinum albums. For many of the people in attendance, the occasion was bittersweet, a homecoming without a king. It was a bit like the fake pub backstage; you hadn't needed props like that when Bon Scott was around, because Bon was a walking, talking one-man party.

A sour note was struck when an unidentified woman in the crowd yelled out for the original members of the band, but AC/DC rewrite their past as it suits them. She might well also have called for Michael Browning; he was going about his business elsewhere in the city, discarded by AC/DC after he'd served his purpose. Mark Evans would eventually win an out-of-court settlement with Alberts over unpaid royalties. "Sometimes," he says, "when I'm in the right mood, seeing Bon on TV looking straight at me can still freak me out."

"All I can really say is that Bon is still around and watching," Brian Johnson said. "I can't tell you anymore because it's all so personal, but at night in my hotel room I had proof that he was there in some form. I know that he approves of what the new line-up is trying to do. He didn't want the band to split up or go into a long period of mourning. He wanted us to build on the spirit he left behind."

The band had to race to Brisbane the next day for the first of two nights at Festival Hall. And it was here that things started to really unravel. A couple of cars got torched after the show. Remarkably, hillbilly dictator Joh Bjelke-Peterson's stormtroopers were caught off guard. That wasn't going to happen in Melbourne, where the police surrounded the Myer Music Bowl, intent on nipping any public drunkenness or petty vandalism in the bud. On the first night, they made 30 arrests as the crowd dispersed after the show.

There was a real sense of closure here, in more ways than one. As Tadhg Taylor put it in *Top Fellas*, his brilliant history of Melbourne's sharpie cult, those two AC/DC gigs at the Myer Music Bowl were "one of the most significant moments in the great sharp epic—the grand finale, the last big night on the town. Sharpie ended that night." Taylor quotes a survivor called "Chris," who recalls that while the cult was then in its dying days, "Every sharp in Melbourne would have been there and they went berserk, smashed all the trains and trams, pulled the cops off their horses, a riot. By this stage I was into punk and so these kids with moccasins and Bon Scott RIP T-shirts weren't sharpies, they were headbangers."

On the second night, the band played as if cowed, but still that didn't stop the cops from arresting another 30 kids—and this in the city that now names a street after AC/DC! For the band, there was a real sense of déjà vu about it, another storm in a teacup like the punk rock shock *Dirty Deeds* tour the last time, and they left Australia again with no particular wish to come back soon. Indeed, they wouldn't return for another seven years.

You would be forgiven, then, for expecting that at this stage the band might take a break, if only to catch their breath, if not reflect on all that happened in the past year. But Malcolm and Angus kept on pushing harder and harder, and that's how it all finally caught up with them.

After Australia, they never even really went off the road; they toured the US from March until June. Atlantic had finally relented and released the initially rejected *Dirty Deeds* in May. Five years old, it soared to number three, where it sat for four weeks. The entire back catalogue was peppering the charts at that point; by now, *Dirty Deeds* and *Highway to Hell* have each sold over three million copies in the US alone.

There was still one height AC/DC hadn't yet scaled, though—the top of the American charts. But they wouldn't have long to wait. In July 1981, the band went to Paris to start recording the follow-up to *Back in Black* with Mutt Lange. The sessions became fraught. The band was drying up. The album that resulted, *For Those About to Rock*, which was released even before the end of that year, was an almost empty vessel. As a consequence, it was the last album Lange cut with the band—even though it became the first AC/DC record to reach number one in the US. It didn't stay there long—in fact, it was the first new AC/DC album that didn't outsell its predecessor—but it got there. There wasn't much now that AC/DC hadn't accomplished.

But if it is indeed a long way to the top, it can be a quick slide down the other side. AC/DC's characteristic insularity degenerated, as it could, into paranoia. For drummer Phil Rudd, it was never the same after Bon died, and after touring *For Those About to Rock* for most of 1982, he started to go off the rails again—but more seriously this time.

The band would bounce back before the decade was out, but the mid-'80s was a testing time, creatively the lowest point of AC/DC's career. 1983's *Flick of the Switch* patently lacked the quality songs the band seemed to turn out at will when Bon was alive. Much had changed, and the production credit—to Malcolm and Angus themselves—was merely the tip of the iceberg. The pair had carried out a purge of the entire band and its support structure. It's a classic syndrome: the successful campaigner who fears his own troops. But Malcolm and Angus never trusted anyone anyway. After sacking Mutt Lange, who had so successfully (literally) engineered their breakthrough (and who would go on to even greater success, practically inventing '80s hair metal via former AC/DC support act Def Leppard), they sacked practically everybody else: Phil Rudd, for starters; Peter Mensch, who had himself usurped Michael Browning; even de facto official photographer Robert Ellis. The replacement of Rudd by Englishman Simon Wright meant there wasn't an Australian-born member left in the band.

The larger disaster of *Fly on the Wall*, the 1985 follow-up to *Flick of the Switch*, prompted Malcolm and Angus to rethink their dictatorship.

When longtime AC/DC fan Stephen King invited the band to contribute to the soundtrack of the film *Maximum Overdrive*, Malcolm and Angus re-enlisted brother George and Harry Vanda and found a born-again energy. The resulting track, "Who Made Who," was a turntable hit in 1986 and served notice that AC/DC were on the comeback trail.

With George and Harry back at the controls, 1988's *Blow Up Your Video* completed their return. The single "Heatseeker" was the band's first bona fide hit (albeit a minor one) since "You Shook Me All Night Long." The album was further helped, ironically, by a set of videos which saw AC/DC finally catch up, for better or worse, with MTV.

The next album, 1990's *The Razor's Edge*—on which George started work only to be sacked once more and replaced by Canadian Bruce Fairbairn—consolidated AC/DC's comeback, yielding the semi-hit single/ad jingle "Thunderstruck." (By now, Brian Johnson had dropped out of the songwriting, leaving it all to the Young/Young axis.)

AC/DC was now a rock'n'roll institution—a living piece of rock'n'roll history, like the Stones, Tina Turner, or Bruce Springsteen. Successive generations of kids keep coming to see them just so they can say they saw them (which is the basis on which the Stones function today, too). And, just like the Stones, for all their imitators nobody does AC/DC better than AC/DC.

Still, when the band more recently contemplated sacking Brian Johnson—for whatever reason—they ultimately thought better of it. Not even AC/DC, they may have feared, could survive losing its singer for the second time.

George and Harry have never again reproduced the sort of magic they managed with ease in the '70s, and Alberts today lives largely on the back of AC/DC and its other former glories. The Midas touch with which George steered the company deserted him not long after AC/DC first left the nest. The Angels left the label to sign to Epic in America. Rose Tattoo became an increasingly erratic proposition, and acts like John Paul Young and the Ted Mulry Gang simply faded away.

Alberts eventually moved out of Kangaroo House, studios and all, into a new building on Sydney's leafy north shore. It was the end of an era. George and Harry found themselves out of time—and out of touch—in the '80s, producing little except their own Flash & the Pan material. Even the Choirboys had left the label before they produced their one classic hit, "Run to Paradise," for Mushroom in 1988.

Ted Albert himself had just bought into a promising stage musical called *Strictly Ballroom* when he died in 1990. The film version of *Strictly Ballroom* became a phenomenal success, and propelled John Paul Young back into the charts with a remixed version of "Love Is in the Air" from the soundtrack—but with Ted's death a cloud descended on what was left of Alberts.

In the 1990s, AC/DC's work rate slowed dramatically, as befitting a band whose members were all at least in their forties by now. Malcolm had already had to take time off to dry out in the late eighties. The official line was that he was suffering from "nervous exhaustion"; nephew Steve Young replaced him on the *Blow Up Your Video* tour and few people seemed to notice. Malcolm bought a house back in Australia, a palace in boho Sydney harborside suburb Balmain. Soon enough Angus also bought a property "back home"; both brothers divided their time between Europe and Australia.

It would be five years before the band followed up *The Razor's Edge* with the Rick Rubin-produced *Ballbreaker* in 1995, by which time a clean and sober Phil Rudd was back in the fold. "The best thing was the return of Phil," Rubin told *Rolling Stone*. "To me, that made them AC/DC again. You can hear it in how he drags behind the beat. It's the same rhythm that first drew me to them in junior high. That groove is timeless."

It would be another five years again before 2000's *Stiff Upper Lip*. *Stiff Upper Lip* was AC/DC's seventeenth album, produced by none other than big brother George. The family ties are still strong, and some of the touch is still there.

Of course, AC/DC could never be the same after Bon died. Not since the first rush of hits off *Back in Black* have they produced much to equal their best earlier songs. But while the Young brothers' suspicion that they were regarded less highly post-Bon fed their paranoia for a long time, with the continuing success they have had, Malcolm and Angus are today much more comfortable with who they are. Like a vintage bluesman, AC/DC deserve the respect and success they enjoy. The energy and commitment they display is the least the punters should expect from any rock'n'roll band. But AC/DC have always been distinguished by their sense of humor and lack of pretension, too, and these are qualities they still retain.

Bon was contemptuous of the critics who misunderstood AC/DC, but the band's critical reputation improved over time as it became clear not only that they weren't going to go away, but that what they'd started had influenced the course of rock'n'roll history. They're now a touchstone, and Bon himself is recognized as one of the great lost figures of rock.

Calling AC/DC a heavy metal band in the seventies was as inaccurate as it is today. To start with, they've never looked like a heavy metal band. Forgetting AC/DC's glam-rock origins, Malcolm once commented, "It's disgusting to see men prancing around with make-up on and hairspray wafting around them." But AC/DC were never anything more or less than a straight rock'n'roll band. The confusion arises today because of the enormous influence they've had. The headbangers loved AC/DC from the very first, because—like Led Zeppelin—they could be embraced as a heavy metal band, even if they transcended the genre. AC/DC were a rock'n'roll band that just happened to be heavy enough for metal—and, as it also turned out, funky enough for hip-hop!

"The other thing that separates AC/DC as a hard rock band is that you can dance to their music," says Rick Rubin. "They didn't play funk, but everything they played was funky. And that beat could really get a crowd going. I first saw them in 1979, before Bon Scott died, opening for Ted Nugent at Madison Square Garden. The crowd yanked all the chairs off the floor and piled them into a pyramid in front of the stage."

Before grunge, there was thrash; before thrash, there was hardcore; and before hardcore, there was punk. Before punk, before metal, there was heavy rock, as it was called in the early '70s. AC/DC never fitted the punk stereotype, but as soon as hardcore came along they were recognized as an influence. And by the time thrash emerged—and remember that Metallica, for example, were called a thrash band when they first appeared in the mid-eighties—AC/DC's influence was pervasive. (And who managed Metallica? And, for that matter, Def Leppard? Peter Mensch . . .) When Henry Rollins guested with Australian trio the Hard-Ons on a 1991 single version of "Let there Be Rock," it was but one of a stream of tributes that continues to this day. The 2004 Australian feature film *Thunderstruck* makes a pilgrimage to Bon's grave, which has become such a tourist attraction that it's now protected by the National Trust.

AC/DC was a band that made their own path, and it was Bon who gave them the character and spirit they've only ever been able to approximate since he died.

"I don't think there would have been an AC/DC if it hadn't been for Bon," says Angus today. "You might have got me and Malcolm doing something, but it wouldn't have been what it was. Bon molded the character and flavor of AC/DC. He was one of the dirtiest fuckers I know."

For all his flesh and blood reality, Bon lent AC/DC a mystique that the band now sorely lacks. Angus still parades in the school uniform he should have grown out of years ago, a cartoon character who comes off stage and admits it's a role he plays. The band has become two-dimensional. They're no less pudgy-faced and red-eyed, no less obviously, honestly human—which is admirable when one of the great failings of so many rock bands is patent, show-business phoniness—but they seem to be set on autopilot. Angus should cut that blues album Atlantic was always pestering him to do.

Bon provided the spark—sweet inspiration!—that ignited the fire, that elevated Malcolm and Angus above mere guitarsmiths, churning out riff after riff in a rote fashion. Malcolm and Angus patched up the band as best they could, and carried on. What else could they do?

ACKNOWLEDGMENTS

This book started life as a film proposal. It was my friend Tim Ferrier's idea, and he's the first person to whom I owe thanks. Tim was already in the film business, and as an old AC/DC fan, he could see the potential in Bon's story. He asked me, as a writer, to help him, and I shared his enthusiasm for the idea. I remember the summer we spent writing a treatment. Even after only cursory research, Tim and I got it right enough to arouse terrific enthusiasm on the part of a producer and potential investors.

But the project went no further than that. The reason was that Alberts Productions, which owns the rights to AC/DC's songs, and with whom we had initially had agreeable meetings, simply stopped taking our calls. We could only assume they weren't going to grant us permission to use AC/DC's music, and this effectively killed the film. With great disappoint-ment, Tim and I shelved the thing. I still believe Bon's story would make a great film.

I refused to let go of the subject, though. Bon's story was such a good one and, I believed, an important one, that I remained determined to tell it in some form. This book is the result.

My intention was only ever to portray Bon through the eyes of the people who knew him best, so I had to seek all these people out. As a result, I got to know a great many people I would otherwise never have met; this was an experience I mostly enjoyed and learned a lot from. I figure I would have liked Bon myself, because I liked so many of his old friends. I have relied on these people, and I extend to them my sincere gratitude for the faith and trust they extended to me, for their time and emotion, and the precious memories and mementos they shared so generously.

Of course, I went to Bon's family first, his mother and father, Isa and

Chick, in Perth. "Ron would have loved this," Isa kept saying, rolling her r's in a still strong Scottish brogue. She and Chick both gave me every assistance they could, and to them I extend my special thanks.

I went back to Alberts in the hope that they might now want to join the party, but my hopes were in vain. I still don't know why—they won't tell me—they simply refuse to talk about their fallen comrade. Even after we agreed that it was in no one's interest that I get the facts wrong, they would not help me check facts. They denied permission to quote from Bon's lyrics. Their lack of grace is astonishing.

Curiously, it was only people who had a purely professional relationship with Bon who were reluctant to talk to me. Plenty of them were keen, but just as many weren't. Is this book authorized? they all asked. Knowing what they were really getting at—whether or not Alberts approved of it. I would reply, Well, it depends what you mean by authorized.

I would think, I would go on, that only Bon's family have the right to authorize a book about him, and certainly I have their blessing. At which point they would all say, No, no, is Alberts going along with it? I would say, No—and they would back off. Alberts seems to generate an atmosphere bordering on fear.

Almost without exception though, Bon's personal friends were delighted that an appropriate tribute was at last being paid to him, and they were unequivocal in their enthusiasm to help.

I am indebted first and foremost to Vince Lovegrove, who not only opened quite a few doors for me—to people, like himself, who were Bon's oldest friends—but also encouraged and inspired me all the way along the line. That he did so during a time when he was under great personal duress is all the more humbling.

Mary Renshaw and Irene Thornton, Bon's wife, let me into their lives, and if a man can be measured by the women in his life, Mary and Irene prove Bon was a fine man. Great thanks also to Mark Evans, Michael Browning, Bruce Howe, and Silver Smith. I kept going back to all these people with questions, and to use them as sounding-boards, and their patience never flagged.

I am also indebted to Pat Pickett, Pam Swain, Chris Gilbey, Anthony O'Grady, Christie Eliezer, Juke, *Rolling Stone*, Mick Cocks, Joe Furey, Peter Head and Mouse, Uncle John Ayers, John Freeman, Helen Carter, Dave Jarrett, Molly Meldrum, Wyn Milson, John Darcy, Doris Howe, Peter Noble, Adrian Driscoll, Terry Serio, Sam See, Maria and Jim Short, Rob Bailey, Hamish Henry, Dennis Laughlin, Anna Baba, Graeme Scott, Keith Glass,

Ian McFarlane, Richard Griffiths, Perry Cooper, Coral Browning, Paul Stewart, Chris Sturt, and Dave Baxter. And to the photographers Philip Morris, Bob King, Peter Carrette, Roger Gould, and Graeme Webber. And to a few people who preferred to remain nameless—they know who they are.

I am indebted, too, to other writers whose research I have plundered, particularly Glenn A Baker, who seems to be the only journalist ever to have "penetrated" Alberts. For months, I went back and forth to the Mitchell Library in Sydney and the Victorian State Library to rifle through old issues of *Go-Set, RAM, Juke, Rolling Stone* and *Digger*, and I salute their creators and often nameless contributors. I also referred continuously to Noel McGrath's *Australian Encyclopaedia of Rock & Pop*, Peter Beilby and Michael Roberts' *Australian Music Directory*, Chris Spencer's *Who's Who of Australian Rock*, and David Day and Tim Parker's *It's Our Music*.

Naturally, I read the two previously published AC/DC biographies— *Hell Ain't No Bad Place To Be* by Richard Bunton, and *Shock to the System* by Mark Putterford—and I only hope I'm not found out repeating any of their mistakes!

In general, quotes presented oral history style I obtained myself through first-hand interviews; those presented otherwise were derived from other sources, usually cited.

Of course, there are also my own friends and associates who have helped in different ways, among them Tony Hayes and all the people we met in Scotland, David McClymont, everyone in Adelaide (the Herzs, the Norwoods, the Harrises), Bleddyn Butcher and Jude Toohey in London, Richard Guilliatt and Susan Bogle in New York, Ken West, Bruce Milne, Robert Forster and Karin, Dave Graney and Clare Moore, Steve and Helen, Matthew and Dianne, Peter Blakeley, and Stuart Coupe and Julie Ogden. Thanks also to my family, especially my mother. And last but most of all, my wife Debbie, who means more to me than words can express.

Special thanks to Penguin Books Australia Ltd for permission to reproduce passages from William Dick's *A Bunch of Ratbags*; and the *Boston Globe* for permission to quote from an October 7, 1970 column by George Frazier. And finally, thanks to Katherine Spielmann and Steve Connell for getting this US edition out.

PHOTO CREDITS

BIOGRAPHIES

TED ALBERT: Head of J Albert & Son, the music publishing company that became a record label, too. In its 1970s heyday, the label was headed by the Vanda/Young production team and included not only AC/DC but also John Paul Young and the Ted Mulry Gang. Ted Albert died suddenly in 1990 … **ANGELS**: They formed a triumvirate at Alberts with AC/DC and Rose Tattoo, and are an Australian pub rock institution … **"UNCLE" JOHN AYERS**: Harmonica player in Fraternity. He subsequently formed Adelaide R&B outfit Mickey Finn … **ANNA BABA**: Lived with Bon in London for the last few weeks of his life. After he died, she returned to Japan and went to work in medical publishing … **ROB BAILEY**: AC/DC's original bassist. He was sacked after the recording of the band's first album. Later involved in new age music … **BLACKFEATHER**: Archetypal progressive rockers of the early '70s. Bon plays recorder on their classic 1971 album *At the Mountains of Madness* … **CORAL BROWNING**: Michael Browning's sister, who worked for him and AC/DC in London, then America, until Peter Mensch took over management of the band in mid-1979. She later worked for Virgin Music in Los Angeles … **MICHAEL BROWNING**: Managed AC/DC from late 1975 to mid-1979. He'd previously run clubs (Sebastians, then the Hard Rock Cafe), and managed Doug Parkinson and Billy Thorpe and the Aztecs, Australia's biggest band in the early '70s. When he was sacked by AC/DC, he returned to Australia and set up Deluxe Records, which gave INXS, among others, its first recording deal. He went on to manage more bands, the most successful of which was Noiseworks … **PHIL CARSON**: General manager of Atlantic Records in London in 1976, and responsible for signing AC/DC to the label. Now based in Los Angeles, where he heads Victory Music, he was reluctant to be interviewed for this book … **HELEN CARTER**: Girlfriend of Bon's in Sydney in 1975/76. She went on to become a musician, initially as bassist/songwriter with Do-Re-Mi, who enjoyed Australian hits such as "Man Overboard" in the '80s … **MICK COCKS**: Rhythm guitarist in Rose Tattoo. After leaving the band in 1979, Mick landed in London, where he saw a lot of Bon before his death. He subsequently returned to Australia and rejoined Rose Tattoo … **COLD CHISEL**: Fronted by Jimmy Barnes—Bon disciple, fellow Scot and replacement for Bon in the last Fraternity lineup—Cold Chisel defined Australian pub rock in the late '70s/early '80s. As if punk never happened. When he went solo, Barnes became an Oz stadium rock icon … **PERRY COOPER**: A newcomer at Atlantic Records in New York in 1977 when AC/DC had just joined the label, as director of special projects he became one of the band's first champions there. He often went out on the road with them, and always roomed with Bon ... **JOHN DARCY**: A roadie for the Valentines in 1969, he remained friends with Bon for years afterward. He later worked with numerous other bands before getting out of the business, and today lives with his family in the hills outside Melbourne ... **MAL EASTICK**: Lead guitarist in Adelaide band Stars, who supported AC/DC on their controversial return Australian tour in 1976. Today, he plays the blues ... **EASYBEATS**: After the Seekers and the BeeGees, Australia's most successful '60s pop export. But the band could not follow up its one international hit, "Friday on My Mind," leaving songwriting/production partnership George Young and Harry Vanda to fend for themselves ... **MARK EVANS**: AC/DC's bass player from 1975 to 1977. Went on to play with other bands, including Finch and Heaven, before retiring from the stage gracefully and working in a music shop, which only interrupts his golfing schedule. Some ten years after being dismissed from AC/DC, won an out-of-court settlement with Alberts over unpaid royalties ... **FLYING CIRCUS**: Classically schizophrenic Australian act of the late '60s: as a singles band they were pure bubblegum but as a live act/album band were progressive folk-country-rock. Found some success in Canada in the early '70s ... **JOHN FREEMAN**: Drummer in Fraternity, went on to play with Uncle and Bruce Howe in Adelaide R&B institution Mickey Finn, and today performs as an acoustic delta-blues guitarist ... **JOE FUREY**: Met Bon and Silver Smith in Sydney in the summer of 1977/78 and, living in London thereafter and working for UFO, remained friends with both of them ... **CHRIS GILBEY**: Worked at Alberts as a promotions man and later general manager between 1973 and 1977. Went on to become one of the most powerful figures in the Australian music industry ... **RICHARD GRIFFITHS**: AC/DC's first booking agent in Britain, now CEO of Epic Records in New York ... **PETER HEAD** (né Beagley): Keyboardist for Headband, and a contemporary and friend of Bon's in Adelaide in the early '70s. Under the name the Mount Lofty Rangers, he cut a number of tracks with Bon in 1974 ... **MAUREEN HENDERSON**: Lived around the corner from the Scotts in Fremantle when Bon was growing up. She taught Bon to kiss ... **HAMISH HENRY**: A wealthy Adelaide patron of the arts who acted as benefactor to Fraternity, and managed the band. He later went back to the family business, but then up and moved to Queensland, where he is now a successful manufacturer of children's playground equipment ... **BRUCE HOWE**: Leader of Fraternity. He steered the band on after Bon left, with Jimmy Barnes as singer, but not for long. Later rejoined Uncle in Mickey Finn, an R&B outfit which later also numbered John Freeman. Summoned by Jimmy Barnes to join his band after Cold Chisel split, he soon returned to Adelaide. He still lives on the Peninsula, just down the road from the Largs Pier Hotel, and plays with the Mega Boys ... **DAVE JARRETT**: Promotions man for WEA Records in London in the late '70s, his responsibilities included AC/DC. Worked for Hot Records in Sydney in the '80s, before moving to Adelaide, where he died in his sleep in 2000 ... **IAN JEFFERY**: AC/DC's tour manager for many years, from 1977 until the mid-'80s, he later went back to work for Peter Mensch, with Metallica. He lives in Japan, and eluded being interviewed for this book ... **ALISTAIR KINNEAR**: Was with Bon on the night he died. After one interview, he faded from public view and moved to Spain's Costa del Sol, where he still lives and plays music. He resurfaced in 2005 and gave a public statement that finally put to rest the conspiracy theories surrounding Bon's death ... **HERM KOVAC**: Played drums in the Ted Mulry Gang. Today, he runs Ramrod Recording Studios in Sydney ... **DENNIS LAUGHLIN**: Original lead singer in Sherbet, and AC/DC's first, short-lived manager. Today, manages a hi-fi store in Geelong ... **LOVED ONES**: The most mercurial of '60s Australian bands, Melbourne's Loved Ones exploded with a handful of classic hits, then fell apart ... **VINCE LOVEGROVE**: Met Bon in Perth in the early '60s, and with him formed the Valentines. They remained friends and both lived in Adelaide in the early '70s, Vince working as a journalist and later an agent, in which capacity he was instrumental in Bon joining AC/DC. Went on to manage Cold Chisel briefly, before moving into TV as a producer, and then back to rock'n'roll, as manager of the Divinyls. In the mid-'80s, his second wife Suzie and son Troy, were stricken with AIDS, and he devoted himself to nursing them—they both subsequently died—and to documenting the experience in films and a book in the hope of raising awareness and understanding of the disease. After working as a journalist in London for some years, has now returned to Australia ... **LOBBY LOYDE**: Australia's Godfather of Punk, guitar anti-hero Lobby Loyde started out in Brisbane blues-boom band the Purple Hearts, went on to help rebuild Billy Thorpe's Aztecs and then formed the Coloured Balls, the missing link between the Aztecs and AC/DC. He died in 2007 ... **MASTERS APPRENTICES**: Led out of Adelaide by Scottish immigrant Jim Keys, the Masters Apprentices were one of the great Australian '60s bands, a chameleon-like act who went from raw R&B through psychedelia and bubblegum back to country-rock and heavy metal, before breaking up in 1971 and giving AC/DC its first drummer, Colin Burgess ... **IAN "MOLLY" MELDRUM**: Media personality, creator of *Countdown*, "the oldest teenager in Australia," and someone whose enthusiasm for rock'n'roll—particularly Australian rock'n'roll—shows no sign of abating ... **PETER MENSCH**: As part of New York management company Leber & Krebs, usurped Michael Browning's position as manager of AC/DC in 1979. Was himself subsequently sacked, but since his other charges have included Def Leppard and Metallica, he has remained successful. He declined to be interviewed for this book ... **WYN MILSON**: Played guitar alongside Bon in his first band, the Spektors, and went on with Bon to join the Valentines. Later became a live sound engineer, a job he still performs at the highest level ... **TED MULRY**: Leader of the Gang, a hitmaker for Alberts throughout the '70s. He died in 2001 ... **PAT PICKETT**: A wicked friend of Bon's who managed to attach himself to both Fraternity and AC/DC. He learnt the ropes as a roadie and today enjoys almost legendary status as one of that breed's elder statesmen ... **ROSE TATTOO**: Recommended to Alberts by Bon, Rose Tattoo were among the most ferocious white blues-rock bands the world has ever seen ... **PHIL RUDD**: The drummer in AC/DC initially between 1976 and 1983. After running a recording studio in New Zealand, he rejoined AC/DC in 1994. He politely declined to be interviewed for this book ... **CHICK & ISA SCOTT**: Bon's parents, who long outlived their oldest boy ... **GRAEME SCOTT**: Bon's youngest brother, left home to go to sea in the late '60s, and dropped in and out of Bon's life according to where either of them was around the world at any one time. Eventually settled in Thailand, where, with his Thai wife, he ran a bar ... **SAM SEE**: Guitarist/keyboardist in Fraternity, after he'd formed Sherbet and left the Flying Circus, and before he rejoined the Circus. He went on to play all around the traps, before recently taking up musical directorship of Australian television Channel 7's *Tonight Live* ... **SHERBET**: Australia's biggest teenybop rock band of the mid-'70s, rivals of Skyhooks and *Countdown* darlings ... **MARIA SHORT**: Bon's first real steady girlfriend, whom he lived with on and off, in both Perth and Melbourne between 1965 and 1968, and with whom he always kept in touch. She lives in Perth with her family, and is highly successful in the rag trade … **SILVER SMITH** (née Margaret Smith): She and Bon lived together in London in 1976 and 1977, and they continued to see each other right up until Bon died. She eventually returned to Adelaide, where she lives in a small bungalow with a large garden, which she shares with her son and two German Shepherds. She has been drug and alcohol free since 1986 … **PAM SWAIN**: Met Bon in 1979 when she was working for radio station 2JJ, and enjoyed a brief fling with him. Today, she works for ABC-TV … **IRENE THORNTON**: Bon's wife. They were married, in Adelaide, in 1972. They separated in 1974, when Bon joined AC/DC, and divorced in 1978, though they remained friends … **BILLY THORPE AND THE AZTECS**: Manchester-born Billy Thorpe was a show-business veteran by the time he migrated to Brisbane as a kid in the fifties. He went on to lead the Aztecs, who succeeded in traversing two distinct eras of Australian rock'n'roll, first as a '60s beat sensation, then as '70s "progressive" blues rockers. Thorpie later moved to the west coast of America where, after recording a few US albums, he became a soft toy manufacturer, before returning to Australia to reclaim his legacy. He published two volumes of memoirs and spearheaded 2002's "Long Way to the Top" tour. He died suddenly of a heart attack in 2007 … **TWILIGHTS**: With dual lead singers Glen Shorrock and Paddy McCartney, the Twilights broke out of Adelaide as the Antipodes' most slavish Beatles acolytes. Shorrock went on to front country-rock supergroup Axiom, then dabbled with the Mount Lofty Rangers, before joining the Little River Band … **HARRY VANDA**: Formerly of the Easybeats, the passive partner to George Young in the production team that shaped the success of not only AC/DC but also William Shakespeare, John Paul Young, Rose Tattoo, the Angels, and their own recording persona, Flash & the Pan. He refused to be interviewed for this book … **MARY WALTON** (née Wasylyk, now Renshaw): A dear friend of Bon's, she met him initially in the '60s, when the Valentines were based in Melbourne. Then a budding fashion designer, she went on to open her own boutique. Still works in the business, and lives with her kids in Melbourne … **ROSS WILSON**: A seminal figure in Australian rock, Ross the Boss's first band, the Party Machine, spawned two early '70s standards, Daddy Cool and Spectrum. He himself went on to produce the ground-breaking Skyhooks, to found Oz Records, and to lead Mondo Rock … **STEVIE WRIGHT**: Former Easybeats frontman. "Little Stevie," Bon's role model in many respects, became one of Australian rock's most infamous casualties. After following up the "Evie" single and *Hard Road* album with *Black-Eyed Bruiser* in 1975, he declined into hardcore heroin addiction … **ANGUS YOUNG**: Lead guitarist in AC/DC, he refused to be interviewed for this book, although the author did interview him for a *RAM* cover story in 1990 … **GEORGE YOUNG**: Formerly of the Easybeats, he was the sixth member of AC/DC, the producer who guided the band from the very first. He refused to be interviewed for this book … **JOHN PAUL YOUNG**: Starting his singing career around the same time and place as Malcolm Young, the unrelated John Paul Young (aka "Mungy," "Squeak," "JPY") almost replaced Dave Evans in AC/DC. He went on to become an Alberts labelmate and sang the unforgettable Vanda-Young disco-pop classic "Standing in the Rain" … **JOHNNY YOUNG**: No relation to the Young clan, he began as a '60s singing sensation, and went on to success as a songwriter and producer (1969's *The Real Thing*, most notably). He also fronted Australian television's much-loved *Young Talent Time* between 1971 and 1986 … **MALCOLM YOUNG**: Rhythm guitarist, he formed AC/DC in 1973. He refused to be interviewed for this book.

DISCOGRAPHY

Entries ranged left are the original Australian issues; those indented are UK/US releases.

THE VALENTINES
Every Day I Have To Cry (Alexander)/I Can't Dance With You (Marriott/Lane)
(Clarion, May 1967)

She Said (Wright/Young)/To Know You Is To Love You (Spector)
(Clarion, August 1967)

Why Me/I Can Hear The Raindrops (Lovegrove/Ward)
(Clarion, February 1968)

Peculiar Hole In The Sky (Vanda/Young)/Love Makes Sweet Music (Ayers)
(Clarion, June 1968)

My Old Man's A Groovy Old Man (Vanda/Young)/Ebeneezer
(Prince/Taylor) (Philips, March 1969)

Nick Nack Paddy Whack (trad. arr. Valentines)/Getting Better (Scott/Milson)
(Philips, August 1969)

Juliette (Milson/Ward/Scott)/Hoochie Coochie Billy (Lovegrove/Ward/Milson)
(Philips, March 1970)

FRATERNITY
Why Did It Have To Be Me? (Ashdown/Stewart)/Questions (Hayward) (Sweet
Peach, September 1970). *Does not feature Bon.*

Seasons Of Change (Robinson/Johns)/Sommerville (Howe/See)
(Sweet Peach, May 1971)

LIVESTOCK (LP, Sweet Peach, June 1971)
Livestock (Bisset/Jurd)/Sommerville/Raglan's Folly (Jurd/Scott)/Cool Spot (Bisset/
Jurd)/Grand Canyon Suite (Jurd)/Jupiter's Landscape/You Have A God (M. Jurd/
C. Jurd)/It

The Race, Part 1/The Race, Part 2 (Ashdown/Stewart)
(Sweet Peach, October 1971)

If You Got It (Fraternity)/Raglan's Folly/You Have a God
(Raven, October 1971)

Welfare Boogie (Fraternity)/Annabelle (Jurd/Bisset) (RCA, March 1972)

FLAMING GALAH (LP, RCA, April 1972)
Welfare Boogie/Annabelle/Seasons Of Change/If You Got It/You Have a God/
Hemming's Farm/Raglan's Folly/Getting Off (Jurd)/Sommerville RIP (Howe/See)/
Canyon Suite (Jurd)

AC/DC

All songs by Young/Scott/Young unless otherwise indicated.

Can I Sit Next To You Girl?/Rockin' In The Parlour (Young/Young) (Alberts, July
1974). *Does not feature Bon.*

HIGH VOLTAGE (LP, Alberts, February 1975)
Baby, Please Don't Go (Williams)/She's Got Balls/Little Lover/Stick Around/Soul
Stripper (Young/Young)/You Ain't Got A Hold On Me/Love Song/Show Business

Baby, Please Don't Go/Love Song (Alberts, March 1975)

High Voltage/Soul Stripper (Alberts, June 1975)

Long Way To The Top/Can I Sit Next To You Girl? (Alberts,
December 1975)

TNT (LP, Alberts, February 1976)
Long Way To The Top/Rock'n'roll Singer/The Jack/Live Wire/TNT/Rocker/Can I
Sit Next to You Girl?/High Voltage/School Days (Berry)

TNT/Rocker (Alberts, March 1976)

> **Long Way to the Top**/Can I Sit Next to You Girl?
> (UK Atlantic, April 1976)
>
> **HIGH VOLTAGE** (LP, UK Atlantic, May 1976)
> Long Way to the Top/Rock'n'roll Singer/The Jack/Live Wire/TNT/
> Rocker/ Can I Sit Next To You Girl?/Little Lover/She's Got Balls/High Voltage

Jailbreak/Fling Thing (Alberts, June 1976)

> **Jailbreak**/Fling Thing (UK Atlantic, August 1976)

Dirty Deeds Done Dirt Cheap/Rock In Peace (Alberts, October 1976)

> **High Voltage**/Live Wire (UK Atlantic, October 1976)

DIRTY DEEDS DONE DIRT CHEAP (LP, Alberts, October 1976)
Dirty Deeds Done Dirt Cheap/Ain't No Fun (Waiting Around to Be a
Millionaire)/There's Gonna Be Some Rockin'/Problem Child/Squealer/Big Balls/
Rock In Peace/Ride On/Jailbreak

> **HIGH VOLTAGE** (LP, US Atco, November 1976)
> Long Way to the Top/Rock'n'roll Singer/The Jack/Live Wire/TNT/ Can I Sit
> Next to You Girl?/Little Lover/She's Got Balls/High Voltage
>
> **High Voltage**/Long Way to the Top (US Atco, December 1976)
>
> **DIRTY DEEDS DONE DIRT CHEAP** (LP, UK Atlantic, December 1976)
> Dirty Deeds Done Dirt Cheap/Love at First Feel/Big Balls/Rocker/Problem
> Child/There's Gonna Be Some Rockin'/Ain't No Fun (Waiting Around to be a
> Millionaire)/Ride On/Squealer

Love At First Feel/Problem Child (Alberts, January 1977)

> **Dirty Deeds Done Dirt Cheap**/Big Balls/The Jack (UK Atlantic, January 1977)

Dog Eat Dog/Carry Me Home (Alberts, March 1977)

LET THERE BE ROCK (LP, Alberts, April 1977)
Go Down/Dog Eat Dog/Let There Be Rock/Bad Boy Boogie/Overdose/Crabsody
In Blue/Hell Ain't A Bad Place To Be/Whole Lotta Rosie

> **Let There Be Rock**/Problem Child
> (UK/US Atlantic/Atco, September 1977)

LET THERE BE ROCK (LP, UK/US Atlantic/Atco, October 1977)
same track listing as Australian LP

Let There Be Rock, Part 1/Let There Be Rock, Part 2
(Alberts, October 1977)

POWERAGE (LP, Alberts, April 1978)
Rock'n'roll Damnation/Down Payment Blues/Gimme A Bullet/Riff Raff/Sin City/
Next To The Moon/Gone Shootin'/Up To My Neck In You/Kicked in the Teeth

> **POWERAGE** (LP, UK/US Atlantic, June 1978)
> *same track listing as Australian LP*
>
> **Rock'n'roll Damnation**/Sin City (UK Atlantic, May 1978)
>
> **Rock'n'roll Damnation**/Kicked in the Teeth
> (US Atlantic, June 1978)

Rock'n'roll Damnation/Cold Hearted Man (Alberts, June 1978)

> **Whole Lotta Rosie (live)**/Hell Ain't a Bad Place to Be (live)
> (UK/US Atlantic, October 1978)

IF YOU WANT BLOOD (LP, Alberts; UK/US Atlantic, October 1978)
Riff Raff/Hell Ain't a Bad Place to Be/Bad Boy Boogie/The Jack/Problem Child/
Whole Lotta Rosie/Rock'n'roll Damnation/High Voltage/Let There Be Rock/
Rocker

Whole Lotta Rosie/Dog Eat Dog (Alberts, November 1978)

HIGHWAY TO HELL (LP, Alberts; UK/US Atlantic, July 1979)
Highway To Hell/Girl's Got Rhythm/Walk All Over You/Touch Too Much/Beating
Around the Bush/Shot Down In Flames/Get It Hot/If You Want Blood/Love
Hungry Man/Night Prowler

Highway to Hell/If You Want Blood (Alberts, August 1979)

> **Highway to Hell**/If You Want Blood (UK Atlantic, August 1979)
>
> **Highway to Hell**/Night Prowler (US Atlantic, August 1979)
>
> **Girl's Got Rhythm**/Get It Hot (UK Atlantic, November 1979)
>
> **Girl's Got Rhythm**/If You Want Blood/Hell Ain't a Bad Place to Be (live)/
> Rock'n'roll Damnation (EP, UK Atlantic, Nov. 1979)
>
> **Touch Too Much (live)**/Live Wire (live)/Shot Down in Flames (live) (UK
> Atlantic, January 1980)
>
> **Touch Too Much (live)**/Walk All Over You (live)
> (US Atlantic, February 1980)
>
> **DIRTY DEEDS DONE DIRT CHEAP** (LP, US Atlantic, May 1981)
> Dirty Deeds/Ain't No Fun/There's Gonna Be Some Rockin'/Love at First Feel/
> Big Balls/Problem Child/Rocker/Ride On/Squealer
>
> **'74 JAILBREAK** (mini-LP, US Atlantic, August 1984)
> Jailbreak/You Ain't Got a Hold on Me/Show Business/Soul Stripper/Baby,
> Please Don't Go

REISSUES

BON SCOTT WITH THE SPEKTORS AND THE VALENTINES
(CD, UK, See for Miles, 1999)
The Spektors: Gloria (Morrison)/It Ain't Necessarily So (Gershwin)/ On My
Mind/Yesterday (Lennon/McCartney)/Interview By Allan Mannings/ **The
Valentines:** To Know You Is To Love You/She Said/Every Day I Have To Cry/I
Can't Dance With You/Peculiar Hole In The Sky/Love Makes Sweet Music/I Can
Hear The Raindrops/Why Me/Sooky Sooky (Covay).

BON SCOTT: THE EARLY YEARS, 1967-72 (CD, UK, See for Miles, 1991)
The Valentines: To Know You Is To Love You/She Said/Every Day I Have To Cry/I Can't Dance With You/Peculiar Hole In The Sky/Love Makes Sweet Music/I Can Hear The Raindrops/Why Me?/Sooky Sooky/Getting Better/Ebeneezer/Hoochie Coochie Billy/My Old Man's A Groovy Old Man/Nick Nack Paddy Wack/Juliette/ **Fraternity:** Annabelle/Welfare Boogie/Hemming's Farm /Sommerville R.I.P./Getting Off/If You Got It/Seasons Of Change/Interview with David Day of 5KA Adelaide.

BON SCOTT & FRATERNITY: THE COMPLETE SESSIONS, 1971-72 (2CD, Australia, Raven, 1996)
Disc One: Sweet Peach, 1971: Seasons of Change/Livestock/ Sommerville/Raglan's Folly/Cool Spot/Grand Canyon Suite/Jupiter's Landscape/You Have A God/It/The Race, Parts One & Two/Why Did It Have to Be Me?/Question. **Disc Two, Raven/ RCA, 1971-1972:** The Shape I'm In (Robertson)/If You Got It/ Welfare Boogie/ Annabelle/Seasons Of Change/If You Got It/You Have A God/Hemming's Farm/ Raglan's Folly/Getting Off/Sommerville RIP/Canyon Suite/If You Got It/Battle of the Sounds/Interview with David Day of 5KA Adelaide.

BON SCOTT [THE MOUNT LOFTY RANGERS] (CD single, Australia, Head Office Records, 1996)
Round and Round and Round (Head/Yanni)/Carey Gulley (Head)/Round and Round (Head)

AC/DC: BONFIRE (4CD box-set, Elektra, 1997)
Disc One, Live from the Atlantic Studios: Live Wire/Problem Child/High Voltage/ Hell Ain't a Bad Place to Be/Dog Eat Dog/The Jack/Whole Lotta Rosie/Rocker. **Disc Two, Let There Be Rock: The Movie:** Live Wire/Shot Down in Flames/Hell Ain't a Bad Place to Be/Sin City/Walk All Over You/Bad Boy Boogie/The Jack/Highway to Hell. **Disc Three, Volts:** Dirty Eyes/Touch Too Much/If You Want Blood/Back Seat Confidential/Get it Hot/Sin City/She's Got Balls/School Days/Long Way to the Top/ Ride On. **Disc Four, Back in Black** (*does not feature Bon*): Hell's Bells/Shoot to Thrill/What Do You Do For Your Money, Honey?/Give the Dog a Bone/Let Me Put My Love Into You/Back in Black/You Shook Me All Night Long/Have a Drink on Me/Shake a Leg/Rock'n'roll Ain't Noise Pollution (Young/Johnson/Young)

ADDITIONAL LISTENING

To contextualize Bon's recordings, sample a cross section of '60s and '70s Australian rock. For many years the definitive compilation of the '60s Australian scene was Glenn A. Baker's two double-album volumes of *So You Wanna Be A Rock'n'roll Star* (Festival): *The "Scream" Years, 1964-66* and *The Psychedelic Years, 1967-70.* Baker's own reissue label, Raven Records (not to be confused with the Raven that released one of Fraternity's singles) has subsequently released no less than four volumes of *Sixties Downunder*, on CD, but Festival/Mushroom has also repackaged *So You Wanna Be a Rock'n'roll Star* in its entirety as a 3CD set; it's still the best source, if you supplement it with Raven's *Ugly Things* CD, a *Pebbles*-like collection of '60s garage bands.

Raven's *Boogie, Balls & Blues* hasn't yet made the transition from vinyl to CD, but the label has two fine CD collections that cover the early-to-mid '70s: *Golden Miles: Australian Progressive Rock 1969-1974* and *Seventies Downunder.* There's also an Alberts double set, *Goodtimes,* on CD, while Raven's *Do Y'self a Favour: The Countdown Years, 1975-1979* includes many Alberts hits of the era plus much more (Raven Records' web site is www.ravenrecords.com.au).

And the absolute completist who wants every note Bon got down on vinyl must have Blackfeather's classic 1971 album *At The Mountains of Madness* (Infinity Records, re-released on CD by Festival). Bon plays recorder on a couple of tracks, including the hit version of the single "Seasons of Change," which Bon's own band Fraternity also covered.

ABOUT THE AUTHOR

Clinton Walker has been hailed as "our best chronicler of Australian grass-roots culture" by the Sydney *Sun-Herald*.

Born in country Victoria in 1957, Walker grew up in Melbourne and, after dropping out of Brisbane Art College in 1976, started writing for student newspapers and his own punk fanzines. After moving to Sydney in 1980 and freelancing for rock magazines such as *RAM* and *Rolling Stone*, he gained a reputations as Australia's most prescient and colorful music critic. His early books *Inner City Sound* (1981; reissued by Verse Chorus Press in 2005) and *The Next Thing* (1984) were the first to champion punk and independent music in Australia, and are now regarded as classics of DIY cultural history.

SUSAN BOGLE

Since *Highway to Hell* was first published in 1994, Walker has written four more works of ground-breaking music and social history: *Stranded: The Secret History of Australian Independent Music, 1977-1992* (1996), *Football Life* (1998), *Buried Country: The Story of Aboriginal Country Music* (2000) and *Golden Miles: Sex, Speed and the Australian Muscle Car* (2005).

Walker was the presenter of late night live-music TV show *Studio 22* on ABC, co-wrote the acclaimed 2001 rockumentary *Long Way to the Top*, and produced soundtrack CDs for both series. He also wrote the documentary film based on *Buried Country* and produced its double-CD soundtrack, as well as *Inner City Soundtrack,* a 2CD set released to coincide with the new edition of that book.

Walker lives with his wife and two children in Sydney's inner western suburbs, just down the road from AC/DC's birthplace.